Medici

PreTest®
Self-Assessment
and Review

Medicine

PreTest®
Self-Assessment
and Review

Seventh Edition

Edited by

Mark I. Taragin, M.D., M.P.H.
Assistant Professor of Medicine
Department of Medicine, Division of General Internal Medicine
University of Medicine and Dentistry of New Jersey—
  Robert Wood Johnson Medical School
New Brunswick, New Jersey

McGraw-Hill, Inc.
Health Professions Division/PreTest® Series

New York   St. Louis   San Francisco   Auckland
Bogotá   Caracas   Lisbon   London   Madrid
Mexico City   Milan   Montreal   New Delhi
San Juan   Singapore   Sydney   Tokyo   Toronto

Medicine: PreTest® Self-Assessment and Review

4 5 6 7 8 9 0   DOCDOC   9 9 8 7 6

ISBN 0-07-052024-0

The editors were Gail Gavert and Bruce MacGregor.
The production supervisor was Gyl A. Favours.
R.R. Donnelley & Sons was printer and binder.
This book was set in Times Roman by Compset, Inc.

Library of Congress Cataloging-in-Publication Data

Medicine : Pretest self-assessment and review. — 7th ed. / edited by
Mark I. Taragin.
    p. cm.
    Includes bibliographical references and index.
    ISBN 0-07-052024-0
    1. National Board of Medical Examiners—Examinations—Study
guides.   2. Federation of State Medical Boards of the United States—
Examinations—Study guides.   3. Educational Commission for foreign
Medical Graduates—Examinations—Study guides.   4. Medicine—
Examinations, questions, etc.   I. Taragin, Mark I.
    [DNLM: 1. Medicine—examination questions.   W 18 M4914 1995]
    R834.5.M4   1995
    616'.0076—dc20
    DNLM/DLC
    for Library of Congress   93-45305

Contents

Contributors

Louis Amorosa, M.D.

Professor of Clinical Medicine
Division of Endocrinology,
Metabolism and Nutrition
UMDNJ—Robert Wood Johnson
Medical School
New Brunswick, New Jersey

Jerry M. Belsh, M.D.

Associate Professor of Neurology
Director, Neuromuscular Center
Department of Neurology
UMDNJ—Robert Wood Johnson
Medical School
New Brunswick, New Jersey

Richard S. Berger, M.D.

Clinical Professor of Medicine
and Acting Chief
Department of Medicine
Division of Dermatology
UMDNJ—Robert Wood Johnson
Medical School
New Brunswick, New Jersey

Mitchell S. Cappell, M.D., Ph.D.

Assistant Professor of Medicine
Director, Gastrointestinal Motility
and Laser Endoscopy Unit
Department of Medicine/
Gastroenterology
UMDNJ—Robert Wood Johnson
Medical School
New Brunswick, New Jersey

Perry Cook, M.D.

Assistant Professor of Medicine
and Director of Lymphoma Service
Department of Medicine
Division of Neoplastic Diseases
New York Medical College
Valhalla, New York

Douglas Hutt, M.D.

Clinical Assistant Professor
of Medicine
Department of Medicine
Division of Pulmonary
and Critical Care
UMDNJ—Robert Wood Johnson
Medical School
New Brunswick, New Jersey

Clifton R. Lacy, M.D.

Associate Professor of Medicine
Department of Medicine
Division of Cardiovascular
Diseases and Hypertension
UMDNJ—Robert Wood Johnson
Medical School
New Brunswick, New Jersey

Catherine A. Monteleone, M.D.

Assistant Professor of Medicine
Department of Medicine
Division of Allergy, Immunology
and Infectious Diseases
UMDNJ—Robert Wood Johnson
Medical School
New Brunswick, New Jersey

Satinder Sachdeo, M.D.

Assistant Professor of Medicine
Department of Medicine
Division of Endocrinology
UMDNJ—Robert Wood Johnson
  Medical School
New Brunswick, New Jersey

Leonard H. Sigal, M.D.

Associate Professor
Departments of Medicine
  and Molecular Genetics
  and Microbiology
Chief, Division of Rheumatology
  and Connective Tissue Research
UMDNJ—Robert Wood Johnson
  Medical School
New Brunswick, New Jersey

Ajay B. Singh, M.D.

Assistant Professor of Medicine
Department of Medicine
Division of Nephrology
UMDNJ—Robert Wood Johnson
  Medical School
New Brunswick, New Jersey

Steven J. Sperber, M.D.

Director of Medical Resident
  Research Program
Hackensack Hospital
Hackensack, New Jersey
Clinical Assistant Professor
  of Medicine
Department of Medicine
Division of Allergy, Immunology
  and Infectious Diseases
UMDNJ—Robert Wood Johnson
  Medical School
Newark, New Jersey

Preface

A physician is entrusted with an awesome responsibility—human life. This commitment is rewarded by the satisfaction of assisting people through difficult circumstances and the fulfillment of developing long-term relationships. To effectively meet this obligation and maintain expertise requires extensive training built upon a strong foundation of knowledge.

Much has transpired in this ever-changing, exciting field of medicine. Therefore, this edition has been extensively revised by the contributors, experts in their respective fields. Not only are they outstanding clinicians, they are also academicians with an awareness of recent developments. I thank them for a job well done. Additionally, I encourage you to provide us with comments and suggestions to improve this text in the future.

This book should provide you with a useful self-assessment of your proficiency while simultaneously expanding your fund of knowledge. May your quest for wisdom be never-ending, yet fulfilling.

Mark I. Taragin, M.D., M.P.H.

Introduction

Medicine: PreTest® Self-Assessment and Review, 7/e, has been designed to provide medical students, as well as physicians, with a comprehensive and convenient instrument for self-assessment and review within the field of medicine. The 500 questions provided have been designed to parallel the format and degree of difficulty of the questions contained in Step 2 of the United States Medical Licensing Examination (USMLE).

Each question in the book is accompanied by an answer, a paragraph explanation, and a specific page reference to either a current journal article, a textbook, or both. A bibliography that lists all the sources used in the book follows the last chapter.

Perhaps the most effective way to use this book is to allow yourself one minute to answer each question in a given chapter; as you proceed, indicate your answer beside each question. By following this suggestion, you will be approximating the time limits imposed by the board examinations previously mentioned.

When you have finished answering the questions in a chapter, you should then spend as much time as you need verifying your answers and carefully reading the explanations. Although you should pay special attention to the explanations for the questions you answered incorrectly, you should read every explanation. The editor of this book has designed the explanations to reinforce and supplement the information tested by the questions. If, after reading the explanations for a given chapter, you feel you need still more information about the material covered, you should consult and study the references indicated.

Allergy and Immunology

DIRECTIONS: Each question below contains five suggested responses. Select the **one best** response to each question.

1. Immunological mechanisms play a role in many hematological disorders. All the following statements about the autoimmune hemolytic anemias are true EXCEPT

(A) warm autoimmune hemolytic anemia is more common than cold autoimmune hemolytic anemia
(B) in warm autoimmune hemolytic anemia, erythrocytes are coated with IgG
(C) in cold autoimmune hemolytic anemia, erythrocytes are coated with IgM
(D) complement is involved in the warm but not in the cold form of autoimmune hemolytic anemia
(E) corticosteroids are the primary therapy for the warm but not the cold form of autoimmune hemolytic anemia

2. Selective IgA deficiency is the most common of all immunodeficiency states. Study of patients who have this problem has revealed that

(A) they may suffer anaphylactic reactions following the administration of serum products
(B) clinical improvement follows regular infusions of fresh plasma
(C) secretory component is usually increased in an attempt to compensate for lack of secretory IgA
(D) there is an increase in 19S IgM in the secretions of certain affected patients
(E) few of them have associated autoimmune disorders

1

3. Which of the following statements about the administration and use of intravenous gamma globulin is correct?

(A) The administration of high doses may produce a remission in idiopathic thrombocytopenic purpura

(B) It must be administered slowly, as concentrated gamma globulin used intravenously has spontaneous anticomplementary activity

(C) Intravenous gamma globulin preparations are safe and effective in the management of patients with selective IgA deficiency

(D) Intravenous gamma globulin preparations have been associated with the development of acquired immune deficiency syndrome (AIDS)

(E) In calculating the dose of intravenous gamma globulin to be administered, the physician should take into account the fact that the half-life of the immunoglobulin in the product is 7 to 12 days in vivo

4. Each of the following statements concerning the stimulation of immunological responses after vaccine administration is true EXCEPT

(A) a primary immunological response is first detected within 1 week of the administration of vaccine

(B) repeat exposure to the antigen present in the vaccine causes a secondary immunological response involving the production of comparable levels of IgM (immunoglobulin M) and IgG

(C) the immunological response to vaccine requires T-cell help to induce B cells to produce IgG

(D) primary exposure to the antigen present in the vaccine causes a weaker immunological response than does secondary or repeat exposure

(E) antibody response peaks 1 to 2 weeks after the initial administration of vaccine

5. True statements concerning the relationship of asthma and immediate hypersensitivity (allergic) reactions include all the following EXCEPT

(A) immediate hypersensitivity reactions to food allergens are involved in provoking asthma in an estimated 20 percent of adult asthmatics

(B) immediate hypersensitivity reactions to aeroallergens are involved in provoking asthma in an estimated 25 percent of adult asthmatics

(C) inhalation of a specific allergen in a sensitive person can increase nonspecific bronchial hyperreactivity

(D) after inhalation of allergens, an isolated, late-phase pulmonary response may occur in up to 50 percent of asthmatics

(E) allergen-provoked asthma is more common in children and young adults than in older adults

6. All the following statements about antigen-presenting cells are true EXCEPT

(A) they include macrophages and dendritic cells

(B) they have class I major histocompatibility complex (MHC) molecules on their surfaces

(C) they present a surface complex of polypeptide antigen and MHC that interacts with the T-cell receptor

(D) they have adhesion ligands on their surfaces that bind accessory adhesion molecules (such as ICAM-1) on T cells

(E) they have surface ligands that bind to T-cell activation antigens (such as CD28) and provide a costimulatory signal

7. During the primary immune response a network of interactions is required for the successful elimination of antigen. During this process, which of the following occurs?

(A) CD8-positive T-lymphocytes stimulate macrophages to release interleukin 2

(B) CD4-positive T lymphocytes stimulate macrophages to release interleukin 1

(C) B lymphocytes react with antigen and interleukin 1 and then secrete immunoglobulin M (IgM)

(D) Antigen-presenting macrophages present antigen to lymphocyte-activating macrophages

(E) IgA antibodies are secreted by plasma cells that have interacted with secretory piece

8. A 55-year-old farmer develops recurrent cough, dyspnea, fever, and myalgia several hours after entering his barn. All the following statements concerning this patient are true EXCEPT

(A) testing of pulmonary function several hours after an exposure will most likely reveal a restrictive pattern

(B) immediate-type IgE hypersensitivity is not involved in the pathogenesis of his illness

(C) the etiological agents may well be thermophilic actinomycete antigens

(D) demonstrating precipitable antibodies to the offending antigen confirms the diagnosis of hypersensitivity pneumonitis

(E) a suppressor-cell functional defect is present

9. Which of the following statements concerning allergic reactions in patients receiving penicillin is true?

(A) Allergic reactions occur in approximately 20 percent of patients receiving penicillin

(B) Approximately 25 percent of patients allergic to penicillin will also experience allergic reactions to cephalosporins

(C) Low titers of IgM antibodies specific for the "major" antigenic determinant can be detected in almost every person who has received penicillin

(D) Immediate allergic reactions to penicillin, including anaphylaxis, are most commonly due to the presence of IgE specific for the "major" determinant

(E) The oral route of administration of penicillin is the most likely to induce anaphylaxis

10. Immediate hypersensitivity or allergic reactions can occur in response to a variety of substances including foods. Which of the following statements about allergic reactions to foods is true?

(A) At least 30 percent of the adult population is believed to be allergic to some food substance

(B) Breast feeding and delaying the introduction of solid foods have no effect on the likelihood that an infant will develop food allergies

(C) The foods most likely to cause allergic reactions include egg, milk, seafood, nuts, and soybeans

(D) The organ systems most frequently involved in allergic reactions to foods in adults are the respiratory and cardiovascular systems

(E) Immunotherapy is a proven therapy for food allergies

11. Each of the following statements concerning allergic responses to latex is true EXCEPT

(A) allergic reactions to latex vary in severity from contact urticaria to anaphylaxis
(B) risk factors include a history of atopy and frequent exposure to latex
(C) diagnostic testing includes both skin tests and radioallergosorbent tests (RASTs)
(D) latex products include surgical gloves, condoms, catheters, and balloons
(E) children with cystic fibrosis are at a greater risk than the general public

12. A 6-year-old white boy presents to his physician with a history of recurrent staphylococcal infections and chronic dermatitis. If the boy has the hyper-IgE syndrome, it is likely that

(A) his IgE level (normally less than 300 ng/mL) will be moderately elevated to between 1000 and 4000 ng/mL
(B) he will have a tendency to develop osteomyelitis
(C) he will have associated asthma or allergic rhinitis
(D) depressed cell-mediated immunity will be discovered
(E) he will respond well to treatment with gamma interferon

13. A 32-year-old woman experiences a severe anaphylactic reaction following a sting from a hornet. Correct statements about this patient include all the following EXCEPT that

(A) she has a strong likelihood of having a similar reaction to a sting from a yellow jacket
(B) she would have a prior history of an adverse reaction to an insect sting
(C) as an adult she is more likely to die as a result of an insect sting than a child with the same history
(D) she should be skin-tested with venom antigens and, if positive, immunotherapy should be started
(E) she most likely began to experience symptoms within 15 min of the sting

14. Atopic dermatitis is a common allergic skin disorder. Which of the following statements concerning this disease is true?

(A) Diagnosis is based on clinical features including pruritus, a typical distribution, and a history of atopy
(B) In adults, the extensor surfaces of the extremities are most commonly affected
(C) Skin involvement often worsens during puberty
(D) Cell-mediated immune function is usually normal
(E) Antihistamines constitute the primary therapy

DIRECTIONS: Each question below contains four suggested responses of which **one or more** is correct. Select

A	if	**1, 2, and 3**	are correct
B	if	**1 and 3**	are correct
C	if	**2 and 4**	are correct
D	if	**4**	is correct
E	if	**1, 2, 3, and 4**	are correct

15. A 15-year-old boy develops painless hematuria, myalgias, and malaise immediately following a viral upper respiratory infection. Renal biopsy reveals a focal and segmental proliferative glomerulonephritis with mesangial matrix increase and hypercellularity; immunofluorescence reveals diffuse staining for IgA and C3 in all mesangial areas. True statements about this boy's condition include that

(1) depressed levels of C3 and C4 are commonly found
(2) subendothelial and subepithelial deposits are associated with more severe disease
(3) early steroid therapy alters the natural history of the illness
(4) after 25 years, 50 percent of patients will have developed end-stage renal disease

16. True statements regarding immunological and inflammatory responses to glucocorticoid therapy include which of the following?

(1) There are fewer infectious complications with alternate-day therapy than with daily steroid therapy
(2) Chronic steroid administration causes lymphocytopenia and eosinopenia, but not monocytopenia
(3) High-dose steroid therapy causes a decrease in immunoglobulin levels
(4) Permanent damage to the immunological system occurs with long-term steroid therapy

17. Allergic bronchopulmonary aspergillosis is associated with which of the following statements?

(1) Forty percent of sputum cultures are negative for *Aspergillus fumigatus*
(2) It may lead to pulmonary fibrosis if left untreated
(3) Sputum and blood eosinophilia are characteristic
(4) IgE levels fluctuate with disease activity

18. Disorders associated with circulating blood eosinophilia include

(1) atopic dermatitis
(2) Addison's disease
(3) helminthic infections
(4) protozoan infections

19. Which of the following medications would have an equal effect on both the early (immediate) asthmatic response and the late asthmatic response?

(1) Corticosteroids
(2) Albuterol
(3) Theophylline
(4) Sodium cromolyn

20. Bone marrow–derived B lymphocytes exhibit which of the following characteristics?

(1) They are the proliferating cells in chronic lymphocytic leukemia
(2) They carry a surface membrane receptor for the Fc portion of IgG
(3) They carry a surface membrane receptor for the breakdown products of the third component of complement
(4) They have a receptor for the Epstein-Barr virus

21. The functions of the complement system include which of the following?

(1) Direct lysis of cells, bacteria, and enveloped viruses
(2) Mediation of the process of opsonization
(3) Anaphylatoxic activity mediated via the generation of active peptide fragments
(4) Chemotactic activity mediated via the generation of active peptide fragments

DIRECTIONS: Each group of questions below consists of lettered headings followed by a set of numbered items. For each numbered item select the **one** lettered heading with which it is **most** closely associated. Each lettered heading may be used **once, more than once, or not at all.**

Questions 22–25

For each of the following immunological diseases, select the immune defect that is most likely to be associated with that disease.

(A) Decreased immunoglobulins
(B) Serum antibodies to IgA in nearly half of cases
(C) Decreased antibodies to Epstein-Barr virus (EBV) nuclear antigen
(D) Giant cytoplasmic lysosomes in white cells
(E) Abnormal phagocytic respiratory burst

22. Selective IgA deficiency

23. Common variable hypogammaglobulinemia

24. Chronic granulomatous disease of childhood

25. X-linked lymphoproliferative disease

Questions 26–30

For each of the following diseases, select the HLA antigen that is most closely associated.

(A) HLA-B27
(B) HLA-DR4
(C) HLA-DR3
(D) HLA-DR2

26. Reiter's syndrome

27. Multiple sclerosis

28. Ankylosing spondylitis

29. Rheumatoid arthritis

30. Systemic lupus erythematosus

Questions 31–35

Match each of the following characteristics with the immunoglobulin type that it best describes.

(A) IgG
(B) IgA
(C) IgM
(D) IgE
(E) IgD

31. Binding to high-affinity receptors on mast cells via the Fc receptor

32. The only class of immunoglobulin that crosses the placenta

33. The most efficient complement-fixing immunoglobulin

34. The predominant immunoglobulin in membrane secretions

35. The class of immunoglobulin that has four subclasses with differences in their heavy chains

DIRECTIONS: Each group of questions below consists of four lettered headings followed by a set of numbered items. For each numbered item select

A	if the item is associated with	(A) **only**
B	if the item is associated with	(B) **only**
C	if the item is associated with	**both** (A) and (B)
D	if the item is associated with	**neither** (A) nor (B)

Each lettered heading may be used **once, more than once, or not at all.**

Questions 36–40

(A) Bullous pemphigoid
(B) Pemphigus vulgaris
(C) Both
(D) Neither

36. Acantholysis

37. Antibodies against the basement membrane zone

38. Positive Nikolsky's sign

39. Treatment with immunosuppressive drugs

40. Autoimmune disorders

Questions 41–44

(A) Nasal polyps
(B) Sinusitis
(C) Both
(D) Neither

41. Increased incidence in patients with asthma

42. Incidence of approximately 50 percent in asthmatics with aspirin sensitivity

43. Increased incidence in patients with cystic fibrosis

44. Increased incidence in patients with allergic rhinitis

Allergy and Immunology
Answers

1. The answer is D. *(Rosenwasser, JAMA 268:2940–2941, 1992.)* In autoimmune hemolytic anemia, patients produce antibodies against antigens on the surfaces of their own red blood cells. These autoantibodies can be either warm-reacting, as is more common, or cold-reacting, depending on the temperature at which they are most active. In warm autoimmune hemolytic anemia, erythrocytes bind IgG, with or without complement. The IgG is specific against Rh antigens. Coating of the erythrocytes with IgG and complement leads to decreased erythrocyte survival as these cells are phagocytized by macrophages in the spleen and liver. Corticosteroids constitute the primary therapy for warm autoimmune hemolytic anemia. Immunosuppressive drugs and splenectomy may also be necessary. Cold autoimmune hemolytic anemia may be primary or secondary and associated with such diseases as infectious mononucleosis. The cold antibody is usually IgM-specific against I/i antigens. These antibodies bind as erythrocytes move through cooler areas of the microvasculature, such as fingers and nose. Subsequently, the bound IgM activates complement, which leads to phagocytosis of the erythrocytes. Treatment consists of keeping the patient warm. In chronic cases, immunosuppressive therapy may be necessary.

2. The answer is A. *(Wilson, 12/e, p 1400.)* IgA deficiency occurs in approximately 1 out of 700 births. Failure to produce this antibody results in recurrent upper respiratory tract infections in 50 percent of affected patients. IgA-deficient patients frequently have autoimmune disorders, atopic problems, and malabsorption and eventually develop pulmonary disease. Replacement therapy is entirely unsatisfactory. If IgA is totally absent, its administration can represent an antigenic challenge that may result in anaphylaxis. Secretory component is normally present, and very few cases of IgA deficiency are due to a lack of this accessory factor. Some patients compensate for IgA deficiency by secreting a low-molecular-weight 7S IgM antibody.

3. The answer is A. *(Stiehm, Ann Intern Med 107:367–382, 1987. Wilson, 12/e, p 1402.)* The availability of concentrated forms of gamma globulin suitable for intravenous use represents a significant advance in the management of immunodeficiency states. Immune serum globulin (ISG) could not be given intravenously, as the aggregates in the material have spontaneous anticomplementary activity and would cause an anaphylactic-like reaction; intravenous preparations of gamma globulin do not have the spontaneous anticomplementary activity but do retain the ability to activate the classic complement cascade after combining with antigen. Intravenous gamma globulin can be administered to premature babies who have low immunoglobulin levels because of poor transplacental passage of maternal IgG. Apart from its obvious use in the management of congenital and acquired hypogammaglobulinemia, intravenous gamma globulin provides the preferable way of replacing gamma globulin in patients who are severely burned, who have hypogammaglobulinemia secondary to chronic lymphocytic leukemia or multiple myeloma, and who need IgG after plasmapheresis. Patients with selective IgA deficiency may make IgE anti-IgA antibodies that could produce an immediate hypersensitivity reaction to intravenous gamma globulin. The product is prepared from pooled plasma obtained at numerous collection sites, which ensures that antibodies to ubiquitous antigens are represented in each batch of the product. AIDS has been associated with its use. The half-life of the IgG in the product is approximately 27 days, so it can be administered on a monthly basis. Although the mechanisms are as yet unknown, it is of interest that high doses of intravenous gamma globulin (1 g/kg over 5 days) will produce remission in both acute and chronic idiopathic thrombocytopenic purpura in many patients. In addition, its administration has led to remission in autoimmune neutropenia.

4. The answer is B. *(Bart, J Allergy Clin Immunol 79:296–315, 1987.)* Active immunization involves the administration of an antigen into a host to induce an immunological response. This antigen may be live organisms, detoxified bacterial toxins, or structural components of the organisms. After the vaccine is administered, there is a several-day latency period before a primary immunological response is detectable. B cells initially produce IgM and later switch to produce IgG. Although some antigens may be T cell–independent, the switch to IgG synthesis requires T-cell help. Upon reintroduction of the same antigen, a secondary immunological response occurs. This response, which consists solely of IgG, occurs sooner and is more intense than the primary response. Measuring the level of circulating antibodies present after vaccination gives an indication of the adequacy of the immunological response. However, the presence of antibodies does not always insure clinical protection.

5. The answer is A. *(Middleton, 4/e, pp 330–342, 1263–1299.)* Asthma is a reversible obstructive airway disease characterized by edema, hypersecretion, and hyperresponsive airways. It can be categorized as intrinsic or extrinsic. Intrinsic asthma is due to nonspecific physical triggers and respiratory infections. In extrinsic asthma, exposure to inhalant allergens and, rarely, to foods triggers an immediate hypersensitivity reaction. Both types of asthma may be present in the same patient. In extrinsic asthma, allergen triggers either immediate or late-phase responses or, more commonly, both. The immediate response involves IgE on mast cells that reacts with allergen and causes mediator release. This reaction begins 10 to 20 min after exposure to allergen and resolves within 1 to 2 h. IgE may also be involved in the late-phase response and cause mediator release, which attracts inflammatory cells to the area. A late-phase response begins 3 to 4 h after exposure and persists for up to 12 h or longer.

6. The answer is B. *(Middleton, 4/e, pp 363–364.)* Unlike B-lymphocyte receptors, T-cell surface antigen receptors do not bind to native antigen. These receptors recognize and bind antigen fragments only if they are complexed with MHC molecules. The function of presenting antigen to T-cells in a recognizable form is performed by antigen-presenting cells (APCs). APCs take up native antigens and degrade them intracellularly in endosomes. The resulting polypeptide fragments are returned to the cell surface, where they bind to class II MHC molecules, which are expressed on APCs. The complex of antigen and "self-MHC" can then bind to the T-cell receptor. The surfaces of APCs also contain adhesion ligands, which bind to accessory molecules on T-cells and thus strengthen the binding between the two cells. Other ligands on APCs bind to T-cell activation antigens and trigger T-cell responses.

7. The answer is B. *(Roitt, 2/e, pp 8.1–8.12. Wilson, 12/e, pp 76–86.)* The primary immune response involves an initial presentation of antigen to a CD4 inducer T cell by an antigen-presenting macrophage. The latter cell is remarkable for the strong expression of HLA-D histocompatibility molecules on its membrane. T cells, in contrast to B cells, are able to recognize antigen only in the presence of HLA molecules. The macrophage is thus able to present both foreignness (antigen) and self (HLA-D) to a CD4 inducer T cell, an essential step in initiating the immune response. T lymphocytes carrying the surface antigen CD4 (detected by monoclonal antibodies) bind to the HLA-D/antigen complex and then activate the macrophages known as lymphocyte-activating macrophages. These cells release interleukin 1, a messenger substance that binds to a receptor on the surface of the CD4-positive T cell. The CD4-positive T cell then releases interleukin 2, a second soluble messenger substance that causes the activated T cell to proliferate and produce other classes of interleukins that act on activated B cells to stimulate antibody production. Interleukin 2 also binds directly to B cells that have recognized antigen and induces them to mature into plasma cells that will secrete antibody.

8.   The answer is D. *(Levy, Ann Allergy 54:167–171, 1985.)* Hypersensitivity pneumonitis is characterized by an immunological inflammatory reaction in response to inhaling organic dusts, the most common of which are thermophilic actinomycetes, fungi, and avian proteins. In the acute form of the illness, exposure to the offending antigen is intense. Cough, dyspnea, fever, chills, and myalgia, which typically occur 4 to 8 h after exposure, are the presenting symptoms. In the subacute form, antigen exposure is moderate, chills and fever are usually absent, and cough, anorexia, weight loss, and dyspnea dominate the presentation. In the chronic form of hypersensitivity pneumonitis, progressive dyspnea, weight loss, and anorexia are seen; pulmonary fibrosis is a noted complication. In most cases, leukocytosis and eosinophilia are present; the finding of IgG antibody to the offending antigen is universal, although it may be present in asymptomatic patients as well and is therefore not diagnostic. While peripheral T-cell, B-cell, and monocyte counts are normal, a suppressor-cell functional defect can be demonstrated in these patients. Inhalation challenge with the suspected antigen and concomitant testing of pulmonary function help to confirm the diagnosis. Therapy involves avoidance; steroids are administered in severe cases. Bronchodilators and antihistamines are not effective.

9.   The answer is C. *(Patterson, 4/e, pp 479–488.)* One to three percent of patients being treated with penicillin will experience an allergic reaction to the drug. The reaction usually occurs in the first 3 weeks of treatment and is most common when therapy is resumed after an interruption. Allergic reactions can occur with any route of administration; however, anaphylactic or severe generalized allergic reactions are more common when penicillin is given parenterally. Penicillin reactions are of three types: (1) immediate reactions begin within 1 h of administering the drug and usually involve urticaria or anaphylaxis; (2) accelerated reactions begin 1 to 72 h after the drug is given and are manifest as urticaria or angioedema; and (3) delayed or late reactions begin more than 72 h after drug administration and typically involve skin eruptions. The degradation products of penicillin bind to serum proteins to form immunogens. Ninety-five percent of penicillin binds with protein to form the benzylpenicilloyl (BPO) group, or "major" determinant. The majority of antibodies formed in penicillin-allergic persons are specific for this determinant. About 5 percent of penicillin is degraded to various "minor" determinants, which include penicilloates and benzylpenicillin itself. In general, immediate reactions, including anaphylaxis, are usually due to IgE antibodies specific for the "minor" determinants. In contrast, accelerated and many late reactions are usually secondary to IgE specific to the "major" determinants. Accelerated reactions involve preformed IgE, while in late reactions, IgE is formed during the course of the treatment. Twenty-five percent of patients with late-reaction skin eruptions have been found to have IgM specific for the "major" determinant. Skin testing to diagnose penicillin allergy is done to both the "major" and "minor" determinants. The "major" determinant is commercially available as benzylpenicilloyl-polylysine (Pre-Pen). The "minor" determinants are tested with either benzylpenicillin G or a "minor" determinant mixture. The mixture is not commercially available. In patients with a positive history of penicillin allergy, approximately 2 percent will experience an allergic reaction to cephalosporins.

10. The answer is C. *(Middleton, 4/e, pp 1661–1681.)* The incidence of true food allergy in the general population is unknown. However, it appears to be less common than is perceived by the general population. Food allergies are considered to be more common in children than in adults. Studies have demonstrated that exclusive breast feeding can decrease the incidence of allergies to food in infants genetically predisposed to developing them. The major identified food allergens are glycoproteins. Those which most frequently cause allergic symptoms are found in eggs, cow's milk, peanuts, nuts, fish and other seafood, soybeans, and wheat. Food allergens cause symptoms most commonly expressed in the gastrointestinal tract and the skin. In addition, respiratory and, in severe reactions, cardiovascular symptoms may occur. Food allergic reactions are diagnosed by the medical history, skin tests or radioallergosorbent tests (RASTs), and elimination diets. The best test, however, remains the double-blind, placebo-controlled food challenge. If the diagnosis of a food allergy is confirmed, the only proven therapy is avoidance of the offending food. At present, there is no role for immunotherapy in the treatment of food allergy.

11. The answer is E. *(Sussman, JAMA 265:2844–2847, 1991.)* In the last few years, IgE-mediated immediate hypersensitivity to latex has been recognized as an important medical problem. Reactions ranging from contact urticaria to systemic reactions with respiratory symptoms or anaphylaxis have been documented. Groups at risk for latex allergy include those with occupational exposure, such as health care workers and rubber industry workers, and children with spina bifida who are at a high risk for sensitization. An atopic history appears to be an independent risk factor. Natural latex is the milky sap from the rubber tree, *Hevea brasiliensis*. Products manufactured from latex include surgical gloves, condoms, balloons, catheters, and rubber bands. At least four polypeptides from natural latex can bind to IgE. Testing for IgE to latex can be done with skin tests or RASTs. The only current effective treatment for latex allergy is avoidance.

12. The answer is D. *Middleton, 4/e, pp 1012–1015.)* The hyper-IgE syndrome (formerly known as Job's syndrome) affects both males and females by causing chronic dermatitis and increased susceptibility to infections with staphylococcal organisms. Sensitivity to candidal and streptococcal infections can also occur. The recurrent infections are found to affect mainly the skin and respiratory tract, where they lead to the formation of abscesses and pneumatoceles. The condition is associated with extremely high serum IgE levels, often greater than 10,000 ng/mL. Blood and sputum eosinophilia also occurs. Most polymorphonuclear cell functions are normal, with defects in chemotaxis discovered in some patients. Most patients have deficient cell-mediated immune function. An autosomal dominant form of inheritance appears to be involved in this syndrome. Treatment consists of penicillinase-resistant penicillin and surgical drainage of abscesses.

13. The answer is B. *(Middleton, 4/e, pp 1511–1517.)* The incidence of insect sting allergy is difficult to determine. Approximately 40 deaths per year occur as a result of Hymenoptera stings. Additional fatalities undoubtedly occur and are unknowingly attributed to other causes. Both atopic and nonatopic persons experience reactions to insect stings. The responses range from large local reactions with erythema and swelling at the sting site to acute anaphylaxis. The majority of fatal reactions occur in adults, with most persons having had no previous reaction to a stinging insect. Reactions can occur with the first sting and usually begin within 15 min. Enzymes, biogenic amines, and peptides are the allergens present in the insects' venom that provoke allergic reactions. Venoms are commercially available for testing and treatment. Within the Vespidae family, which consists of hornets, yellow jackets, and wasps, cross-sensitivity to the various insect venoms occurs. The honeybee, which belongs to the Apid family, does not show cross-reactivity with the vespids. Patients with systemic reactions are skin-tested with venom concentrations of up to 1 μg/mL. Greater concentrations tend to cause nonspecific skin reactions. Venom immunotherapy is indicated for patients with a history of sting anaphylaxis and positive skin tests.

14. The answer is A. *(Horan, JAMA 268:2862–2864, 1992.)* Atopic dermatitis is a chronic, relapsing, inflammatory skin condition. There are no pathognomonic histological or laboratory features; therefore, the diagnosis is based on clinical features. The diagnostic criteria include pruritus, a typical morphology and distribution, a chronic or chronically relapsing course, and a personal or family history of atopy. In infancy, skin lesions are most commonly distributed on the face and extensor surfaces of the extremities, while in adults the flexor surfaces of the extremities are most often affected. Atopic dermatitis usually begins during infancy and can be classified into the three stages of infancy, childhood, and adulthood. Improvement is often seen during puberty. Various immunological abnormalities are associated with this disorder. Eighty percent of patients have elevated IgE levels, and studies have demonstrated that cell-mediated immunity is defective. The natural history of atopic dermatitis is variable. The more severely affected children have the greatest likelihood of residual disease in adulthood. Topical corticosteroids are the primary treatment of this disorder. Antihistamines can be used to provide additional relief of pruritus.

15. The answer is C (2, 4). *(Wilson, 12/e, p 1179.)* Berger's disease (IgA nephropathy), the most common cause of recurrent hematuria of glomerular origin, usually affects young adult males. It is typically preceded by a viral illness. The hematuria may be gross or microscopic and the proteinuria is usually less than 3.5 g per day, although the nephrotic syndrome is occasionally seen. Diagnosis is based on finding diffuse mesangial deposition of IgA usually accompanied by C3 and less frequently by IgG; C1q and C4 are not found. Fifty percent of patients have elevated levels of IgA, while serum complement levels remain normal. A poor prognosis is associated with azotemia, hypertension, and the nephrotic syndrome at the time of diagnosis and subepithelial and subendothelial deposits on renal biopsy. The disease generally progresses slowly and no form of therapy has been shown to be effective.

16. The answer is B (1, 3). *(Felig, 2/e, pp 548–551, 795.)* In general terms, glucocorticoids affect cellular processes, leukocyte distribution, and macrophages more than they affect humoral processes, leukocyte function, and polymorphonuclear leukocytes. Circulating lymphocytes, monocytes, and eosinophils are decreased secondary to redistribution of these cells into other compartments, while blood polymorphonuclear cells are increased. Within 2 h of administration of steroids, there is a decrease in inflammatory cell accumulation at sites of injury. Lymphocyte proliferation, mediator production, autologous and allogenic mixed leukocyte reactions, and cutaneous delayed hypersensitivity are all suppressed. While there is no evidence that complement components are lowered, a small decrease in immunoglobulins secondary to decreased synthesis and increased catabolism is observed. Because precursor cells are steroid-resistant, permanent damage to the immunological system does not occur. The cushingoid effects of glucocorticoid therapy can be minimized by administering the full 48-h dose as a *single* dose of intermediate-acting steroid on the morning of every other day. However, this transition from daily to alternate-day administration should be attempted only after the manifestations of the disease are reasonably under control and is best made gradually.

17. The answer is E (all). *(Greenberger, Ann Allergy 56:444–448, 1986.)* Aspergillus is a ubiquitous fungus that is usually acquired by inhalation of its spores. While exposure is almost universal, disease is uncommon. Allergic bronchopulmonary aspergillosis is usually a complication of preexisting asthma and is characterized by transient pulmonary infiltrates, sputum and blood eosinophilia, elevated serum IgE, and an immediate-type skin-test response to *Aspergillus* antigen. Patients present complaining of fevers, chills, malaise, and a productive cough. If allergic bronchopulmonary aspergillosis is left untreated, bronchiectasis and pulmonary fibrosis are possible complications. Corticosteroids are the mainstay of therapy. Because evidence indicates that elevations in IgE occur prior to clinical exacerbations, prevention of acute flares is possible with early use of steroids.

18. The answer is A (1, 2, 3). *(Middleton, 4/e, pp 1077–1078.)* Increased numbers of eosinophils in circulating blood are associated with various inflammatory, neoplastic, infectious, and allergic diseases. Normal, healthy adults have a blood eosinophilia of approximately 100 to 125 cells per cubic millimeter. Obvious conditions that are associated with increased blood eosinophilia include hypereosinophilic syndrome and eosinophilic gastroenteritis. Eosinophilia may be a manifestation of an adverse reaction to drugs such as penicillin, phenytoin, sulfonamides, and L-tryptophan. Parasitic infections due to helminths provoke eosinophilic reactions, while protozoan infections do not. The parasites must have a phase in their life cycles in which they invade tissue in order to provoke this reaction. Eosinophilia frequently accompanies atopic disorders such as asthma and atopic dermatitis. In addition, peripheral eosinophilia is seen with endocrine disorders, such as Addison's disease, and with various connective tissue diseases that involve fascia, muscle, or synovium.

19. The answer is D (4). *(O'Byrne, Am Rev Respir Dis 136:740–751, 1987.)* Inhalation of an allergen by a sensitized person leads to a distinct series of events. Within 10 min of the exposure, bronchoconstriction occurs, which continues for 1 to 3 h. This is termed the early, or immediate, asthmatic response. In most asthmatics, this is followed 3 to 4 h after exposure by the late asthmatic response, which may last for 24 h or more. The immediate response occurs secondary to the interaction of allergen with mast cell–bound IgE, which causes mediator release. The late asthmatic response is also believed to be IgE-dependent. However, in addition to the effects of mast cell or basophil mediators, the late response involves airway inflammation with eosinophils and neutrophils predominating. The difference in mechanisms of the early and late responses accounts for their different reactions to various medications. Albuterol and other β-receptor agonists inhibit the early asthmatic response, but have little or no effect on the late response. Theophylline slightly decreases the immediate response and has a significant effect on the late response. Corticosteroids have a minimal effect on the immediate response, while they inhibit the late response. In contrast, sodium cromolyn inhibits both the early and late responses.

20. The answer is E (all). *(Roitt, 2/e, pp 2.6–2.7. Wilson, 12/e, p 79.)* B lymphocytes are cells that mature in the bone marrow and have surface receptors that bind the Fc portion of IgG, some complement components, the Epstein-Barr virus, and, most importantly, specific antigen. The last is accomplished via a specific immunoglobulin receptor molecule. The cells have a short half-life (days) and are thus quite different from T cells that live for years. Oncogenic influence may cause these cells to proliferate and produce chronic lymphocytic leukemia or lymphomas. B cells bind antigen and then divide to form plasma cells. The cells secrete an antibody product identical to that of the receptor on the B cell from which it was derived.

21. The answer is E (all). *(Stites, 7/e, pp 161–173.)* The complement system is composed of a cascade of more than 25 plasma proteins.

These proteins or their cleavage products bind to receptors and thus mediate immune and inflammatory responses. Activation of complement proteins occurs through one of two pathways: the classical pathway or the alternative pathway. The classical pathway is usually activated by the binding of antigen by antibody of either the IgM or IgG class. This antigen-antibody complex then binds to and activates the first complement component (C1). The alternative pathway does not require antibody for activation. It is in a constant state of "low-level" activation beginning with the third complement component (C3). Activators of this pathway include bacteria, yeast, and virus-infected cells, which bind to protect C3 from inhibitory factors. Both the classical and alternative pathways culminate in the formation of the membrane attack complex, which comprises C5b, C6, C7, C8 and C9. The membrane attack complex inserts itself into a cell membrane and allows extracellular water to enter into the cell and cause lysis.

Cleavage products of complement proteins mediate many of the responses to complement activation. For example, foreign particles may be coated with C3b, a cleavage product of C3, which is recognized by receptors on phagocytic cells. Cleavage products of C3 and C5 (C3a, C5a) are anaphylatoxins and bind to receptors on various cells to cause release of histamine, smooth muscle contraction, and increased vascular permeability. In addition, C5a is a potent chemotactic factor for neutrophils and mononuclear phagocytes.

22–25. The answers are 22-B, 23-A, 24-E, 25-C. *(Buckley, JAMA 268:2797–2806, 1992.)* IgA is present in serum as a monomer and in secretions as a polymer consisting of two basic IgA units, a J chain and a secretory component. The secretory component is synthesized by epithelial cells near mucous membranes and may function to transport IgA across the mucosa and into secretions. Selective IgA deficiency is the most common, well-defined immunodeficiency. The most common infections occur in the respiratory, gastrointestinal, and urogenital tracts. Serum antibodies to IgA are found in 44 percent of these patients.

Patients with common variable hypogammaglobulinemia are usually well until 15 to 35 years of age. They then develop pyogenic infections and have an increased incidence of autoimmune diseases. Other associated conditions include a spruelike syndrome, gastric atrophy, bronchiectasis, and pernicious anemia. Most patients with this disease have a defect in B-cell differentiation. Normal numbers of circulating immunoglobulin-bearing B cells are present but they do not differentiate into immunoglobulin-producing plasma cells. About 10 percent of patients with this condition have associated T-cell abnormalities.

Chronic granulomatous disease of childhood is an X-linked disorder with onset of symptoms during the first 2 years of life. Neutrophils and monocytes from these patients have a normal ability to phagocytize organisms but have abnormal O_2-dependent killing of catalase-positive organisms (e.g., *Staphylococcus aureus, Proteus*) owing to a defect in the intracellular respiratory burst enzyme complex. Defects in both cytochrome b-245 and NADPH oxidase have been identified. Patients develop pneumonia, skin infections, draining adenopathy, osteomyelitis, and liver abscesses.

X-linked lymphoproliferative disease, or Duncan's syndrome, is characterized by a poor immune response to infection with Epstein-Barr virus (EBV). Patients with this disease are well until they develop infectious mononucleosis; two-thirds have a fatal outcome. Of those surviving the acute infection, a majority will develop hypogammaglobulinemia, B-cell lymphomas, or both. Patients have an impaired antibody response to EBV nuclear antigen. Other immune defects occur, such as decreased natural killer cell function and depressed antibody-dependent, cell-mediated cytotoxicity against EBV-infected cells.

26–30. The answers are 26-A, 27-D, 28-A, 29-B, 30-C. *(Wilson, 12/e, pp 86–92.)* The major histocompatibility complex is contained on the short arm of chromosome 6 and codes for three classes of cell-surface antigens. Class I antigens—HLA-A, -B, and -C—are found on virtually all nucleated cells. Class II antigens, referred to as HLA-D/DR, are expressed on B lymphocytes, activated T lymphocytes, and monocytes. Another group of antigens, belonging to class III, consists of the C2, C4, and factor B components of complement. HLA antigens play a role in immune recognition. For example, T lymphocytes recognize antigen in conjunction with HLA antigens. There is an increased risk of susceptibility to certain diseases in people who possess particular HLA antigens. For example, HLA-B27 is found in only 7 percent of people of Western European ancestry, yet is present in 80 to 90 percent of patients with ankylosing spondylitis.

31–35. The answers are 31-D, 32-A, 33-C, 34-B, 35-A. *(Stites, 7/e, pp 109–121.)* Mature plasma cells produce immunoglobulins capable of combining with antigenic determinants on diverse substances. Immunoglobulins constitute approximately 20 percent of all plasma proteins. They have a basic structure composed of four polypeptide chains—two light and two heavy chains. Light chains are of two types, kappa and lambda. There are five classes of heavy chains—gamma, alpha, mu, delta, and epsilon. The type of heavy chains an immunoglobulin possesses determines its class. The various classes of immunoglobulins are present in serum in different amounts and have different properties. IgG constitutes 75 percent of the total serum immunoglobulins and is present as four subclasses. IgG is capable of crossing the placenta and fixing serum complement. It is the major immunoglobulin involved in secondary immune responses. IgA represents 15 percent of the total serum immunoglobulins and is the predominant immunoglobulin in membrane secretions. It provides primary immune protection at the mucosal level. IgM exists as a pentameric structure and accounts for 10 percent of normal immunoglobulins. It plays a major role in early immune responses and efficiently activates the classic complement pathway. IgE is present in only trace amounts in serum, but is bound avidly to Fc receptors on mast cells and basophils. When cell-surface IgE is cross-linked by antigen, mediator release occurs and an immediate hypersensitivity reaction ensues. IgD represents less than 1 percent of normal serum immunoglobulins. Many circulating B lymphocytes have IgD on their surfaces, where its function is unclear.

36–40. The answers are 36-B, 37-A, 38-B, 39-C, 40-C. *(Patel, Ann Allergy 50:144–149, 1984.)* Bullous pemphigoid is characterized by large, tense bullae that have a predilection for the inner thighs, flexor surfaces of the forearms, axillae, groin, and lower abdomen; mucous membranes may be involved, as well. Direct immunofluorescence reveals the presence of autoantibodies against the perilesional epidermal basement membrane zone in the lamina lucida where cleavage takes place. A mild vasculitis in lesional skin is also noted. While the disease is generally benign and self-limited, therapy with steroids, sometimes in combination with immunosuppressive drugs, is often used to control eruptions; relapses are infrequent. Healing generally takes place without scarring.

Pemphigus refers to a group of bullous diseases that includes pemphigus vulgaris, pemphigus vegitans, pemphigus foliaceus, and fogo selvagem. Pemphigus vulgaris is the most common type seen in North America and is characterized by acantholysis and the presence of IgG directed against cell surface antigenic determinants on keratinocytes. The bullae tend to spread on pressure (positive Nikolsky's sign), involve large areas, and heal poorly. Therapy involves corticosteroids along with steroid-sparing cytotoxic drugs. Recurrences are not infrequent and patients should be followed every 4 to 6 months after cessation of therapy for clinical or serological recurrence of pemphigus.

41–44. The answers are 41-C, 42-A, 43-C, 44-C. *(Middleton, 4/e, pp 1455–1470.)* Nasal polyps are outgrowths of the nasal mucosa and arise most often from the ethmoid sinus. The incidence of nasal polyps in the general population is unknown, but several groups are particularly susceptible to their formation. For instance, in a study of patients with cystic fibrosis, 26 percent developed nasal polyposis. In another study, 32 percent of asthmatic patients had nasal polyps with the incidence increasing to 49 percent in asthmatic patients with aspirin sensitivity. The pathogenesis of nasal polyps is not known, but both allergic and infectious causes have been postulated. Treatment involves either medications or surgery with a high recurrence rate noted.

There are four pairs of paranasal sinuses surrounding the nasal cavities: the maxillary, ethmoid, frontal and sphenoid sinuses. Factors that predispose to infection of the sinuses include allergic rhinitis, immunodeficiency, and cystic fibrosis. Sinusitis is frequently associated with asthma, although the mechanism for this relationship remains undefined. Treatment of sinusitis involves antibiotics and other medications; persistent or recurrent episodes require surgery.

Infectious Disease

DIRECTIONS: Each question below contains five suggested responses. Select the **one best** response to each question.

45. All the following statements concerning Rocky Mountain spotted fever are true EXCEPT

(A) fulminant cases leading to death in 5 days have been described
(B) the causative organism creates a vasculitis of small arteries and veins
(C) patients may present with severe abdominal pain
(D) the disease usually begins with a rash
(E) patients recovering from the disease are resistant to reinfection

46. Toxic shock syndrome is characteristically associated with each of the following EXCEPT

(A) fever
(B) hypotension
(C) rash
(D) hypercalcemia
(E) *Staphylococcus aureus*

47. All the following statements concerning cryptococcal meningoencephalitis are true EXCEPT

(A) it may be a presenting manifestation of AIDS
(B) it may occur in patients with no identifiable immunological defect
(C) urine or blood culture may be positive for the organism
(D) the India ink preparation usually reveals gram-negative bacteria
(E) detection of cryptococcal polysaccharide antigen in cerebrospinal fluid (CSF) is useful in making the diagnosis

48. Patients with cellular immune dysfunction are particularly susceptible to infection with all the following organisms EXCEPT

(A) cytomegalovirus
(B) *Haemophilus influenzae*
(C) *Mycobacterium tuberculosis*
(D) *Pneumocystis carinii*
(E) *Histoplasma capsulatum*

49. A 30-year-old man who has spent 5 of the last 10 years in prison in New York City is referred from the prison because of hemoptysis. He has a history of tuberculosis diagnosed 3 years ago and took isoniazid and rifampin for about a month. A cavitary lesion is seen on chest x-ray. One should do all the following EXCEPT

(A) obtain sputum for acid-fast bacilli (AFB) stain, culture, and sensitivity
(B) start supervised isoniazid and rifampin administration
(C) start a supervised multiple-drug combination to treat multidrug-resistant tuberculosis
(D) place the patient in respiratory isolation
(E) perform routine screening of inmates and staff for tuberculosis

50. A 43-year-old previously healthy man is admitted to the hospital in September with a fever and a cough productive of nonbloody purulent sputum. The patient states he had an allergic reaction to penicillin as a child and has not taken any antibiotics since then. On physical examination, his temperature is 38.89°C (102°F), the respiratory rate is 22 breaths per minute, and he has signs of right lower lobe consolidation. You examine the sputum Gram stain, which reveals many white blood cells and gram-positive cocci in pairs. Which of the following is the most appropriate action and rationale?

(A) Begin ciprofloxacin to treat *Streptococcus pneumoniae*
(B) Begin erythromycin to treat pneumonia caused by organisms such as *Legionella* and *Mycoplasma*
(C) Begin erythromycin to treat *Streptococcus pneumoniae*
(D) Begin vancomycin to treat *Staphylococcus*
(E) Withhold antibiotics until the organism has been identified

51. A recent outbreak of severe diarrhea is currently being investigated. Several children developed bloody diarrhea and one remains hospitalized with acute renal failure. A preliminary investigation has determined that all the affected children ate at the same restaurant. The food they consumed was most likely to be

(A) pork chops
(B) hamburger
(C) gefilte fish
(D) sushi
(E) soft boiled eggs

52. Infection with *Plasmodium falciparum* is associated with all the following EXCEPT

(A) hemoglobinuria and renal failure
(B) hypoglycemia
(C) cerebral malaria
(D) high-density parasitemia
(E) effective prevention by chloroquine

53. A 40-year-old female nurse was admitted to the hospital because of fever to 39.44°C (103°F). Despite a thorough workup in the hospital for over 2 weeks, no etiology has been found and she continues to have temperature elevations up to 39.44°C. All the following should be considered in the differential diagnosis and further evaluation of the patient EXCEPT

(A) occult bacterial infection
(B) influenza
(C) lymphoma
(D) adult Still's disease
(E) factitious fever

54. In a patient who has mitral valve insufficiency, prophylactic antibiotic treatment is recommended for all the following procedures EXCEPT

(A) cardiac catheterization
(B) prostatectomy
(C) cystoscopy
(D) tonsillectomy
(E) periodontal surgery

55. Rabies, an acute viral disease of the mammalian central nervous system, is transmitted by infective secretions, usually saliva. Which of the following statements about this disease is the most accurate?

(A) The disease is caused by a reovirus that elicits both complement-fixing and hemagglutinating antibodies useful in the diagnosis of the disease

(B) The incubation period is variable and, although 10 days is the most common elapsed time between infection and symptoms, some cases remain asymptomatic for 30 days

(C) Only 30 percent of infected patients will survive

(D) In the United States, the skunk and the raccoon have been important recent sources of human disease

(E) Wild animals that have bitten and are suspected of being rabid should be killed and their brains examined for virus particles by electron microscopy

56. All the following statements concerning herpes simplex encephalitis are true EXCEPT that

(A) it is the most common identified form of nonepidemic adult encephalitis in the United States

(B) the causative virus can usually be isolated from cerebrospinal fluid

(C) the cerebrospinal fluid in affected patients often contains red blood cells during acute illness

(D) it may result in necrosis of brain tissue and high fatality

(E) evidence of a localized brain lesion may be found on electroencephalography

57. All the following may be associated with group A streptococci EXCEPT

(A) scarlet fever
(B) acute rheumatic fever
(C) acute glomerulonephritis
(D) bullous myringitis
(E) toxic shock–like syndrome

58. Medical personnel who have just completed mouth-to-mouth resuscitation on a patient with known meningococcemia should receive chemoprophylaxis with which of the following antibiotics?

(A) Penicillin
(B) Rifampin
(C) Sulfadiazine
(D) Erythromycin
(E) None of the above

DIRECTIONS: Each question below contains four suggested responses of which **one or more** is correct. Select

A	if	**1, 2, and 3**	are correct
B	if	**1 ad 3**	are correct
C	if	**2 and 4**	are correct
D	if	**4**	is correct
E	if	**1, 2, 3, and 4**	are correct

59. A lifelong resident of Connecticut traveled to Arizona to work on a water project in the desert. Shortly after beginning work he developed fever, cough, and shortness of breath. He was diagnosed as having *Coccidioides immitis* by urine wet smear and culture. Other findings that he might be expected to develop include

(1) erythema nodosum
(2) arthralgias   \
(3) pneumonia
(4) erythema multiforme

60. Resistance to antiviral drugs has been demonstrated for

(1) herpes simplex
(2) cytomegalovirus (CMV)
(3) influenza A
(4) human immunodeficiency virus (HIV)

61. Immunizations that would be recommended for a healthy adult over age 65 who has not been immunized for at least the past 15 years include

(1) pneumococcal vaccine
(2) influenza vaccine
(3) tetanus and diphtheria toxoids (Td)
(4) oral polio vaccine (OPV)

62. Correct statements regarding herpes zoster (shingles) include which of the following?

(1) It probably results from reactivation of latent infection in persons who previously have had chickenpox
(2) It usually causes a bilateral skin eruption in a dermatomal distribution
(3) It is often associated with depression of delayed hypersensitivity by immunosuppressive chemotherapy
(4) Severe pain in an affected dermatome usually precedes the onset of the vesicular lesions and lasts until the skin manifestations clear

SUMMARY OF DIRECTIONS

A	B	C	D	E
1, 2, 3 only	1, 3 only	2, 4 only	4 only	All are correct

63. A previously healthy 25-year-old medical student consults you prior to leaving for work in a hospital in tropical Africa. Appropriate topics for discussion include

(1) chemoprophylaxis of malaria
(2) foods and beverages to avoid
(3) measures to reduce exposure to insects
(4) immunization against hepatitis B

64. Infection with influenza A virus may be

(1) treated with an antiviral drug such as amantadine
(2) prevented by an antiviral drug such as amantadine
(3) prevented by immunization
(4) acquired by immunization

65. A diabetic patient who requires insulin is seen in the emergency room with a painfully swollen eye, proptosis, and loss of external eye movements. She is acidotic. Tenderness is elicited over the frontal sinus of the affected side. Rapid involvement of the other eye would suggest which of the following disorders?

(1) Osteomyelitis
(2) Orbital cellulitis
(3) Mucormycosis
(4) Cavernous sinus thrombosis

66. *Streptococcus pneumoniae* is responsible for a significant number of deaths. A vaccine containing capsular polysaccharides from the 23 pneumococcal types responsible for 90 percent of bacteremic pneumococcal infections in the United States is available. Patients who should receive this vaccine include

(1) children who experience, in the first year of life, three attacks of otitis media caused by the pneumococcus
(2) patients with functional or anatomical asplenia
(3) patients with sickle cell disease who have not received a booster dose of vaccine for 2 years
(4) patients over 55 years of age who have chronic cardiovascular disease

67. A 28-year-old woman is brought to an emergency room with an infection in a foot wound sustained 7 days earlier. Examination reveals a moderate degree of cellulitis associated with the wound. Primary immunization at 4 years of age had consisted of three doses of tetanus toxoid and one booster 8 years later. She should now be treated with

(1) wound debridement
(2) diphtheria-pertussis-tetanus vaccine (DPT)
(3) tetanus-diphtheria toxoids (Td)
(4) hyperimmune antitetanus gamma globulin

68. A 36-year-old woman has recently returned to the U.S. after a vacation in Egypt that included several swims in the Nile River. She has developed dysuria and hematuria; eggs of *Schistosoma haematobium* are found in her urine. Correct statements concerning this patient include that

(1) sexual partners are at risk of acquiring infection
(2) praziquantel is the drug of choice
(3) she should use separate toilet facilities until the infection has cleared
(4) if she is not treated, hydronephrosis may occur

69. A 60-year-old man is diagnosed as having *Streptococcus bovis* endocarditis. Appropriate evaluation and treatment should include

(1) throat culture
(2) intravenous penicillin
(3) evaluation for development of rheumatic fever
(4) colonoscopy

70. *Histoplasma capsulatum* is associated with which of the following conditions?

(1) Pneumonia
(2) Pulmonary cavities
(3) Meningitis
(4) Febrile hepatosplenomegaly

71. Antibiotics contraindicated during pregnancy include

(1) trimethoprim-sulfamethoxazole
(2) chloramphenicol
(3) erythromycin estolate
(4) tetracycline

72. Antibiotics associated with pseudomembranous colitis include

(1) gentamicin
(2) ampicillin
(3) tetracycline
(4) clindamycin

DIRECTIONS: Each group of questions below consists of lettered headings followed by a set of numbered items. For each numbered item select the **one** lettered heading with which it is **most** closely associated. Each lettered heading may be used **once, more than once, or not at all.**

Questions 73–76

Match each clinical description with the appropriate infectious agent.

(A) Herpes simplex virus
(B) Epstein-Barr virus
(C) Parvovirus B19
(D) *Staphylococcus aureus*
(E) *Neisseria meningitidis*

73. "Slapped-cheek" rash

74. Desquamation of skin on hands and feet

75. Petechiae on trunk

76. Diffuse rash after administration of ampicillin

Questions 77–79

For each description below, select the most appropriate drug.

(A) Penicillin
(B) Clindamycin
(C) Tetracycline
(D) Ciprofloxacin
(E) Metronidazole

77. Ill feeling when taken with alcohol

78. Poor absorption when taken with antacids

79. Increased theophylline levels

Questions 80–84

Match the following diseases with their appropriate signs.

(A) Koplik's spots
(B) Agammaglobulinemia
(C) A vesicular and pustular eruption that begins when the patient is afebrile
(D) Acute cerebellar ataxia
(E) Pancreatitis

80. Mumps

81. Chickenpox

82. Smallpox

83. Echovirus infection

84. Measles

Questions 85–89

Match the clinical illness with the appropriate opportunistic pathogen in patients with AIDS.

(A) *Pneumocystis carinii*
(B) *Toxoplasma gondii*
(C) *Cryptosporidium*
(D) Cytomegalovirus
(E) *Salmonella*

85. Pneumonia

86. Retinitis

87. Seizures

88. Bacteremia

89. Diarrhea diagnosed by direct examination of stool

Questions 90–95

Match the results of sputum examination with the appropriate clinical setting.

(A) Pneumococcal pneumonia
(B) *Haemophilus influenzae* pneumonia
(C) *Staphylococcus aureus* pneumonia
(D) Tuberculosis
(E) Poor sputum specimen

90. Gram stain shows few epithelial cells, many neutrophils, gram-positive cocci in clusters

91. Gram stain shows few epithelial cells, many neutrophils, gram-positive cocci in pairs

92. Gram stain shows many epithelial cells, few neutrophils, gram-negative rods

93. Gram stain shows few epithelial cells, many neutrophils, gram-negative rods

94. Positive acid-fast stain

95. Positive quellung reaction

Questions 96–100

Match the clinical presentation with the proper helminth.

(A) *Ascaris lumbricoides*
(B) *Necator americanus*
(C) *Onchocerca volvulus*
(D) *Trichinella spiralis*
(E) *Strongyloides stercoralis*

96. Periorbital edema

97. Blindness

98. Gram-negative bacteremia

99. Iron-deficiency anemia

100. Intestinal obstruction

Questions 101–105

For each of the sexually transmitted diseases listed below, select the treatment of choice.

(A) Penicillin
(B) Doxycycline
(C) Ceftriaxone plus doxycycline
(D) Metronidazole
(E) Acyclovir

101. Presumed gonococcal urethritis

102. Nongonococcal urethritis

103. Severe primary genital herpes

104. Trichomoniasis

105. Syphilis

Questions 106–109

Identify the antimicrobial agent associated with the adverse effects listed below.

(A) Gentamicin
(B) Imipenem
(C) Tetracycline
(D) Clindamycin
(E) None of the above

106. Photosensitivity

107. Acute tubular necrosis

108. Progressive weakness in a patient with myasthenia gravis

109. Seizures

Questions 110–115

Match the clinical presentation with the proper helminth.

(A) *Trichuris trichiura*
(B) *Enterobius vermicularis*
(C) *Diphyllobothrium latum*
(D) *Taenia solium*
(E) *Taenia saginata*

110. Vitamin B_{12} deficiency

111. Cysticercosis

112. Perianal pruritus

113. Rectal prolapse

114. Illness following ingestion of raw fish

115. Illness following ingestion of raw pork

Infectious Disease

Answers

45. The answer is D. *(Mandell 3/e, pp 1465–1471.)* Rocky Mountain spotted fever is a disease transmitted by ticks and is the most common rickettsial infection in the U.S. More than 50 percent of cases occur in the South Atlantic region with a prevalence in the spring and summer. The infection is caused by the deposition of rickettsiae into the skin by ticks. A vasculitis of the small vessels is then produced, which may cause infarction in regions of the heart, brain, kidney, skin, and adrenal gland. Patients typically present with fever, chills, headache, and myalgias; a peripherally located, macular rash then appears on the third to fifth day of illness. Gastrointestinal symptoms such as nausea, vomiting, abdominal pain, or diarrhea may dominate the early presentation and suggest an acute surgical abdomen or gastroenteritis.

46. The answer is D. *(Stein, 3/e, pp 1432–1433.)* Toxic shock syndrome is a multiple organ system syndrome with a clinical picture of shock associated with fever and a characteristic sunburnlike rash with subsequent desquamation. Among the many laboratory abnormalities is hypocalcemia, which may be severe. This syndrome is caused by a toxin elaborated by *Staphylococcus aureus*; similar syndromes have less commonly been described in association with other bacteria, including group A streptococci.

47. The answer is D. *(Stein, 3/e, pp 1573–1577.)* Meningitis or meningoencephalitis is the most common clinical manifestation of infection with the fungus *Cryptococcus neoformans*. The majority of patients are immunocompromised (i.e., they are receiving corticosteroid or immunosuppressive therapy or are infected with HIV), but about 35 percent have no identifiable predisposing immunological defect. The diagnosis is confirmed by examination of the CSF. The India ink preparation of CSF will reveal budding yeast in about three-fourths of cases. Cryptococcal polysaccharide antigen is present in CSF in over 90 percent of cases; in most cases this antigen is also present in serum. Culture of CSF is usually positive; cultures of blood and urine are each positive for cryptococci in about one-fourth of patients.

48. The answer is B. *(Mandell, 3/e, pp 2258–2265.)* Patients with Hodgkin's disease or AIDS or those receiving corticosteroid and cytotoxic agents all have in common a dysfunction of cellular immunity that leaves them particularly susceptible to infection with such pathogens as *Listeria monocytogenes, Legionella, Nocardia, Salmonella,* varicella-zoster virus, herpes simplex virus, *Toxoplasma gondii,* and *Strongyloides stercoralis,* as well as those listed in the question. Patients with humoral immune dysfunction, in contrast, lack opsonizing antibodies in their serum and therefore cannot adequately defend against encapsulated organisms such as *Haemophilus influenzae* and *Streptococcus pneumoniae.* Granulocytopenic patients and those with defective leukocyte phagocytic activity are prone to infection with *Candida, Aspergillus,* agents of mucormycosis, *Pseudomonas aeruginosa,* and certain other bacteria.

49. The answer is B. *(CDC, MMWR 42:48–51, 1993.)* Multidrug-resistant tuberculosis (TB) has become an increasing problem in several settings including correctional facilities and health-care institutions. Noncompliance or poor compliance with prescribed anti-TB medications is the major factor in the development of multiple drug resistance. When the disease is suspected, patients should be placed in respiratory isolation and sputum should be obtained for AFB stain, culture, and sensitivity. Treatment of high-risk patients, such as this patient, should be supervised and the possibility of multidrug-resistance should be considered. Regular screening of inmates and staff for TB is important for preventing the spread of TB within the facility and for early diagnosis of new infections.

50. The answer is C. *(Stein, 3/e, pp 1263–1270.)* *Streptococcus pneumoniae* is the etiological agent for the majority of pneumonias that are acquired in the community and severe enough to warrant hospitalization. Antibiotics should be initiated after baseline studies are obtained and should be directed against the most likely pathogen(s). The Gram stain of the sputum in this case confirms that the etiology is most likely to be *Streptococcus pneumoniae.* The drug of choice for pneumococcal pneumonia remains penicillin. In the penicillin-allergic patient, erythromycin is an effective alternative. Erythromycin is also effective in treating pneumonia caused by *Legionella pneumophila* and *Mycoplasma pneumoniae.* These organisms might be suspected where the sputum Gram stain is not suggestive of any one causative agent and in other clinical settings. Ciprofloxacin, which has a broad spectrum of antimicrobial activity, is not the drug of choice for the treatment of pneumococcal pneumonia, even in a penicillin-allergic patient, because of its relatively poor activity against streptococci. Vancomycin is the drug of choice to treat staphylococcal infections that are resistant to agents such as nafcillin, oxacillin, and methicillin and in the penicillin-allergic patient. Staphylococcal pneumonia occurs with increased frequency in the community during and after influenza outbreaks; the sputum Gram stain in such cases reveals gram-positive cocci in clusters.

51. The answer is B. *(CDC, MMWR 42:258–263, 1993.)* The outbreak described is similar to those previously attributed to *Escherichia coli* 0157:H7. Ingestion and infection with this organism may result in a spectrum of illnesses including mild diarrhea, hemorrhagic colitis with bloody diarrhea, acute renal failure, and death. Infection has been associated with ingestion of contaminated beef, in particular ground beef, but also raw milk and contamination via the fecal-oral route. Cooking ground beef so that it is no longer pink is an effective means of preventing infection, as are handwashing and pasteurization of milk.

52. The answer is E. *(Stein, 3/e, pp 1577–1583.)* Infection with *Plasmodium falciparum* should be regarded as a medical emergency. Patients may present with a shaking chill followed by fever and then diaphoresis. Examination may reveal scleral icterus, jaundice, or splenomegaly (but vigorous palpation should be avoided). The parasite load in *Plasmodium falciparum* malaria may be high. Patients with the highest degree of parasitemia are at greatest risk for severe hemolytic anemia and hemoglobinura. This syndrome is called "blackwater fever." Renal failure may occur as a result of hemoglobinuria or hypovolemia or may be medication-related. Cerebral malaria also occurs in patients infected with *Plasmodium falciparum* and may be manifest by a change in mental status, psychosis, or seizures. Serum glucose levels should be monitored in patients with *Plasmodium falciparum* malaria because hypoglycemia may result from a high parasite load or secondary to treatment with quinine. Chloroquine was previously an effective drug for preventing *Plasmodium falciparum* infection. In most areas of the world, *Plasmodium falciparum* is now resistant to chloroquine, and alternative agents are recommended.

53. The answer is B. *(Stein, 3/e, pp 1240–1246.)* Patients may develop fever as a result of infectious and noninfectious diseases. The term "fever of unknown origin" (FUO) is applied when significant fever persists without a known cause after an adequate evaluation. Several studies have found the leading causes of FUO to include infections, malignancies, collagen vascular diseases, and granulomatous diseases. As the ability to more rapidly diagnose some of these diseases increases, their likelihood of causing undiagnosed persistent fever lessens. Infections such as intrabdominal abscesses, tuberculosis, hepatobiliary disease, endocarditis (especially if the patient had previously taken antibiotics), and osteomyelitis may cause FUO. In immunocompromised patients, such as those infected with HIV, a number of opportunistic infections or lymphoma may cause fever and escape early diagnosis. Self-limited infections such as influenza should not cause persistent fever for many weeks. Neoplastic diseases such as lymphomas and some solid tumors (e.g., hypernephroma and primary or metastatic disease of the liver) are associated with FUO. A number of collagen vascular diseases may cause FUO. Since conditions such as systemic lupus erythematosus are more easily diagnosed today, they are less frequent causes of this syndrome. Adult Still's disease, however, is often difficult to diagnose. Other causes of FUO include granulomatous diseases (which include giant cell arteritis, regional enteritis, sarcoidosis, and granulomatous hepatitis), drug fever, and peripheral pulmonary emboli. Factitious fever is most common among young adults employed in health-related positions. A prior psychiatric history or multiple hospitalizations at other institutions may be clues to this condition. Such patients may induce infections by self-injection of nonsterile material with resultant multiple abscesses or polymicrobial infections. Alternatively, some patients may manipulate their thermometers. In these cases, a discrepancy between temperature and pulse or between oral temperature and witnessed rectal temperature will be observed.

54. The answer is A. *(Mandell, 3/e, pp 716–721.)* Although no evidence exists that prophylactic antibiotic therapy prevents endocarditis, prophylaxis is recommended for all procedures that may generate bacteremias. Following cardiac catheterization, blood cultures obtained from a distal vein rarely are positive. Thus, prophylactic antibiotics are not currently recommended for cardiac catheterization. Bacteremia occurs commonly following other procedures such as periodontal surgery, tonsillectomy, and prostate surgery.

55. The answer is D. *(Mandell, 3/e, pp 1291–1303.)* Rabies is caused by a bullet-shaped rhabdovirus. In the United States, dogs seldom are rabid. The animals that represent the most danger are wild skunks and bats; foxes also are possible carriers. Raccoons are responsible for an increasing number of cases in the mid-Atlantic states. The incubation period ranges from 4 days to many years but is usually between 20 and

90 days. The incubation period is usually shorter with a bite to the head than with one to an extremity. In humans, only three definite recoveries from established infection have been reported. Nonimmunized animals that have bitten should be killed and their brains submitted for virus immunofluorescent antibody examination. A negative fluorescent test removes the need to treat the bite victim, either actively or passively.

56. The answer is B. *(Mandell, 3/e, p 764. Wyngaarden, 19/e, pp 2182–2183.)* In active cases of herpes simplex encephalitis, it is rare to culture herpesvirus from the cerebrospinal fluid. Once found, the virus is easily grown; a biopsy specimen from an affected part of the brain, procured early in the course of the disease, is the best means of isolating it. When the index of suspicion is high, treatment with an agent such as acyclovir should be initiated early, even without confirmation of the diagnosis, because a favorable outcome correlates with early initiation of therapy.

57. The answer is D. *(Wilson, 12/e, pp 563–569.)* Group A streptococci cause the majority of cases of pharyngitis of bacterial origin. Infections due to group A streptococci may be complicated because of the production of one or more toxins. Scarlet fever results from infection of a susceptible host with a strain that produces erythrogenic toxin. The rash may be accompanied by a facial flush, characteristic circumoral pallor, and confluent petechiae along skin folds known as Pastia's lines. Another toxin is responsible for causing a severe toxic shock–like syndrome. Pharyngitis and bullous myringitis may be seen in patients infected with *Mycoplasma pneumoniae.*

Treatment of streptococcal pharyngitis is directed primarily at prevention of acute rheumatic fever and suppurative sequelae. Treatment of acute pharyngitis, even as late as 9 days into the course of infection, is adequate to prevent acute rheumatic fever. Whereas group A streptococcal pharyngitis may lead to acute rheumatic fever or acute glomerulonephritis, streptococcal pyoderma due to group A streptococci does not lead to rheumatic heart disease.

58. The answer is B. *(Stein, 3/e, pp 1468–1472.)* Meningococci are gram-negative cocci or diplococci whose natural habitat is the nasopharynx; transmission from person to person is through inhalation of droplets of infected nasopharyngeal secretions. Meningococci may cause either epidemic or sporadic disease. While some people harbor meningococci for years, nasopharyngeal infection is usually transient. Between epidemics, 5 to 15 percent of the people in urban centers carry meningococci in the nasopharynx. In closed populations, the carrier state in close contacts approaches 80 percent. Nasopharyngeal carriage results in production of antibodies in 7 to 10 days. When invasive disease occurs after acquisition of carriage, it usually occurs before the development of specific antibodies. Because carriers, not patients, are the foci from which disease is spread, chemoprophylaxis should be administered to intimate contacts of sporadic cases of meningococcal disease. Rifampin in dosages of 600 mg every 12 h for 2 days for adults and 10 mg/kg body weight every 12 h for children will eradicate the carrier state temporarily and minimize the spread of meningococci.

59. The answer is E (all). *(Mandell, 3/e, pp 2008–2017. Wilson, 12/e, pp 746–747.)* *Coccidioides immitis* has been found in certain semiarid and arid regions of Arizona, Texas, and New Mexico, as well as in Mexico and some parts of Central and South America. Persons entering these regions from nonendemic areas are liable to become infected with this organism, which causes fever, malaise, dry cough, chest pain, night sweats, and anorexia. Erythema nodosum or erythema multiforme and arthralgias may occur 3 days to 3 weeks after the onset of symptoms. The combination of erythema nodosum, arthralgias, and pneumonia represents the classic syndrome of valley fever (primary coccidioidomycosis). Headache and stiff neck occur much less commonly during primary infection. Risk of dissemination from a pulmonary focus is very high in Filipinos, blacks, and pregnant women.

60. The answer is E (all). *(Mandell, 3/e, pp 370–393.)* Antiviral drugs are becoming increasingly available to treat a variety of viral infections. Unfortunately resistance to antiviral therapy has been observed with increasing frequency in the clinical setting, especially in immunocompromised patients who receive medication for prolonged periods. Antiviral resistance has been demonstrated in patients who receive acyclovir for herpes simplex infections, patients who take ganciclovir for CMV infections, and those on zidovudine (AZT) for HIV infection. Resistant virus has also been isolated from patients with acute influenza A infection after just several days' treatment with rimantadine (a drug related to amantadine). This would certainly argue for the prudent use of such agents.

61. The answer is A (1, 2, 3). *(Wyngaarden, 19/e, pp 55–61.)* Adults over age 65 should receive the influenza vaccine on an annual basis. This vaccine is reformulated yearly to include the virus strains most likely to cause epidemics during the following winter. Pneumococcal vaccine should be administered once, although the duration of immunity is not known. Booster immunizations with Td (tetanus and diphtheria toxoids, adult type) should be performed every 10 years.

62. The answer is B (1, 3). *(Mandell, 3/e, pp 1153–1159. Stein, 3/e, pp 1406–1407.)* Herpes zoster (shingles) usually is *unilateral* in distribution. It causes a vesicular skin eruption that often halts abruptly at the midline of its dermatomal pattern. Despite a distinct association with Hodgkin's disease, zoster is not limited to patients with this disease. Frequently, pain along affected dermatomes persists for many weeks after the skin lesion has disappeared.

63. The answer is E (all). *(Stein, 3/e, pp 1345–1347.)* Advice to travelers requires an understanding of the diseases likely to be encountered as a result of the journey in the setting of that particular patient's medical and immunization history. Not only should the physician give the traveler advice as to how to prevent certain illnesses (such as malaria and traveler's diarrhea) and administer any required immunizations, but this is also a good opportunity to review and update the patient's immunization record. Since the medical student is likely to have exposure to blood or other secretions of patients in a region where the carriage rate of hepatitis B is high, hepatitis B immunization would be recommended if it has not already been administered.

64. The answer is A (1, 2, 3). *(Stein, 3/e, pp 1370–1371.)* Amantadine has been demonstrated to be effective in the treatment of uncomplicated influenza A illness when administered early in the course of infection. It will also prevent about 70 percent of influenza A illness if administered prophylactically. The influenza virus vaccine should not be administered to persons with allergy to eggs or egg products. Since vaccine is produced from inactivated viruses, it does not cause infection. The newer drug rimantadine has activity similar to that of amantadine.

65. The answer is D (4). *(Wilson, 12/e, pp 748–749, 2028.)* Patients who have cavernous sinus thrombosis with obstruction of the ophthalmic vein and involvement of cranial nerves III, IV, V, and VI are acutely ill and present characteristic eye findings of proptosis, chemosis, edema, and pain. Extension of the lesion through the intercavernous sinus to the contralateral sinus can be rapid. Although the commonest offending organism is *Staphylococcus aureus*, antibiotic therapy also should include coverage for *Proteus* and *Pseudomonas*. While mucormycosis and orbital cellulitis both enter the initial differential diagnosis of the patient discussed in the question, rapid spread of the lesion to the other eye in these disorders is uncommon.

66. The answer is C (2, 4). *(Mandell, 3/e, pp 1539–1550.)* The fatality rate in patients over the age of 12 with bacteremic pneumococcal pneumonia is about 20 percent. The rate is significantly higher in patients who are over the age of 50, especially patients with chronic disorders including cardiovascular disease, chronic bronchopulmonary and hepatic disease, diabetes, and renal insufficiency. The vaccine is recommended for all patients with sickle cell disease who are more than 2 years old. Unfortunately, the vaccine is of little use in children under the age of 2, who respond poorly to polysaccharide antigens, a circumstance that makes it difficult to protect them from many of the serious bacterial diseases that particularly affect this age group (e.g., *Haemophilus influenzae,* group B *Streptococcus, Meningococcus*). The vaccine is also recommended for adults with chronic cardiovascular or pulmonary disease and adults with splenic dysfunction or other immune suppression, including persons with alcoholism, cirrhosis, renal failure, and CSF leaks.

67. The answer is B (1, 3). *(Mandell, 3/e, p 2325. Stein, 3/e, pp 1461–1465.)* Tetanus toxin, produced by *Clostridium tetani,* causes prolonged muscle spasms of flexor and extensor muscle groups. The masseter and respiratory muscles may be involved and produce lockjaw and respiratory paralysis, respectively. Patients with any type of wound must be considered for tetanus prophylaxis and adequate debridement of the wound. Adults are considered adequately immunized if they have completed a three-dose primary immunization series within 10 years, or if they have received such a series earlier and been given a booster within 10 years. Inadequately immunized adults should receive a booster of Td (tetanus and diphtheria toxoids, adult type) if they completed the primary series, or a series of boosters if they did not. Hyperimmune antitetanus gamma globulin should be given only to patients who either have tetanus or have tetanus-prone wounds and have received either no previous immunization or only a single dose. The pertussis vaccine is usually not recommended for adults because the risk of infection seems to be lower and because vaccine reactions may be more frequent.

68. The answer is C (2, 4). *(Mandell, 3/e, pp 2145–2149.)* Schistosomes are endemic to Puerto Rico, Brazil, the Middle East, and the Philippines and require an appropriate snail intermediate host, which is absent in the U.S., for transmission. The patient in the question, then, is not a threat for spreading infection. Unlike *S. mansoni* and *S. japonicum,* which cause hepatomegaly and diarrhea, *S. haematobium* affects the ureters and bladder, where granulomatous reactions to the eggs occur and may lead to urinary obstruction. Praziquantel is a broad-spectrum antihelminthic agent and is the drug of choice for all human schistosome species; it is well tolerated and only occasionally causes fever, headache, and abdominal discomfort. Other agents effective against schistosomes include metrifonate, which is effective against *S. haematobium,* and oxamniquine, which is effective against *S. mansoni.*

69. The answer is C (2, 4). *(Stein, 3/e, pp 1447–1448.)* Streptococcus *bovis* is a nonenterococcal group D streptococcus that is susceptible to penicillin. Between 5 and 10 percent of normal adults will have *S. bovis* in their stools. Because of an association between *S. bovis* endocarditis and occult colonic neoplasms, persons diagnosed with this infection should undergo colonoscopy or barium enema or both. Unlike infection with group A streptococci, infection with group D streptococci is not associated with sequelae such as rheumatic fever.

70. The answer is E (all). *(Wyngaarden, 19/e, pp 1887–1890.)* Histoplasma capsulatum is an airborne microorganism that causes primary infection of the lung. Lymphatic spread to regional lymph nodes and hematogenous spread to the liver and spleen are common. Infection in all these sites is suppressed by the immune response. A small number of affected patients may suffer relapse associated with hepatosplenomegaly and fever. This type of chronic disseminated histoplasmosis may be mistaken for a lymphoma. Disseminated infection may involve the adrenals, endocardium, pericardium, oropharynx, and larynx, as well as the meninges. Chronic pulmonary histoplasmosis resembles chronic pulmonary tuberculosis and may be associated with cavities.

71. The answer is E (all). *(Chow, Rev Infect Dis 7:287–313, 1985.)* In terms of maternal toxicity, both erythromycin estolate and tetracycline are associated with hepatotoxicity, trimethoprim-sulfamethoxazole with vasculitis, and chloramphenicol with bone marrow aplasia. No known fetal damage occurs as a result of erythromycin estolate administration. In contrast, chloramphenicol is associated with the gray baby syndrome; tetracycline, because it avidly binds to developing bone, with inhibition of bone growth; and trimethoprim-sulfamethoxazole with various congenital anomalies. Essentially all antibiotics are excreted in breast milk, which is an important concern especially in relation to premature infants and those with hereditary enzyme defects.

72. The answer is E (all). *(Wilson, 12/e, pp 581–582.)* A relatively common complication of antibiotic therapy is diarrhea. The diarrhea may result from changes in microbial flora or production of a toxin produced by *Clostridium difficile.* Colonoscopic examination may reveal colitis and pseudomembranes (pseudomembranous colitis). Whereas it was previously believed that only clindamycin caused pseudomembranous colitis, it has more recently been appreciated that this complication may result from virtually any antibiotic.

73–76. The answers are 73-C, 74-D, 75-E, 76-B. *(Stein, 3/e, pp 1231–1233, 1272–1285.)* Parvovirus B19 is the agent responsible for erythema infectiosum, also known as *fifth disease.* This most commonly affects children between ages 5 and 14, but it can also occur in adults. The disease is characterized by a "slapped-cheek" rash, which may follow a prodrome of low-grade fever. A lacelike, diffuse rash may also occur. Complications in adults include arthralgias, arthritis, aplastic crisis in patients with chronic hemolytic anemia, spontaneous abortion, and hydrops fetalis.

Desquamation of the skin usually occurs during or after recovery from toxic shock syndrome (associated with a toxin produced by *Staphylococcus aureus*). Peeling of the skin is also seen in Kawasaki disease, scarlet fever, and some severe drug reactions.

Petechial rashes are often seen with potentially life-threatening infections including meningococcemia, gonococcemia, rickettsial disease, infective endocarditis, atypical measles, and disseminated intravascular coagulation (DIC) associated with sepsis.

Infectious mononucleosis is the usual manifestation of infection with Epstein-Barr virus. Since it is a viral disease, antibiotic therapy is not indicated. A diffuse maculopapular rash has been observed in over 90 percent of patients with infectious mononucleosis who are given ampicillin.

77–79. The answers are 77-E, 78-C, 79-D. *(Wilson, 12/e, pp 478–493.)* Combinations of drugs may have unexpected effects, including effects on absorption of one drug by another, increased or decreased metabolism of one drug by another drug, or interactions between drug metabolites. Metronidazole, which has activity against anaerobic bacteria and certain parasites, may cause a disulfiram-type reaction in patients who drink alcohol. Thus, patients taking metronidazole should be advised to avoid alcohol. Metronidazole may also inhibit the metabolism of oral anticoagulant drugs; thus clotting times need to be carefully monitored, often with a reduction in the anticoagulant dosage. The absorption of tetracyclines from the gastrointestinal tract is decreased by milk-containing products and many antacid preparations. A number of drugs, including erythromycin and most quinolones, may cause elevation of theophylline levels. The quinolones may also increase, to varying degrees, the half-life of caffeine.

80–84. The answers are 80-E, 81-D, 82-C, 83-B, 84-A. *(Mandell, 3/e, pp 1261, 1354–1355, 1375–1376. Wilson, 12/e, pp 686–689, 705–707, 709–711, 715–716, 717–720.)* Although salivary adenitis is the most prominent feature of the communicable disease of viral-origin mumps, it is not uncommon to have involvement of the gonads, meninges, and pancreas. Males who develop mumps after the age of puberty have a 20 to 35 percent chance of developing a painful orchitis. Central nervous system involvement is common but usually mild, with 50 percent of cases having an increase in lymphocytes detectable in the CSF. Myocarditis, thrombocytopenic purpura, and polyarthritis may also occur as complications of this disease. An inflammatory change in the pancreas, however, is a potentially serious problem; symptoms consist of abdominal discomfort and a gastroenteritis-like illness.

Although a polyneuritis and a transverse myelitis have been described, the most common manifestation of CNS infection with varicella is acute cerebellar ataxia. While chickenpox is usually a benign illness in children, other complications such as myocarditis, iritis, nephritis, orchitis, and hepatitis may occur. Pneumonitis occurs more commonly in adults than children.

It can be difficult to distinguish between the vesicular lesions of smallpox and chickenpox. Classically, however, a history of rash with vesicles that develop over a few hours would be typical of a chickenpox infection; vesiculation that develops over a period of days is the rule in smallpox. While fever is characteristic of the prodrome of smallpox, it subsides prior to focal eruptions. Lesions of smallpox are typically all at the same stage of development, in contrast to the various stages seen in a patient with chickenpox. Preparations of vesicular fluid under electron microscopy show characteristic brick-shaped particles with poxvirus. A more readily available test, the Tzanck smear, performed by scraping the base of the lesion, should reveal multinucleated giant cells microscopically in a patient with chickenpox.

Humoral immunity appears to be very important in the recovery from enteroviral infections. One of the most common complications for patients with sex-linked or acquired agammaglobulinemia is a chronic central nervous system infection with an echovirus. In the absence of the ability to produce antibodies, this virus spreads rapidly and usually produces a fatal illness. The administration of intravenous preparations of gamma globulin intraventricularly has controlled this serious complication of immune deficiency in some patients.

It may take from 9 to 11 days for the first symptoms of measles to develop after exposure. Malaise, irritability, and a high fever often associated with conjunctivitis with prominent tearing are common symptoms. This prodromal syndrome may last from 3 days to a week before the characteristic rash of measles develops. One or two days before the onset of the rash, characteristic Koplik's spots—small, red, irregular lesions with blue-white centers—may be visible on the mucous membranes and occasionally on the conjunctiva. Classically, the measles rash will begin on the forehead and spread downward and the Koplik's spots will rapidly resolve.

85–89. The answers are 85-A, 86-D, 87-B, 88-E, 89-C. *(Wyngaarden, 19/e, pp 1928–1957.)* The number of opportunistic infections in patients with AIDS continues to grow. Pneumonia due to *Pneumocystis carinii* was among the first recognized manifestations of AIDS. The chest radiograph typically shows a diffuse bilateral interstitial pattern, but other patterns including a normal radiograph may occur. *Pneumocystis* infection may also occur at extrapulmonary sites.

Cytomegalovirus (CMV) is a frequent disseminated pathogen that causes retinitis that may lead to blindness. CMV may also cause pneumonitis, adrenalitis, and hepatitis, as well as colitis with significant diarrhea.

The protozoa *Cryptosporidium* may cause a chronic diarrhea that leads to malabsorption and wasting. It can be diagnosed by direct examination of the stool with special concentration or staining techniques or both.

Salmonella infections have been recognized with increased frequency in patients with HIV. These patients are typically bacteremic and develop bacteremic relapse; they do not usually present with a diarrheal illness.

Patients who present with seizures warrant an evaluation for toxoplasmosis. CNS lymphoma and certain other infections may also cause seizures. Patients with toxoplasmic encephalitis may also have toxoplasmic chorioretinitis, although CMV remains the most common identified cause of retinitis in patients with AIDS.

90–95. The answers are 90-C, 91-A, 92-E, 93-B, 94-D, 95-A. *(Stein, 3/e, p 1266.)* Examination of a freshly collected sputum specimen is crucial to the early bacteriologic diagnosis of pneumonia and aids greatly in selection of initial antibiotic therapy. An adequate specimen should not be contaminated by oropharyngeal flora, as would be suggested by the presence of many squamous epithelial cells. Knowledge of the appropriate microscopic morphology allows for identification of pathogens: staphylococci, gram-positive cocci in clusters; pneumococci, gram-positive cocci in pairs; *H. influenzae,* small gram-negative rods. The presence of pneumococci can be confirmed by a positive quellung test (a refractory halo around each organism after the addition of serum that contains antibodies to the capsular polysaccharide). Tuberculosis may be suggested by a positive acid-fast stain.

96–100. The answers are 96-D, 97-C, 98-E, 99-B, 100-A. *(Stein, 3/e, pp 1605–1613.)* *Trichinella spiralis* is the cause of trichinosis. Humans become infected after eating larvae in raw or undercooked meat. The typical presentation of periorbital edema, myalgias, petechial hemorrhages, and eosinophilia occurs after an incubation period of 1 to 2 weeks.

Onchocerca volvulus is a major cause of blindness worldwide. The disease onchocerciasis is also known as *river blindness* because it is caused by the bite of an infected blackfly that breeds in rivers and streams.

Strongyloides stercoralis causes a potentially fatal disseminated infection (hyperinfection) in immunocompromised patients. Such patients may present with gram-negative bacteremia and involvement of multiple organ systems. This diagnosis should be excluded before a patient with eosinophilia is begun on immunosuppressive therapy.

Patients with *Ascaris lumbricoides* infection may present with intestinal or biliary obstruction.

Iron-deficiency anemia may be detected in asymptomatic persons infected with hookworm (*Necator americanus* or *Ancylostoma duodenale*).

101–105. The answers are 101-C, 102-B, 103-E, 104-D, 105-A. *(CDC, MMWR 38:1–43, 1989.)* Treatment of gonococcal infections in the 1990s should be guided by the increasing frequency of antibiotic-resistant

Neisseria gonorrhoeae and high frequency of coinfection with *Chlamydia trachomatis*. Because of the increased frequency of resistance to penicillin and tetracyclines, ceftriaxone is recommended as the treatment of choice. Doxycycline is added to treat chlamydial and other causes of nongonococcal urethritis.

First episodes of genital herpes may be particularly severe. Oral acyclovir will accelerate the healing but will not reduce the risk of recurrence once the drug is stopped.

Trichomoniasis is usually diagnosed by a wet preparation microscopic examination or by culture. Both the patient and sexual partner should be treated with metronidazole.

Penicillin remains the drug of choice for treatment of syphilis. The route of administration and duration of therapy depend on the stage of disease and presence of CNS involvement and may also be influenced by the HIV-serostatus of the patient.

106–109. The answers are 106-C, 107-A, 108-A, 109-B. *(Stein, 3/e, pp 1210–1217, 1456–1458.)* The tetracyclines are associated with photosensitization, and patients taking these antibiotics should be warned about exposure to the sun.

Imipenem, a carbapenem, may cause central nervous system toxicity such as seizures, especially when administered at high dosages.

The major toxicity of gentamicin, an aminoglycoside, is acute tubular necrosis; thus, drug levels should be closely monitored. The aminoglycosides may be ototoxic, with effects on vestibular or auditory function or both. This class of drugs can also produce neuromuscular blockade, especially when administered with concomitant neuromuscular blocking agents or to patients with impairment of neuromuscular transmission, such as myasthenia gravis.

110–115. The answers are 110-C, 111-D, 112-B, 113-A, 114-C, 115-D. *(Stein, 3/e, pp 1602–1615.)* The intestinal worms, for the most part, produce disease localized to or resulting from their presence in the gastrointestinal tract. A notable exception occurs with the ingestion of eggs from the pork tapeworm, *Taenia solium*. Larval migration and dissemination throughout the body occur with the formation of fluid-filled cysts. This stage of disease, cysticercosis, can involve almost any tissue in the body, including the central nervous system. Unlike the other helminth infections, such as *Taenia saginata* (beef tapeworm) infection, which are not associated with tissue migration, eosinophilia does occur in cysticercosis and may be very pronounced in association with cyst degeneration.

Trichuris trichiura, the whipworm, may produce rectal prolapse and diarrhea, although most infected patients are asymptomatic.

The adult pinworm, *Enterobius vermicularis,* resides in the intestines. The female worm, after migrating to the rectum at night, deposits her ova on the perirectal mucosa. These eggs are irritative and lead to perianal pruritus.

The fish tapeworm, *Diphyllobothrium latum,* has an affinity for vitamin B_{12} and its ingestion may lead to megaloblastic anemia.

Rheumatology

116. A 55-year-old man awakens with excruciating pain in the first metatarsophalangeal joint of his right foot. His physician identifies needle-shaped, negatively birefringent crystals in white blood cells found in synovial fluid aspirated from the affected joint. The most desirable therapy for this patient would be

(A) allopurinol, 300 mg
(B) colchicine, 3 mg twice a day
(C) sulfinpyrazone, 400 mg daily
(D) indomethacin, 200 mg daily in divided doses
(E) salicylate, 3800 mg daily in divided doses

117. Common manifestations of Henoch-Schönlein purpura include all the following EXCEPT

(A) palpable purpura over the buttocks and lower extremities
(B) colicky abdominal pain, occasionally with diarrhea that contains blood or mucus
(C) bronchospasm
(D) IgA glomerulonephritis
(E) polyarthralgia, often with true inflammatory disease of the joints

118. Ankylosing spondylitis is associated with all the following features EXCEPT

(A) peripheral arthritis
(B) abnormalities of cardiac conduction
(C) uveitis
(D) pulmonary fibrosis
(E) Sjögren's syndrome

119. Deposition of calcium pyrophosphate dihydrate crystals may cause local damage. Such crystals may cause all the following EXCEPT

(A) acute monarticular inflammation (pseudogout)
(B) pseudorheumatoid arthritis
(C) pseudo-osteoarthritis
(D) asymptomatic chondrocalcinosis
(E) pseudoankylosing spondylitis

120. Statements true of gonococcal arthritis include all the following EXCEPT

(A) polyarthralgia and tenosynovitis may occur prior to the onset of arthritis
(B) necrotic or pustular skin lesions are frequent
(C) Thayer-Martin medium should be used to culture the joint fluid
(D) there is a relatively small likelihood that blood cultures will be positive, especially more than 48 h into the illness
(E) there is a female predominance

121. A 65-year-old woman who has a 12-year history of symmetrical polyarthritis is admitted to the hospital. Physical examination reveals splenomegaly, ulcerations over the lateral malleoli, and synovitis of the wrists, shoulders, and knees. Splenomegaly, but no hepatomegaly, is noted. Laboratory values demonstrate a white blood cell count of 2500/mm³ and a rheumatoid factor titer of 1:4096. This patient's white blood cell differential count is likely to reveal

(A) pancytopenia
(B) lymphopenia
(C) granulocytopenia
(D) lymphocytosis
(E) basophilia

122. A 17-year-old girl with a diagnosis of systemic lupus erythematosus (SLE) is referred to you for further evaluation. Among the problems you might expect her to experience would be all the following EXCEPT

(A) Coombs-positive hemolytic anemia
(B) proteinuria
(C) seizures or psychotic episodes or both
(D) deforming arthritis
(E) fever, fatigue, or weight loss or all three

123. All the following statements about inflammatory muscle disease are true EXCEPT

(A) acute rhabdomyolysis and myoglobinuria are rare
(B) childhood dermatomyositis/polymyositis is often associated with vasculitis of the skin or other organs
(C) the classic heliotrope (lilac-colored) rash of dermatomyositis is found on the eyelids, the bridge of the nose, and over the knuckles
(D) ocular muscle disease is common in polymyositis but not dermatomyositis
(E) neoplasia—especially of the lung, ovary, breast, and gut—can be associated with either dermatomyositis or polymyositis

124. A 36-year-old white woman complains of painful joints and morning stiffness that has developed over the last 6 months. Findings compatible with the diagnosis of rheumatoid arthritis include all the following EXCEPT

(A) hot, red, swollen, and tender knees, wrists, and hands in a bilaterally symmetrical distribution
(B) the presence of a firm nodule in the olecranon bursa
(C) a family history of rheumatoid arthritis
(D) inflammation of distal interphalangeal joints
(E) wasting of dorsal interosseous muscle

125. All the following statements about scleroderma are correct EXCEPT that

(A) skin telangiectasias are frequent and may be numerous
(B) weakness and atrophy of the distal muscle groups usually occur
(C) pulmonary interstitial fibrosis independent of pulmonary hypertension is common in advanced disease
(D) stricture of the large bowel secondary to fibrosis in the wall of the intestine may lead to intestinal obstruction
(E) the patient with CREST syndrome rarely has cardiac involvement

126. Viral arthritis can occur in all the following situations EXCEPT

(A) as part of a serum sickness syndrome in the preicteric phase of infection with hepatitis B virus
(B) as a self-limited feature of parvovirus infection, especially in females
(C) as a destructive disease, especially after recurrent infections with related viruses
(D) after either natural infection with rubella or after inoculation with the attenuated vaccine
(E) after resolution of the parotitis of mumps infection, especially in young men

127. Well-described features of Sjögren's syndrome include all the following EXCEPT

(A) pseudolymphoma
(B) keratoconjunctivitis
(C) autoimmune hypothyroidism
(D) immune complex–related glomerulonephritis
(E) vasculitis, most often palpable purpura

128. All the following statements about Lyme disease are true EXCEPT

(A) lymphocytic meningitis, peripheral neuropathy, and cranial nerve palsies may occur days to weeks after the tick bite
(B) Lyme arthritis typically affects the small joints of the hands and feet with onset within days to weeks of the tick bite
(C) hematogenous spread of the organism occurs shortly after the initial inoculation (tick bite)
(D) fatigue, lethargy, and noninflammatory musculoskeletal pain may persist for months after antibiotic therapy has concluded
(E) late neurological features of Lyme disease can include an organic brain syndrome, encephalopathy, and peripheral neuropathy

DIRECTIONS: Each question below contains four suggested responses of which **one or more** is correct.' Select

A	if	**1, 2, and 3**	are correct
B	if	**1 and 3**	are correct
C	if	**2 and 4**	are correct
D	if	**4**	is correct
E	if	**1, 2, 3, and 4**	are correct

129. Correct statements about psoriatic arthritis include which of the following?

(1) Arthritis occurs in 20 to 25 percent of patients with psoriasis

(2) HLA-B27 is strongly associated with sacroiliitis and spondylitis, but not peripheral arthritis, in patients with psoriatic arthritis

(3) Seventy percent of patients with psoriatic arthritis have seronegative symmetrical polyarthritis

(4) The flexor tendon sheaths in the fingers are often inflamed and swollen ("sausage" digits)

130. Joints typically affected in osteoarthritis include

(1) distal interphalangeal joints of the hands

(2) wrists

(3) proximal interphalangeal joints of the hands

(4) elbows

131. Local causes of shoulder pain include bursitis and tendinitis. True statements about these disorders include which of the following?

(1) Rheumatoid arthritis may be a predisposing factor in bursitis

(2) Of the rotator cuff muscles, the most commonly affected by tendinitis is the supraspinatus

(3) A crystal-induced cause of shoulder pain is the "Milwaukee shoulder syndrome," caused by calcium hydroxyapatite crystals

(4) Following rotator cuff inflammation, a "frozen shoulder," or adhesive capsulitis, may occur with near universal permanent disability

132. True statements regarding the inflammatory joint disease seen in inflammatory bowel disease include

(1) axial disease is associated with HLA-B27 positivity
(2) the activity of peripheral joint disease usually correlates with that of the colitis
(3) peripheral arthritis is usually not associated with the presence of rheumatoid factor or antinuclear antibodies in the serum
(4) arthritis is more common in ulcerative colitis than in Crohn's disease

133. Correct statements about the etiology and pathogenesis of osteoarthritis include which of the following?

(1) Osteoarthritic cartilage undergoes increased metabolic activity and increased cell division, which indicates that increased degradation and increased synthesis of cartilage matrix occur concurrently
(2) Routine laboratory tests show no abnormalities in osteoarthritis
(3) Extensive osteoarthritis may be found late in the course of acromegaly
(4) Compensatory changes in subchondral bone in osteoarthritic joints include softening and increased water content, which serve to cushion the articular cartilage

134. A 17-year-old white male high school student seeks medical advice because of recurrent low back pain and stiffness that last for a few days after each football game and practice. No morning stiffness is noted. The patient is otherwise healthy and has no family history of joint problems and no abnormal physical findings. Radiographic examination of his spine and sacroiliac joint reveals no abnormalities. Serological studies are not helpful and the patient's erythrocyte sedimentation rate is 13 mm/h (Westergren method). However, the patient is found to have the histocompatibility antigen HLA-B27 on his leukocytes. With this information, the physician can now advise the patient that

(1) he should have an x-ray examination of his large bowel
(2) he should have a slitlamp examination of his eyes
(3) he should have gold therapy for the next year while his physician observes him closely for signs of developing spondylitis
(4) he has a 25 percent or less chance of developing significant spondylitis

DIRECTIONS: Each group of questions below consists of four lettered headings followed by a set of numbered items. For each numbered item select the **one** lettered heading with which it is **most** closely associated. Each lettered heading may be used **once, more than once, or not at all.**

Questions 135–139

For each condition select the drug with which it is closely associated.

(A) Acetylsalicylic acid (aspirin)
(B) Gold
(C) Prednisone
(D) Chloroquine
(E) None of the above

135. Gastrointestinal bleeding

136. Osteoporosis

137. Retinopathy

138. Proteinuria

139. Stomatitis

Questions 140–144

Match each description with the appropriate disease.

(A) Polyarteritis nodosa
(B) Wegener's granulomatosis
(C) Giant cell arteritis
(D) Multiple cholesterol embolization syndrome
(E) Takayasu's arteritis

140. Involvement of the upper and lower respiratory tracts; a cause of glomerulonephritis

141. Ecchymoses and necrosis in extremities in elderly patients

142. Inflammation of small- to medium-size muscular arteries, which may cause kidney, heart, liver, gastrointestinal, and muscular damage

143. Patients above the age of 55, who may experience fever, weight loss, scalp pain, headache, and visual changes

144. Inflammation of the aorta and its branches in young women; also known as "pulseless disease"

DIRECTIONS: The group of questions below consists of four lettered headings followed by a set of numbered items. For each numbered item select

A	if the item is associated with	(A) **only**
B	if the item is associated with	(B) **only**
C	if the item is associated with	**both** (A) and (B)
D	if the item is associated with	**neither** (A) nor (B)

Each lettered heading may be used **once, more than once, or not at all.**

Questions 145–149

    (A) Gonococcal arthritis
    (B) Reiter's syndrome
    (C) Both
    (D) Neither

145. Uveitis

146. Balanitis

147. Arthritis involving predominantly joints of the upper extremities

148. HLA-B27–positive patients in 6 to 8 percent of cases

149. Stomatitis

Rheumatology

Answers

116. The answer is D. *(Wilson, 12/e, pp 1834–1841.)* Appropriate therapy of acute gouty arthritis can be divided into two phases. In the first phase, the acute gouty inflammation is controlled by anti-inflammatory agents or by giving colchicine, orally or intravenously. In the second phase, the serum urate level is lowered by uricosuric agents or drugs designed to inhibit the development of uric acid. Traditionally, acute gouty inflammation has been controlled by giving colchicine on an hourly basis until a therapeutic response occurs. However, as many as 80 percent of gout patients cannot achieve satisfactory therapeutic levels with colchicine because of the toxicity of the drug. Certainly, colchicine 3 mg twice a day would be too high a dose, although 2 mg given intravenously may give very good results. Anti-inflammatory drugs such as indomethacin or phenylbutazone have been found to be as effective as colchicine and to have fewer of the gastrointestinal side effects frequently associated with colchicine. Sulfinpyrazone and probenecid, both uricosuric agents, are not effective in acute flare. Allopurinol, a xanthine oxidase inhibitor, and the uricosuric agents probenecid and sulfinpyrazone effectively reverse hyperuricemia, but do not relieve inflammation associated with acute attacks of gouty arthritis. Allopurinol would be inappropriate therapy during an acute flare because this drug can precipitate further activity of gout, e.g., polyarticular gout.

117. The answer is C. *(Wilson, 12/e, pp 1458–1459.)* Henoch-Schönlein purpura, also known as anaphylactoid purpura, is a small vessel (leukocytoclastic) vasculitis that causes purpura of the lower extremities and buttocks, colicky abdominal pain, arthritis, and glomerulonephritis (usually with the finding of IgA in the glomerulus and often with IgA-containing immune complexes in the serum). Lung disease is not part of the features of this syndrome. Churg-Strauss disease (allergic angiitis and granulomatosis), which is a vasculitis that affects small to medium arteries, is seen in patients who often have a history of atopy and prior asthma, and this vasculitic syndrome can include bronchospasm.

118. The answer is E. *(Wilson, 12/e, pp 1451–1455.)* Ankylosing spondylitis, an inflammation of the spine, also involves the hip, shoulder, and, in 25 percent of patients, the peripheral joints. It is often associated with aortic regurgitation, conduction abnormalities that may require pacemaker therapy, acute anterior uveitis in 30 percent of patients, and, in long-standing disease, bilateral pulmonary fibrosis of the upper lobe. HLA-B27 is found in the vast majority of patients; the linkage is weaker in nonwhite persons. Ankylosing spondylitis must be differentiated from other diseases associated with spondylitis, such as inflammatory bowel disease, psoriatic arthritis, and Reiter's syndrome. The clinical course is characterized by remissions and exacerbations, although a persistently progressive course may occur. Symptomatic relief may be achieved using nonsteroidal anti-inflammatory drugs. Pain often disappears after total ankylosis of the joint occurs. The uveitis is treated with intraocular steroids. The progression of the disease is not halted, however, by any of these measures. Sjögren's syndrome is not seen in ankylosing spondylitis.

119. The answer is E. *(Wilson, 12/e, pp 1480, 1826, 1834–1841, 1904.)* Calcium pyrophosphate dihydrate (CPPD) deposition disease may produce an asymptomatic calcification in cartilages (especially the knees, symphysis pubis, and triangular ligament of the wrists) called chondrocalcinosis. This is relatively common in older persons and by itself causes no damage. Monarticular inflammation, resembling a flare of gout and called *pseudogout,* can be seen in CPPD deposition and be diagnosed by synovial fluid analysis. Clinically, pseudogout is identical to gout. A pattern of joint disease resembling rheumatoid arthritis, called *pseudorheumatoid arthritis,* may occur. Inflammation is present by history and on clinical examination, but these patients do not have circulating rheumatoid factor and their joints show a pattern of destruction more like extensive osteoarthritis than the classic pattern of rheumatoid arthritis. CPPD deposition disease can be associated with extensive osteoarthritic changes that appear to be virtually identical to those of osteoarthritis on x-ray, but occur in an atypical distribution, e.g., affecting the metacarpophalangeal joints, wrists, elbows, shoulders, and ankles. When this clinical picture occurs, the clinician should suspect CPPD deposition disease and consider the metabolic causes of CPPD deposition disease, which include hyperparathyroidism and hemochromatosis, most notably. The clinical course of pseudorheumatoid arthritis and pseudo-osteoarthritis may be punctuated by flares of pseudogout. CPPD deposition disease is not associated with spine disease, or anything resembling ankylosing spondylitis.

120. The answer is C. *(Wilson, 12/e, pp 544–548, 596–597.)* Gonococcal arthritis is a manifestation of a disseminated infection and is often spread from an asymptomatic primary genital, anal, or oral infection. Tenosynovitis and polyarthralgia may occur before the onset of frank arthritis, often in association with cutaneous features like pustules or necrotic lesions. Blood cultures are infrequently positive once the arthritis has begun, but may be positive in the earlier polyarthralgia/ tenosynovitis phase, which is felt to be due to hematogenous spread of the organism. Female predominance of disseminated gonococcal infection is noted and spread of the infection during menses often occurs. Thayer-Martin (TM) medium was designed for culturing the organism from cervical secretions; this medium contains antibiotics to suppress the growth of the normal cervical flora. Since there is no normal flora in joint fluid (or cerebrospinal fluid), the antibiotics in TM medium are not necessary and in fact may interfere with the growth of gonococcus. TM medium can be of value, however, for anal or oral swabs.

121. The answer is C. *(Wilson, 12/e, pp 357–359, 1439.)* Felty's syndrome consists of a triad of rheumatoid arthritis, splenomegaly, and leukopenia. In contrast to the lymphopenia observed in patients who have systemic lupus erythematosus, the leukopenia of Felty's syndrome is related to a reduction in the number of circulating polymorphonuclear leukocytes. The mechanism of the granulocytopenia is poorly understood. Felty's syndrome tends to occur in people who have had active rheumatoid arthritis for a prolonged period. These patients commonly have other systemic features of rheumatoid disease such as nodules, skin ulcerations, the sicca complex, peripheral sensory and motor neuropathy, and arteritic lesions.

122. The answer is D. *(Wilson, 12/e, pp 1432–1437.)* Hematological disease is frequent in SLE, with lymphopenia, leukopenia, anemia, or thrombocytopenia serving as one of the American College of Rheumatology criteria for the diagnosis of SLE. Other criteria include proteinuria or cellular casts (there are a number of different histological patterns on kidney biopsy), neurological disease (seizures or psychosis or both; peripheral neuropathy and organic brain syndromes also occur, but are not on the criteria list), cardiopulmonary disease (pleurisy and pericarditis—the old name for SLE was *polyserositis*), cutaneous lesions (malar rash in a "butterfly" distribution, discoid lesions, photosensitivity rash, and oral ulcers are each a separate criterion), and arthritis. The arthritis of SLE is typically a nonerosive, nondeforming polyarthritis; the hand deformities, rarely seen, are due to ligamentous laxity at the metacarpophalangeal joints that causes pseudosubluxation—so called Jaccoud's arthritis. Fever, fatigue, malaise, anorexia, nausea, and weight loss are frequent systemic manifestations of SLE and often quite difficult to treat. SLE is more common in people of African, Asian, and Hispanic descent than in whites in the U.S.; 90 percent of all cases occur in women. Patients with SLE usually have antinuclear antibodies in their serum (although this test is *not* specific for SLE), as well as an ever-increasing number of other autoantibodies, including antibodies that bind to neurons, lymphocytes, erythrocytes, platelets, and many cellular and nuclear components.

123. The answer is D. *(Wilson, 12/e, pp 321–322, 2108–2111.)* Inflammatory muscle disease is usually a subacute process and rarely causes acute rhabdomyolysis. The childhood variant may be associated with cutaneous or inner organ vasculitis and occasionally with subcutaneous calcifications. The skin changes that occur with dermatomyositis include the heliotrope rash, which is found over the bridge of the nose, the eyelids, and the knuckles, and Gottron's sign, which consists of violaceous, flat-topped papules found over the distal interphalangeal joints. The relationship of myositis to neoplasia has been accepted; the tumors implicated are those seen in the population over 55 years old. In the absence of coexisting myasthenia gravis or other muscle or neurological diseases, the ocular muscles are usually spared in polymyositis.

124. The answer is D. *(Wilson, 12/e, pp 1437–1443.)* Rheumatoid arthritis (RA) occurs in the third through fifth decades of life and affects women about three times as often as men. There is often a family history of RA. Insidious onset of inflammation of multiple joints, anorexia, fever, weight loss, and weakness occur in about two-thirds of patients; about one-third of patients will have disease in one or only a few joints. Where polyarticular disease occurs, it is usually found in a bilaterally symmetrical distribution and usually affects the metacarpophalangeal, wrist, elbow, knee, ankle, and metatarsophalangeal joints. The proximal interphalangeal joints are also often affected, but the distal interphalangeal joints are not; inflammation at the latter location suggests another disease, e.g., psoriatic arthritis. Patients with high-titer rheumatoid factor are predisposed to developing extraarticular manifestations of *rheumatoid disease* (this term, preferable to *rheumatoid arthritis,* accents the multisystem nature of the disease), such as rheumatoid nodules, which often occur near the olecranon bursa. Other extraarticular manifestations include nodular and fibrotic lung disease, scleritis, and vasculitis. Wasting of dorsal interosseous muscle is common when the metacarpophalangeal joints are inflamed; atrophy often occurs in muscles near inflamed joints, e.g., the quadriceps muscle.

125. The answer is B. *(Wilson, 12/e, pp 1443–1448.)* Scleroderma, or progressive systemic sclerosis, is a disease in which many organs may be damaged by the relentless deposition of fibrous connective tissue. Most frequently affected are the skin and blood vessels, but the gastrointestinal tract, lungs, kidneys, and heart are also commonly involved. Although scleroderma that is localized to the skin may be compatible with a normal life span, systemic involvement is often fatal. Gradual thickening of the skin is associated with loss of mobility that will eventually make it difficult to flex the finger joints normally. In addition and classically, telangiectasias are prominent. When muscles are involved in the sclerodermatous destructive process, they are usually proximal muscle groups in a polymyositis-like syndrome. There has been much recent interest in the lung disease that commonly complicates the course of scleroderma. Pulmonary hypertension is common and may lead to cor pulmonale when pulmonary blood vessels are affected by the fibrotic process. However, interstitial pulmonary fibrosis can develop with alveolar involvement. Although this may represent the direct effects of the disease process, esophageal reflux is so common that a number of studies have demonstrated fibrotic changes in the lung secondary to the aspiration of gastric contents, particularly while the patient sleeps at night. In such cases surgical intervention may be necessary to protect the lungs. As fibrosis destroys the autonomic nerve supply to the intestinal tract, hypomotility and dilatation of the intestinal tract occur. Slowing the passage of food content through the intestinal tract may lead to a malabsorption syndrome. Obstruction due to intestinal fibrosis may occur. The CREST syndrome involves the deposition of Calcium in the skin, the presence of Raynaud's phenomenon, Esophageal hypomotility, Sclerodactyly, and Telangiectasis. It is of interest that while extensive myocardial dysfunction can occur secondary to fibrotic changes in the heart, this is extremely unusual in the CREST syndrome. Serological evidence would suggest a different immunological mechanism may be responsible for the CREST syndrome. Three forms of antinuclear antibody appear to be specific for scleroderma. Antibody to Scl-70 antigen as well as to the nuclear centromere and nucleolar antigens has been demonstrated. The anticentromere antibody is primarily seen in patients with the CREST form of the disease. Treatment of the disease is mainly symptomatic. Steroids do not help, but the malabsorption syndrome is frequently helped by the use of broad-spectrum antibiotics. Captopril, the oral angiotensin-converting enzyme inhibitor, has helped a number of patients with serious hypertension, and in severe ischemic crises sympathectomy has reversed some of the effects of the Raynaud's phenomenon.

126. The answer is C. *(Wilson, 12/e, p 547.)* Before causing jaundice, there may be a phase of disease caused by the immune response to hepatitis B virus rather than the direct effects of the infection. Immune complexes formed at this stage of the infection may cause serum sickness or even a true systemic necrotizing vasculitis indistinguishable from polyarteritis nodosa. Arthritis may be a manifestation of the serum sickness seen in this infection. Parvovirus can cause a self-limited arthritis that is usually seen in women and occasionally affects multiple joints in a symmetrical distribution suggestive of the diagnosis of rheumatoid arthritis, although parvovirus arthritis resolves spontaneously and is usually not associated with rheumatoid factor positivity. Rubella and mumps can also cause arthritis, as can Epstein-Barr virus. In general, however, viral arthritis does not cause erosive, deforming, or nodular disease and usually resolves spontaneously.

127. The answer is D. *(Wilson, 12/e, pp 1449–1450.)* Sjögren's syndrome is a multisystem inflammatory disease often seen in association with other "autoimmune" diseases, like lupus, rheumatoid arthritis, and occasionally Hashimoto's thyroiditis. Dryness of the eyes and mouth, or sicca complaints, are common; the loss of tears causes a pathognomonic keratinization of the cornea, keratoconjunctivitis sicca. Vasculitis can occur, as can central nervous system manifestations. Renal features of Sjögren's syndrome do not include glomerulonephritis, as seen in lupus, but an interstitial nephritis, the manifestation of which is most often a renal tubular acidosis. Diminution of renal function can occur, usually in the presence of extreme interstitial fibrosis in longstanding cases. Pseudolymphomas can occur. They represent an aggregation of normal lymphocytes into masses in the lymph node, parotid gland, or lung. While they appear clinically to be lymphoma, they have none of the hallmarks of malignancy on histological evaluation. Approximately 10 percent of all patients with pseudolymphoma in Sjögren's syndrome will go on to develop a non-Hodgkin's lymphoma.

128. The answer is B. *(Wilson, 12/e, pp 667–669.)* Lyme disease occurs after the inoculation of the causative agent, *Borrelia burgdorferi,* into the skin by the bite of an infected tick. A local rash, erythema migrans, occurs in 50 to 80 percent of patients. Hematogenous spread probably occurs within days. Therapy with oral antibiotics in the early phases of the infection is usually curative, but some patients may experience a few months of nonspecific complaints after the termination of therapy; these complaints, including headache, fatigue, and pain, resolve spontaneously without any further antibiotics. Meningitis and neuropathy can occur within days to weeks of the start of Lyme disease. Arthritis usually occurs months to many years later, occasionally in association with late neurological features, which are now termed *tertiary neuroborreliosis*.

129. The answer is C (2, 4). *(Wilson, 12/e, pp 1453–1455, 1482–1484.)* Five percent of patients suffering from psoriasis develop an arthritic syndrome. Usually the psoriasis is present for many years before joint inflammation develops, but occasionally arthritis may occur before the skin disease. The different syndromes associated with psoriatic arthritis are subgrouped according to the joints involved. At least 70 percent of patients with psoriatic arthritis have a monarticular or asymmetrical oligoarticular arthritis. The smaller joints in the hands and feet can be involved and a classic finding is the sausage-shaped digits produced when the flexor tendon sheaths in the fingers become swollen and inflamed. Fifteen percent of patients with psoriatic arthritis present with a seronegative rheumatoid arthritis–type picture. A third group of patients suffer from arthritis that is limited to the distal interphalangeal joints, and with this form pitting of the fingernails is characteristic. A rare form of psoriatic arthritis is associated with a destructive arthropathy. This form tends to occur in men more than women, although psoriatic arthritis in general is more common in females. Sacroiliitis and spondylitis also occur in association with psoriasis. There is a linkage with HLA-B27 but not as strongly as is seen in ankylosing spondylitis (65 percent in psoriatic disease, up to 95 percent in ankylosing spondylitis). Between 10 and 20 percent of patients with psoriatic arthritis have hyperuricemia, but this rarely leads to crystal formation in joints and is more a reflection of the severity of the skin disease. The treatment of this form of arthritis is similar to that of rheumatoid arthritis.

130. The answer is B (1, 3). *(Wilson, 12/e, pp 1475–1479.)* The joints most frequently affected in osteoarthritis include the distal and proximal interphalangeal joints, the first carpometacarpal joint, the knees, and the hips. Elbows, wrists, and metacarpophalangeal joints are commonly affected in rheumatoid arthritis but are essentially never affected in osteoarthritis unless there has been prior joint damage, e.g., infection, trauma, overuse, or underlying calcium pyrophosphate dihydrate deposition disease.

131. The answer is A (1, 2, 3). *(Wilson, 12/e, pp 101, 122–123, 1488–1489.)* All that hurts in and near a joint is not arthritis; another cause of pain may be inflammation of periarticular structures, like the bursa or tendons. Inflammatory joint disease may predispose to tendinitis, especially if previous damage or splinting of the joint causes changes in the biomechanics of the shoulder apparatus. The rotator cuff consists of the supraspinatus, infraspinatus, teres minor, and subscapularis muscles (SITS). The supraspinatus is a long, thin muscle, whose central portion is poorly vascularized and often compressed by the underlying humeral head—a prime target for local damage and inflammation. Rotator cuff tendinitis may lead to "frozen shoulder." Most such patients will improve spontaneously within about 2 years. Hydroxyapatite crystals in the glenohumeral joint or in the tendons may occur and cause inflammation and ultimately rotator cuff rupture or shoulder osteoarthritis. This is called the "Milwaukee shoulder syndrome," named after the city where it was first described.

132. The answer is E (all). *(Wilson, 12/e, pp 1264–1278.)* Two kinds of inflammatory joint disease have been associated with inflammatory bowel disease: axial (spine and sacroiliac disease) and peripheral joint disease. The former is often seen in association with HLA-B27 in the affected person. Axial disease does not wax and wane in parallel with the activity of the colitis. Peripheral arthritis, however, usually does vary with the colitis. Arthritis is more common in colonic disease than in small bowel disease. Rheumatoid factor and antinuclear antibodies are usually not found in these patients.

133. The answer is A (1, 2, 3). *(Wilson, 12/e, pp 1475–1479.)* The term *degenerative joint disease* is to be eschewed and replaced by the more proper *osteoarthritis*. The major characteristics of osteoarthritis are loss of joint cartilage and hypertrophy of bone, including subchondral sclerosis and osteophyte formation. Within osteoarthritic cartilage, there is a marked increase in metabolic activity owing to the increased rate of destruction of cartilage accompanied by an increased synthesis of cartilage matrix. The increased proteolytic activity in the joint space is associated with higher-than-normal levels of proteases, particularly cathepsin D and similar hydrolases. As the disease progresses, cartilage is steadily lost from the joint because anabolic processes are unable to keep up with catabolism. Thus, there is evidence to suggest that osteoarthritis involves active metabolic processes and is not merely the end result of "wear and tear." Because routine laboratory tests cannot detect the abnormalities, radiological observation of changes in joints still provide the most useful information for arriving at a diagnosis of osteoarthritis. The excessive secretion of growth hormone in patients with acromegaly is thought to be responsible for the thickening of synovial tissues and the overgrowth of joint cartilage that characterize the articular changes seen early in this disease. This cartilage is abnormal and is unable to effectively bear weight. If acromegaly is untreated, marked changes will occur in joints. The subchondral bone in the osteoarthritic joint becomes metabolically active and new bone is produced. This leads to osteophyte formation and sclerosis of the subchondral bone. The result is stiffening of the bone beneath the cartilage, which decreases the bone's ability to absorb forces produced in joint loading; this loss of cushioning may contribute to cartilage damage.

134. The answer is C (2, 4). *(Wilson, 12/e, pp 90–92, 1451–1453, 1483–1484.)* The HLA-B27 antigen is found on the leukocytes of 90 percent of patients with ankylosing spondylitis, but is also present in 7 percent of normal whites. Therefore, the routine use of this test in an individual is usually not valuable for diagnosing inflammatory joint disease. However, in population studies, 25 percent of those who are B27-positive will go on to experience clinical or roentgenographic evidence of spondylitis or sacroiliitis or both. B27 is also associated with psoriatic spondylitis, the spondylitis seen in inflammatory bowel disease, Reiter's syndrome, and anterior uveitis. The exact means by which B27 confers a risk of spondylitis is not known. Occasionally, anterior uveitis may be the first manifestation of ankylosing spondylitis. In the absence of any evidence of inflammation on x-ray or by erythrocyte sedimentation rate (ESR) or of any symptoms referrable to the gastrointestinal tract, an x-ray of the large bowel is not indicated. The diagnosis of ankylosing spondylitis cannot be made in this patient at this time, and, at any rate, gold has not been notable as an effective form of therapy in ankylosing spondylitis. Evidence of ankylosing spondylitis may develop over the course of time. No symptoms at this time suggest an inflammatory joint disease. No morning stiffness is noted and the pain occurs after strenuous exercise; if this were an inflammatory disease, morning stiffness and relief after exercise might be expected.

135–139. The answers are 135-A, 136-C, 137-D, 138-B, 139-B. *(Wilson, 12/e, pp 314–317, 330, 375–379, 1144–1145, 1186, 1436–1437, 1441–1443, 1447, 1845, 1880.)* Drugs used in the treatment of rheumatoid arthritis are broadly classified as anti-inflammatory or remission-inducing (remittive) agents. Aspirin, a nonsteroidal anti-inflammatory agent that inhibits prostaglandin synthesis, is a commonly used first-line drug. The most frequent side effect is gastrointestinal distress.

Gold therapy is effective in many patients with rheumatoid arthritis, especially in those whose disease is of recent onset. Side effects, however, are significant and include a dermatitis that may lead to exfoliative dermatitis if treatment is not discontinued, stomatitis, the nephrotic syndrome, and bone marrow suppression. Patients' response to gold may be only temporary.

Low-dose prednisone may be very useful in controlling an acute flare of arthritis or in controlling the disease while waiting for a remittive agent to begin working. However, prednisone has significant toxicity, including osteoporosis.

The most significant side effect of chloroquine is deposition of the drug in the pigmented layer of the retina. Irreversible retina degeneration may develop, and this has limited the use of this drug. Hydroxychloroquine (Plaquenil) is less frequently associated with retinopathy. Ophthalmic examinations are required every 6 months of therapy.

140–144. The answers are 140-B, 141-D, 142-A, 143-C, 144-E. *(McCarty, 11/e, pp 1189–1196. Wilson, 12/e, pp 1040–1043, 1438–1445, 1457–1462.)* Wegener's granulomatosis is a granulomatous vasculitis of small arteries and veins that affects the lungs, sinuses, nasopharynx, and the kidneys, where it causes a focal and segmental glomerulonephritis. Other organs can also be damaged, including the skin, eyes, and nervous system. A recently described blood test, which identifies antibodies to the cytoplasm of neutrophils, may prove to be of use in making the diagnosis. Treatment has been successful with steroids and cyclophosphamide. Recent evidence suggests that trimethoprim-sulfamethoxazole may also be effective, which raises the possibility that this drug combination may be killing a causative microorganism or may be modifying the immune response in some way.

Elderly people may have extensive atherosclerosis. Especially after an endovascular procedure (like vascular catheterization, grafting, or repair), some of the atheromatous material may embolize, usually to the skin, kidneys, and brain. This material is capable of fixing complement and thus causing vascular damage. The skin lesions—ecchymoses and necrosis—look much like vasculitis. Differentiation between cholesterol embolization and idiopathic vasculitis is important, since not only is the former not steroid-sensitive but there have been reports of increasing damage after the institution of steroid therapy.

Polyarteritis nodosa is a multisystem necrotizing vasculitis that, prior to the use of steroids and cyclophosphamide, was uniformly fatal. In 30 percent of patients, antecedent hepatitis B virus infection can be demonstrated; immune complexes containing the virus have been found in such patients and are likely pathogenetic.

Giant cell arteritis is a disease of elderly patients that classically affects the temporal arteries (thus, the old name, temporal arteritis). Giant cell arteritis, named for the presence of giant cells and granulomata that disrupt the internal elastica of the vessel, may present with headache, anemia, a high ESR (although a normal ESR does *not* rule out the diagnosis), and occasionally a syndrome known as polymyalgia rheumatica. This includes stiffness, aching, and tenderness of the proximal muscles. These patients describe weakness of the hip and shoulder girdles, but there is no objective weakness of the muscles and the muscle enzymes are normal. Giant cell arteritis usually responds to steroid therapy, 45 to 60 mg per day of prednisone; polymyalgia rheumatica typically responds to low-dose prednisone, 10 to 15 mg per day.

First described in Japan and then in Turkey, Takayasu's arteritis is a granulomatous inflammation of the aorta and its main branches. Symptoms are due to local vascular occlusion; aortic regurgitation and systemic and pulmonary hypertension, as well as general symptoms of arthralgia, fatigue, malaise, anorexia, and weight loss may occur. Surgery may be necessary to correct occlusive lesions.

145–149. The answers are 145-C, 146-B, 147-A, 148-A, 149-B. *(Wilson, 12/e, pp 546, 1453–1455.)* Reiter's syndrome is characterized as a triad of seronegative, oligoarticular, asymmetrical arthritis; conjunctivitis; and urethritis. The arthritis coupled with urethritis or cervicitis may be sufficient for the diagnosis. It is the most common cause of arthritis in young men. The syndrome develops in up to 3 percent of males with nongonococcal urethritis, in 2 to 3 percent of patients with bacillary dysentery, and in 20 percent of persons with the HLA-B27 antigen. While the pathogenesis is unclear, an infectious process of the urogenital tract (postvenereal Reiter's) or gut (postdysentery Reiter's) together with a particular genetic background may trigger the development of Reiter's syndrome.

The disorder usually begins with urethritis followed by conjunctivitis, which is usually minimal, and rheumatological findings. The arthritis is usually acute, asymmetrical, and oligoarticular and involves predominantly the joints of the lower extremities; tenosynovitis, dactylitis, and plantar fasciitis also occur. Painless, superficial lesions of the mucosa and glans penis occur in a third of patients; keratosis blennorrhagica occurs in up to 30 percent of postvenereal Reiter's syndrome patients but does not occur in postdysentery patients; circinate balanitis is a characteristic dermatitis of the glans penis.

The diagnosis of gonococcal arthritis is made if the organism is cultured from a mucosal site, typical pustular or hemorrhagic lesions are distributed primarily on the extremities, and a therapeutic antibiotic trial resolves the fevers and arthritis. The course is typically acute, typically involves joints of the upper extremities, and may be associated with uveitis. There is no linkage of HLA-B27 with this disease; thus, the frequency of HLA-B27 is the same as in the general population, 6 to 8 percent.

Pulmonary Disease

DIRECTIONS: Each question below contains five suggested responses. Select the **one best** response to each question.

150. A 64-year-old woman is found to have a left-sided pleural effusion on chest x-ray. Analysis of the pleural fluid reveals a ratio of concentration of total protein in pleural fluid to serum of 0.38, a lactic dehydrogenase (LDH) level of 125 IU, and a ratio of LDH concentration in pleural fluid to serum of 0.46. Which of the following disorders is most likely in this patient?

(A) Uremia
(B) Congestive heart failure
(C) Pulmonary embolism
(D) Sarcoidosis
(E) Systemic lupus erythematosus

151. A patient is found to have an unexpectedly high value for diffusing capacity. This finding is consistent with which of the following disorders?

(A) Anemia
(B) Cystic fibrosis
(C) Emphysema
(D) Intrapulmonary hemorrhage
(E) Pulmonary emboli

152. All the following statements regarding pulmonary complications of the acquired immunodeficiency syndrome (AIDS) are true EXCEPT

(A) pneumococcal pneumonia is common in patients with AIDS
(B) *Pneumocystis carinii* pneumonia (PCP) is more difficult to diagnose in patients who are receiving aerosolized pentamidine prophylaxis
(C) tuberculosis (*Mycobacterium tuberculosis*) is diagnostically and clinically similar in AIDS patients and immunologically normal hosts
(D) Kaposi's sarcoma can occasionally be isolated in the lung
(E) pulmonary fungal infections are more common in patients with AIDS

153. All the following statements concerning the pulmonary effects of radiation therapy are true EXCEPT

(A) symptoms of radiation pneumonitis usually become evident 2 to 3 months after the completion of radiation therapy
(B) frank hemoptysis is an uncommon symptom of radiation pneumonitis
(C) concomitant use of radiation and chemotherapy does not increase the risk of developing pulmonary toxicity from radiation
(D) the earliest radiological change after irradiation of the thorax is a radiolucency of the irradiated area
(E) a second course of radiation therapy to the lung is more likely to precipitate acute radiation pneumonitis than the first

154. All the following are indicative of a *severe* asthmatic attack EXCEPT

(A) silent chest
(B) hypercapnia
(C) thoracoabdominal paradox (paradoxical respiration)
(D) pulsus paradoxus of 5 mmHg
(E) altered mental status

155. All the following statements regarding ventilatory management of critically ill patients are true EXCEPT

(A) studies have shown that newer methods of mechanical ventilation including high-frequency ventilation and pressure-controlled, inverse-ratio ventilation have produced lower mortality in adult respiratory distress syndrome (ARDS) when compared with standard positive-pressure mechanical ventilation
(B) tracheostomy after 21 days of endotracheal intubation is not considered essential to reduce the morbidity of continued mechanical ventilation
(C) long-term mechanical ventilation, either with a tracheostomy or an endotracheal tube, increases the risk of developing tracheal stenosis and tracheomalacia
(D) high levels of positive endexpiratory pressure (PEEP) can adversely affect cardiac output
(E) the risk of barotrauma (i.e., pneumothorax) is correlated with the peak inspiratory airway pressure

156. A 32-year-old black woman without a significant past medical history is referred for a dry cough of 3 weeks' duration. She is afebrile, and physical examination yields normal findings except for the presence of several palpable anterior cervical lymph nodes. A chest roentgenogram reveals significant bilateral hilar adenopathy and clear lung fields. A serum Ca^{2+} is 9.5 mg/dL and a purified protein derivative (PPD) test is nonreactive. A lymph node biopsy reveals granulomas and a stain for acid-fast bacilli (AFB) is negative. All the following statements regarding this patient's current medical condition are true EXCEPT

(A) the angiotensin converting enzyme (ACE) level is a good predictor of the severity of the illness and determines the overall prognosis

(B) approximately 70 percent of patients with this disorder will improve or remain stable without medical therapy

(C) pulmonary function tests in this patient are likely to be abnormal

(D) other organs that may become involved in the disease process in this patient include the skin, heart, liver, spleen, and eye

(E) the etiological agent responsible for this patient's medical problem is not known

157. A 40-year-old man without a significant past medical history comes to the emergency room with a 3-day history of fever, shaking chills with a 15-min episode of rigor, nonproductive cough, and anorexia, as well as the development of right-sided pleuritic chest pain and shortness of breath over the last 12 h. A chest roentgenogram reveals a consolidated right middle lobe infiltrate and a CBC shows an elevated neutrophil count with many band forms present. Which of the following statements regarding pneumonia in this patient is correct?

(A) Sputum culture is more helpful than sputum Gram stain in choosing empiric antibiotic therapy

(B) If the Gram stain revealed numerous gram-positive diplococci, numerous white blood cells, and few epithelial cells, penicillin would be adequate empiric therapy

(C) Although *Streptococcus pneumoniae* is the agent most likely to be the cause of this patient's pneumonia, this diagnosis would be very unlikely if blood cultures were negative

(D) The absence of rigors would rule out a diagnosis of pneumococcal pneumonia

(E) The absence of clinical improvement after 72 h of penicillin therapy would rule out the diagnosis of pneumococcal pneumonia

158. A 57-year-old man develops acute shortness of breath shortly after a 12-h automobile ride. The patient consults his internist, and findings on physical examination are normal except for tachypnea and tachycardia. An electrocardiogram reveals sinus tachycardia but is otherwise normal. All the following statements regarding this patient's disease process are true EXCEPT

(A) an arterial blood gas measurement (ABG) is likely to reveal a partial pressure of oxygen (Pa_{CO_2}) of less than 80 torr

(B) an ABG is likely to reveal a respiratory alkalosis (an elevated pH and reduced partial pressure of carbon dioxide [Pa_{CO_2}])

(C) the patient should be admitted to the hospital, and if there is no contraindication to anticoagulation, intravenous heparin should be started pending further testing

(D) normal findings upon examination of the lower extremities are extremely unusual in this clinical setting

(E) the mortality for this condition, when untreated, is very high

159. The hallmark of asthma that distinguishes it from other obstructive airway diseases is that in asthma

(A) hyperinflation is present on chest roentgenogram

(B) airway obstruction is reversible

(C) hypoxia occurs as a consequence of ventilation-perfusion mismatch

(D) the FEV_1/FVC ratio is reduced

(E) exacerbation often occurs as a result of an upper respiratory tract infection.

160. Factors known to exacerbate obstructive sleep apnea include all the following EXCEPT

(A) consumption of ethanol

(B) benzodiazepines taken orally at bedtime

(C) weight gain

(D) orally administered tricyclic antidepressants

(E) supine body position

161. A 32-year-old white woman is found to have a widened medias-tinum on a routine chest roentgenogram. She is completely asymptom-atic. A CT scan demonstrates that a mass is in the anterior medias-tinum. The best approach to managing this patient would be to

(A) do nothing at this time since most anterior mediastinal masses are benign and she is presently asymptomatic

(B) refer the patient to an oncologist since most anterior mediastinal masses are malignant and not resectable at the time of presenta-tion

(C) perform a Tensilon test since most anterior mediastinal tumors in this age group are thymomas associated with myasthenia gravis

(D) refer the patient to a thoracic surgeon for thoracotomy and re-moval of the mediastinal mass

(E) perform radiation therapy initially to shrink the tumor, then fol-low with thoracotomy

DIRECTIONS: Each question below contains four suggested responses of which **one or more** is correct. Select

A	if	**1, 2, and 3**	are correct
B	if	**1 and 3**	are correct
C	if	**2 and 4**	are correct
D	if	**4**	is correct
E	if	**1, 2, 3, and 4**	are correct

162. True statements concerning theophylline include that

(1) at therapeutic concentrations, inhibition of phosphodiesterase activity is insignificant

(2) cimetidine causes a marked decrease in theophylline clearance

(3) it augments the ventilatory response to hypoxia

(4) patients with congestive heart failure will frequently require higher doses of theophylline to achieve the desired therapeutic effect

163. True statements concerning Wegener's granulomatosis include that

(1) hilar adenopathy is commonly the initial chest x-ray abnormality

(2) the disease is never limited solely to the respiratory tract

(3) disease involvement in organs other than the kidney and respiratory tract is a rare finding

(4) multiple, bilateral nodular infiltrates are typical

164. Lung abscesses are characterized by which of the following statements?

(1) They are most commonly caused by a single anaerobic bacterium

(2) They are most commonly caused by aspiration

(3) Surgical resection reduces the length of antibiotic therapy

(4) They are more commonly noted in the lower lobes, particularly the superior segments

SUMMARY OF DIRECTIONS

A	B	C	D	E
1, 2, 3	1, 3	2, 4	4	All are
only	only	only	only	correct

165. A 28-year-old man enters the hospital with cough and fever. His admission x-ray is shown below. Acid-fast organisms, subsequently identified as *Mycobacterium tuberculosis,* are seen on a smear. Correct statements regarding the pathophysiology of this patient's infection include which of the following?

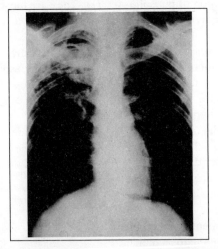

1. The initial exposure probably occurred at a time remote from the current symptoms

2. The location of the current process probably resulted from inspiration of aerosolized droplets into the upper lobe

3. Necrosis of the pulmonary lesion with cavity formation is a common complication of his condition

4. Although coughing is the most common way of spreading this infection, sneezing and even talking have been implicated in disease transmission

DIRECTIONS: Each group of questions below consists of lettered headings followed by a set of numbered items. For each numbered item select the **one** lettered heading with which it is **most** closely associated. Each lettered heading may be used **once, more than once, or not at all.**

Questions 166–170

For each clinical picture below, select the arterial blood gas and pH values with which it is most likely to be associated.

	pH	P_{O_2}	P_{CO_2}
(A)	7.50	75	28
(B)	7.15	78	92
(C)	7.06	36	95
(D)	7.06	108	13
(E)	7.39	48	54

166. A 30-year-old obese female bus driver develops sudden pleuritic left-sided chest pain and dyspnea

167. A 60-year-old heavy smoker has severe chronic bronchitis and peripheral edema and cyanosis

168. A 22-year-old drug-addicted man is brought to the emergency room by friends who were unable to awaken him

169. A 62-year-old man who has chronic bronchitis and chest pain is given oxygen via mask in the ambulance en route to the hospital and becomes lethargic in the emergency room

170. A 20-year-old man with diabetes mellitus comes to the emergency room with diffuse abdominal pain, tachypnea, and a fever of 104°F (40°C)

Questions 171–175

For each set of findings below, select the disease with which it is most likely to be associated.

(A) Asthma
(B) Rheumatoid arthritis
(C) Alpha$_1$-antitrypsin
(D) Cystic fibrosis
(E) Sarcoidosis

171. Low levels of glucose in pleural effusions

172. Bronchiectasis and severe hemoptysis as frequent complications of clinical course

173. Presence of the mucoid strain of *Pseudomonas aeruginosa*

174. Development of severe liver disease that is usually associated with, but may be independent of, lung disease

175. Development of symptoms after ingestion of tartrazine yellow or aspirin

Questions 176–179

For each pulmonary disorder below, select the disease with which it is most likely to be associated.

(A) Scleroderma
(B) Systemic lupus erythematosus (SLE)
(C) Rheumatoid arthritis
(D) Sjögren's syndrome

176. Pulmonary lymphoma

177. Pulmonary hypertension

178. Pulmonary nodules

179. Pleuritis and pericarditis

Pulmonary Disease

Answers

150. The answer is B. *(Murray, pp 1707–1711.)* Classifying a pleural effusion as either a transudate or an exudate is useful in identifying the underlying disorder. Pleural fluid is exudative if it has any one of the following three properties: a ratio of concentration of total protein in pleural fluid to serum greater than 0.5, an absolute value of LDH greater than 200 IU, or a ratio of LDH concentration in pleural fluid to serum greater than 0.6. Causes of exudative effusions include malignancy, pulmonary embolism, pneumonia, tuberculosis, abdominal disease, collagen vascular diseases, uremia, Dressler's syndrome, and chylothorax. Exudative effusions may also be drug-induced. If none of the aforementioned properties are met, the effusion is a transudate. Differential diagnosis includes congestive heart failure, nephrotic syndrome, cirrhosis, Meigs's syndrome, and hydronephrosis.

151. The answer is D. *(Fishman, 2/e, p 2497.)* The carbon monoxide (CO) diffusing capacity provides an estimate of the rate at which oxygen moves by diffusion from alveolar gas to combine with hemoglobin in the red blood cells. It is interpreted as an index of the surface area engaged in alveolar-capillary diffusion. Measurement of diffusing capacity of the lung (DL_{CO}) is done by having the person inspire a low concentration of carbon monoxide. The rate of uptake of the gas by the blood is calculated from the difference between the inspired and expired concentrations. The test can be performed during a single 10-s breath-holding or during a minute of steady-state breathing. The diffusing capacity is defined as the amount of carbon monoxide transferred per minute per millimeter of mercury of driving pressure and correlates with oxygen transport from the alveolus into the capillaries. Primary parenchymal disorders, anemia and removal of lung tissue decrease the diffusing capacity. Conversely, polycythemia, congestive heart failure, and intrapulmonary hemorrhage tend to increase the value for diffusing capacity.

152. The answer is C. *(Murray, pp 950–960, 1931–1941. Clin Chest Med, June 1991, pp 357–360. Crit Care Clin, Jan. 1993, pp 31–44.)* AIDS has become a common clinical entity with multiple pulmonary complications. Most of these complications are infectious and include bacterial and fungal organisms. A common and often fatal infection is PCP, which in recent years has had a lower initial mortality probably because of earlier detection and more aggressive chemoprophylaxis with oral sulfamethoxazole-trimethoprim (Bactrim) and aerosolized pentamidine. Aerosolized pentamidine appears to change the clinical course of PCP. It leads to predominant upper lobe disease and occasional pneumothorax, as well as making the diagnosis of PCP by bronchoscopy more difficult. Fungal infections in AIDS, particularly histoplasmosis, appear to be on the rise. Several reports have indicated that bacterial infections are more common in AIDS and have indicated a tenfold increased chance of developing pneumococcal pneumonia. Tuberculosis (TB) is more common in AIDS, but in comparison to TB in an immunologically normal host, granulomas are rare, the number of organisms seen in sputum or lung biopsy are high, and the disease is often more difficult to treat medically. A relatively common noninfectious complication of AIDS is Kaposi's sarcoma, which is usually a systemic disease of lung, skin, and gastrointestinal tract. In a small percentage of cases, Kaposi's sarcoma can be isolated in the lung.

153. The answer is C. (*Gross, Ann Intern Med 86:81–92, 1977.*) Radiation administered to the thorax in the treatment of patients with breast cancer, lung cancer, Hodgkin's disease, or lymphoma may result in adverse effects on lung and pleura. The incidence and severity of damage are related to two major factors: the greater the volume of lung irradiated, the greater the likelihood of clinical disturbance; and the amount of damage produced is more a function of the rate at which the total dose is delivered than of the total dose, as increasing fractionation allows repair of sublethal damage. The clinical syndrome is divided into two phases: radiation pneumonitis, which occurs 2 to 6 months after radiation therapy, and radiation fibrosis, which follows it and is usually established by 12 months. Symptoms of radiation pneumonitis begin insidiously and usually consist of a harsh cough and dyspnea; frank hemoptysis in uncommon. Nearly all patients with radiation pneumonitis will develop radiation fibrosis and in most cases this will be asymptomatic. However, in severe cases, dyspnea, orthopnea, cyanosis, and clubbing may occur. Concomitant chemotherapy, repeat courses of radiation, and steroid withdrawal all may potentiate the damaging effects of radiation.

154. The answer is D. (*Murray, pp 1047–1050.*) It is extremely important to accurately determine the severity of an exacerbation of asthma since the major cause of death from asthma is the underestimation of the severity of a particular episode either by the patient or the physician. Silent chest is a particularly ominous finding because the airway constriction is so great that airflow is insufficient to generate wheezing. Hypercapnia and thoracoabdominal paradox almost always are indicative of exhaustion and respiratory muscle failure or fatigue and generally need to be aggressively treated with mechanical ventilation. Altered mental status is frequently seen with severe hypoxia or hypercapnia, and ventilatory support is usually required. An increased pulsus paradoxus may also be a sign of severe asthma, as it increases with greater respiratory effort and generation of more negative intrathoracic pressures during inspiration. However, a pulsus paradoxus of up to 8 to 10 mmHg is considered normal; thus, a value of 5 mmHg would not be indicative of a severe episode of asthma.

155. The answer is A. *(Crit Care Clin, July 1990, pp 489–502.)* In recent years, many new modalities of mechanical ventilation have become available for the treatment of critically ill patients with respiratory failure. These include high-frequency ventilation, pressure-support ventilation, and volume-controlled and pressure-controlled, inverse-ratio ventilation (IRV). A problem with these new modalities is that they have been clinically used before provision of adequate documentation of well-controlled clinical trials that show they are efficacious either in reducing mortality or morbidity. Thus there is no adequate study that demonstrates a reduced mortality in ARDS when IRV is used. Major complications of mechanical ventilation include barotrauma, which is a function of the peak inspiratory airway pressure; oxygen toxicity, which may occur when inspired oxygen concentrations exceed 60%; and tracheal injury, which is a direct result of pressure from the tube cuff on the tracheal endothelium. Generally, the risk of tracheal injury (tracheal stenosis and tracheomalacia) is the same for tracheostomy tubes and endotracheal tubes, as both use a low-pressure, high-compliance cuff; therefore, the old "rule" of performing a tracheostomy after 21 days of endotracheal intubation is not strictly correct. Other complications from mechanical ventilation may occur when PEEP is used. PEEP may increase the risk of barotrauma and significantly diminish cardiac output, especially when pressures greater than 5 cmH$_2$O are used.

156. The answer is A. *(Murray, pp 1486–1497.)* The patient has a history, physical examination, chest roentgenogram, and lymph node biopsy consistent with sarcoidosis. No etiological agent responsible for sarcoidosis has been identified, although it has been suggested that transmissible, airborne substances and genetic factors may be involved.

The hallmark of the disease is a granuloma with inflammatory regions that may occur in any area of the body. This leads to a varied presentation in this disorder. Most typically, sarcoidosis presents as an abnormal chest roentgenogram with hilar and paratracheal lymphadenopathy. The lung fields may be clear or demonstrate parenchymal disease. Occasionally, patients may present without lymphadenopathy and with parenchymal disease alone ("burned-out" sarcoidosis). Despite the significant abnormalities on chest roentgenogram, physical examination of the lungs generally reveals normal findings and the major abnormality on examination, if present, is lymphadenopathy. In symptomatic patients, the affected organ or organs dictate the presentation of the disease. Since pulmonary involvement is most common, dry cough and mild dyspnea are the symptoms most often noted, although nonspecific constitutional symptoms, such as weight loss, fatigue, and anorexia are occasionally seen. Other organ systems involved in sarcoidosis include the skin, eye, heart, nervous system, gastrointestinal tract, and kidney.

Diagnosis of sarcoidosis is generally accomplished with tissue biopsy that confirms granuloma without evidence of tuberculosis or other infectious granulomatous diseases. Transbronchial biopsy of the lung during the fiberoptic bronchoscopy is an excellent way of making the diagnosis, as a positive result will be obtained in 85 to 90 percent of patients with parenchymal radiographic abnormalities and in 50 to 60 percent of patients with hilar adenopathy alone. Lymph node biopsy may also provide an excellent and reasonably noninvasive way of establishing the diagnosis, although a number of false positive results have been reported. An accurate but more invasive method of making the diagnosis is mediastinoscopy. The use of angiotensin converting enzyme (ACE) in establishing the diagnosis and in determining prognosis has not proved reliable since there is a wide variation in ACE levels in patients and elevations of ACE have been noted in various other illnesses. However, following the ACE level in an individual patient may occasionally be helpful in determining response to medical treatment.

Approximately 70 percent of patients with sarcoidosis either spontaneously remit or have a stable disease course over an extended period of time. Only about 30 percent show progression of symptoms, usually over a period of 5 to 10 years, although some patients may have a rapid downhill course with death due to respiratory failure in several months. Therefore, only a minority of patients need to be medically treated, usually with high-dose oral steroids. Patients are usually treated only if they are symptomatic (uncontrolled cough, anorexia) or have hypercalcemia, involvement in organ systems in which granulomata may lead to dangerous sequelae (heart, liver, and eye), or evidence of worsening pulmonary status. Pulmonary function studies are frequently abnormal in these patients, even when they are minimally symptomatic. The carbon monoxide–diffusing capacity is most often abnormal. In more severely affected patients, there is evidence of pulmonary restriction with a decrease in lung volumes, and serial lung volumes and diffusing capacity may aid in determining optimal steroid dose and length of therapy.

157. The answer is B. *(Murray, pp 811–814.)* Pneumonia is a common disorder and is a major cause of death, particularly in hospitalized, elderly patients. Before choosing empiric therapy for presumed pneumonia, it is necessary to know the age of the patient, whether the infection is community-acquired or nosocomial, and whether there are any underlying debilitating illnesses. Community-acquired pneumonias in patients over the age of 35 are most likely due to *Streptococcus pneumoniae, Legionella* species (e.g., *pneumophila*), and *Haemophilus influenzae*. In the case outlined, the history is strongly consistent with pneumococcal pneumonia, manifest by a short prodrome, shaking chills with rigor, fever, chest pain, sparse sputum production associated with cough, and a consolidated lobar infiltrate on chest roentgenogram. The most reliable method of making an elderly diagnosis of pneumococcal pneumonia is seeing gram-positive diplococci on an adequate sputum (many white cells, few epithelial cells). Sputum culture is often not reliable in this disorder, since the organism may be easily overgrown. Blood cultures are positive in only about 20 percent of patients, and when positive, may be indicative of a more severe case. Although rigors are common and may be indicative of pneumococcal bacteremia, the absence of rigors does not rule out the diagnosis. Intravenous penicillin is usually the treatment of choice, and the classic response is rapid clinical improvement, frequently within 24 to 48 h. However, it has been appreciated with greater frequency that many patients, particularly older or debilitated patients, may not show clinical improvement for up to 7 days after beginning appropriate antibiotic therapy.

158. The answer is D. *(Murray, pp 1299–1327.)* The clinical situation described is characteristic of pulmonary embolic disease. Pulmonary emboli in greater than 80 percent of cases arise from thromboses in the deep venous circulation (DVTs) of the lower extremities. DVTs often begin in the calf, where they rarely, if ever, cause clinically significant pulmonary embolic disease. However, thromboses that begin below the knee frequently "grow," or propagate, above the knee; clots that dislodge from above the knee cause clinically significant pulmonary emboli, which, if untreated, cause mortality exceeding 80 percent. Interestingly, only about 50 percent of patients with DVT of the lower extremities have clinical findings of swelling, warmth, erythema, pain, or "cords." As long as the superficial venous system, which has connections with the deep venous system, remains patent, none of the "classic" clinical findings of DVT will occur because blood will drain from the unobstructed superficial system. When a clot does dislodge from the deep venous system and travels into the pulmonary vasculature, the most common clinical findings are tachypnea and tachycardia; chest pain is less likely and is more indicative of concomitant pulmonary infarction. The ABG is usually abnormal and a high percentage of patients exhibit hypoxia, hypocapnia, alkalosis, and a widening of the alveolar-arterial gradient ($P[A-a]_{O_2}$). The ECG is frequently abnormal in pulmonary embolic disease. The most common finding is sinus tachycardia, but atrial fibrillation, pseudoinfarction in the inferior leads, and right and left axis deviation are also occasionally seen. Initial treatment for suspected pulmonary embolic disease includes prompt hospitalization and institution of intravenous heparin provided there are no contraindications to anticoagulation. Then, further testing to document pulmonary emboli—including ventilation-perfusion scans, duplex scans of the lower extremities, and, if clinically indicated, pulmonary angiography—can be performed.

159. The answer is B. *(Murray, pp 1032–1068.)* Asthma is an incompletely understood inflammatory process that involves the lower airways and results in bronchoconstriction and excess production of mucus, which lead to increased airway resistance and occasionally respiratory failure and death. During acute exacerbations of asthma and in other obstructive lung diseases, such as chronic obstructive pulmonary disease, hyperinflation may be present on chest roentgenogram, hypoxia is common and usually a result of ventilation-perfusion mismatch, the FEV_1/FVC is reduced, and exacerbations are frequently precipitated by upper airway infections. Only in asthma is the airway obstruction reversible.

160. The answer is D. *(Murray, pp 1845–1850.)* Obstructive sleep apnea (OSA) is a disease of abnormal respiratory control that has only been recognized for about 15 years. It is a very common disorder and may affect as many as 5 percent of the adult male population between the ages of 40 and 65. The typical presentation is an obese, middle-aged man with a short neck, a history of heavy snoring and excessive daytime sleepiness (hypersomnolence), and occasionally evidence of right heart failure. The etiology of OSA is not entirely known but is felt to involve a relative relaxation of upper airway dilator muscles during sleep, which leads to pharyngeal airway collapse during inspiration, when there is a negative intraluminal upper airway pressure. When the airway collapses there is no airflow (apnea); this leads to hypercapnia and hypoxia, which cause constant arousals from sleep (sleep fragmentation), inadequate deep sleep and rapid-eye-movement (REM) sleep time, and thus hypersomnolence. Until recently, there were few treatment options, with bypass of the upper airway by tracheostomy reserved for severe cases. Tricyclic antidepressants have been tried with limited success and probably work by reducing REM sleep time, a period of sleep in which obstructive apneic events are common. The most promising results have come from the recent use of nasal continuous positive airway pressure (nasal CPAP), which acts as a pneumatic splint to prevent pharyngeal airway collapse. Approximately 80 percent of patients with OSA respond to this treatment; however, many patients become noncompliant with nasal CPAP as their symptoms begin to dissipate. Uvulopalatopharyngoplasty (UPPP) is a procedure in which excess upper airway tissue is surgically removed in an attempt to increase the baseline size of the pharynx. The short-term results have been somewhat disappointing, with a success rate of about 50 percent and significant postoperative morbidity. Dental appliances have not had consistent results in treating OSA and are not usually employed in the initial treatment plan. Perhaps the best and often overlooked treatment strategy is weight loss, which may end the obstructive episodes entirely in certain subjects. Treatment is also aimed at avoidance of exacerbating factors of OSA. Ethanol and benzodiazepines both relax the genioglossus (tongue) muscle, a major pharyngeal dilator, and worsen OSA. In addition, supine body position seems to exacerbate sleep apnea by passively allowing the tongue to fall backward, which makes the pharyngeal airway smaller and more likely to become obstructed.

161. The answer is D. *(Murray, pp 1819–1829.)* The mediastinum represents the space between the two pleural cavities and contains numerous structures from different organ systems. Therefore, there is a wide range of mediastinal pathology. When considering mediastinal masses, as in the case illustrated, the most useful method of characterizing the potential pathology is to divide the mediastinum into anterior, middle, and posterior and then localize the mass into one of these compartments. Both malignant and benign neoplasms arise in each segment of the mediastinum, but tumor type and frequency of malignancy are dependent upon both the location of the tumor in the mediastinum and the age of the patient. Tumors arising in the anterior mediastinum, the region most common for malignancy, include thymomas, germ-cell tumors, lymphomas, thyroid and parathyroid tumors, and mesenchymal tumors. It should be noted that with the exception of lymphomas, these tumors may be malignant or benign. Thymomas are the most common anterior mediastinal mass, and the association with myasthenia is reported to be between 10 and 50 percent. Therefore, patients with anterior mediastinal masses and symptoms consistent with myasthenia gravis should have appropriate testing to establish the diagnosis. Lesions in the middle mediastinum are usually benign and consist of developmental cysts, vascular enlargements, and diaphragmatic hernias, although enlarged lymph nodes from both benign and malignant processes can occur. In the posterior mediastinum, almost all lesions arise from neural tissue and are classified according to the specific tissue of origin. Most of these lesions are benign in adults, but up to 50 percent of these neoplasms may be malignant in children. Benign lesions may produce symptoms, including chest pain from nerve or bone erosion, dyspnea from tracheal compression, and neurological deficits secondary to spinal cord compression.

Since mediastinal masses may be malignant or benign, and since even benign lesions may have significant symptoms, the goal of therapy has in general been surgical removal. In certain cases, closed chest biopsy may be appropriate as a diagnostic tool (tuberculosis, sarcoidosis) and may obviate the need for thoracotomy.

The outcome from mediastinal masses is generally favorable, since a majority of these lesions are benign. However, the results for many of the malignant neoplasms are also good, especially if the tumor is well encapsulated at the time of thoracotomy. Preoperative radiation or chemotherapy is not usually performed for most mediastinal masses.

162. The answer is A (1, 2, 3). *(Murray, pp 253–255.)* Theophylline, a methylxanthine, is a frequently used drug in airway obstruction. One of its effects is to inhibit phosphodiesterase activity; however, at therapeutic concentrations, this inhibition is minimal and inadequate to explain the bronchodilation seen. Thus the mechanism responsible for bronchodilation from theophylline is unknown. Other effects of theophylline include improvement of diaphragmatic contractility and augmentation of the ventilatory response to hypoxia. Theophylline metabolism is altered by many drugs. Cimetidine, erythromycin, and birth control pills all reduce its clearance, while phenobarbital and phenytoin increase its clearance. In addition, theophylline dosage must be reduced in liver disease and congestive heart failure and must be increased in cigarette smokers and children.

163. The answer is D (4). *(Fishman, 2/e, pp 1128–1136.)* Wegener's granulomatosis is characterized by glomerulonephritis together with a granulomatous vasculitis of the upper and lower respiratory tracts. Many other organ systems may typically be involved, including eyes, ears, skin, heart, and nervous system. Patients typically present with an upper airway illness related to persistent rhinorrhea and bilateral pulmonary infiltrates. Rarely is there functional renal impairment on presentation. Lung biopsy reveals the presence of granulomata and vasculitis, although, rarely, either may exist alone. The characteristic lung findings are multiple, bilateral nodular infiltrates that tend to cavitate. Twenty percent of patients have pleural effusions. Pulmonary calcifications are rare and hilar adenopathy is not a feature. On pulmonary function testing, airflow obstruction, reduced lung volumes, and an abnormal diffusing capacity are common findings. Without therapy, mortality is 90 percent in 2 years. A variant of systemic Wegener's granulomatosis, called *limited Wegener's,* has disease limited to the respiratory tract. This variant may have a better overall prognosis than the systemic variety. Treatment for systemic Wegener's granulomatosis is with prednisone, frequently with the addition of cyclophosphamide or azathioprine, especially if there is evidence of renal involvement. In limited Wegener's granulomatosis, there are several records of arrest of the disease process with trimethoprim-sulfamethoxazole alone.

164. The answer is C (2, 4). *(Fishman, 2/e, pp 1505–1515.)* Lung abscess is characterized by destruction of lung parenchyma secondary to a suppurative inflammatory process that results in cavitary lesions. Frequent predisposing factors include aspiration, periodontal disease, bronchiectasis, bacteremia, and intraabdominal infection. Anaerobic abscesses, which are most common and are usually caused by more than one organism, typically have an indolent course, while those caused by *Staphylococcus aureus, Streptococcus pyogenes,* or *Klebsiella* have a more sudden presentation. Lung abscesses secondary to another process such as bacterial endocarditis or subphrenic infection may be dominated by the clinical presentation of the underlying pathology. Approximately one-third of lung abscesses are complicated by empyema. Treatment involves 2 to 4 months of antimicrobial therapy for complete resolution; surgical resection is contraindicated early in the disease process. A new treatment modality, currently under investigation, is percutaneous drainage of the abscess under radiological guidance.

165. The answer is B (1, 3). *(Fishman, 2/e, pp 1821–1840.)* The patient described in the question has active tuberculosis. The causative organism is initially inhaled by droplet aerosol into the lower lobes. A primary, usually asymptomatic infection ensues. Organisms are spread subsequently by hematogenous or lymphatic dissemination or both to other foci and grow best in those areas with a high oxygen tension, such as the upper lobe. Necrosis is part of the characteristic tissue reaction to infection. Symptomatic disease may then occur at these distant locations later in life. As the organism spreads by droplet aerosol, isolation of the patient becomes mandatory, preferably in a room with ultraviolet radiation. Coughing is usually the most effective method of spreading infection, as droplet nuclei of a size that can be inhaled are generated. Sneezing and talking usually produce droplet nuclei too large to reach the alveoli, where they would be infectious.

166–170. The answers are 166-A, 167-E, 168-C, 169-B, 170-D. *(Murray, pp 211–230.)* The blood gas values associated with pulmonary embolism may vary tremendously. The most consistent finding is acute respiratory alkalosis. It is important to note that hypoxemia, although frequently found, need not be present.

In severe chronic lung disease, the presence of hypercapnia leads to a compensatory increase in serum bicarbonate. Thus, significant hypercapnia may be present with an arterial pH close to normal, but will never be *completely* corrected.

Acute respiratory acidosis may occur secondary to respiratory depression after drug overdose. Hypoventilation is associated with hypoxia, hypercapnia, and severe, uncompensated acidosis.

In the presence of long-standing lung disease, respiration may become regulated in hypoxia rather than by altered carbon dioxide tension and arterial pH, as in normal people. Thus, the unmonitored administration of oxygen may lead to respiratory suppression, as in the patient described in the question, that results in acute and chronic respiratory acidosis.

Young patients with type I diabetes mellitus may present with rapid onset of diabetic ketoacidosis (DKA), usually secondary to a systemic infection. These patients usually are maximally ventilating, as indicated by a very low arterial P_{CO_2}; however, they remain acidotic secondary to the severe metabolic ketoacidosis associated with this process. In general, these patients are not hypoxic unless the underlying infection is pneumonia.

171–175. The answers are 171-B, 172-D, 173-D, 174-C, 175-A. *(Wilson, 12/e, pp 1047–1053, 1072–1076, 1343, 1437–1443, 1463–1469.)* Asthma is predominantly an inflammatory lower airway process. Frequent triggers of airway inflammation and thus asthma include infection, inhaled allergens, and processes that cool or dry the airways, such as exercise and exposure to cold weather. In addition, certain chemicals, such as aspirin (but not sodium or magnesium salicylate) and tartrazine yellow, have been implicated in the development of bronchospasm in certain patients.

Pleural effusions are not unusual in patients with rheumatoid arthritis. A history of pleurodynia that would suggest an antecedent inflammatory pleuritis is not always obtained, but characteristically the pleural fluid, which is sterile, will contain a high level of lactic dehydrogenase and a low glucose concentration. Other pulmonary phenomena associated with rheumatoid arthritis include diffuse interstitial fibrosis and the occurrence of individual or clustered nodules in the lung parenchyma.

The fatality rate for patients with cystic fibrosis is lower today than in previous years; the average life span of patients afflicted with this disease has been significantly increasing. Chronic lung infections, however, are almost universal. The most common and difficult to treat of such infections is caused by the mucoid strain of *Pseudomonas aeruginosa*. It is doubtful whether any form of antibiotic combination is effective in such patients. Chronic coughing is one of the major and most distressing problems of patients with cystic fibrosis. Liver disease, particularly biliary cirrhosis, may develop in these patients. Common pulmonary complications include bronchiectasis, severe hemoptysis, and allergic bronchopulmonary aspergillosis.

The incidence of liver disease associated with a deficiency of alpha$_1$-antitrypsin is very high. Patients with liver disease secondary to alpha$_1$-antitrypsin deficiency usually, but not always, have accompanying panacinar emphysema.

Sarcoidosis is a nonspecific granulomatous disease of unknown etiology. Blacks and Mediterranean peoples appear to be predisposed. The most commonly involved organs—after the lungs—are liver, eye, spleen, skin, and kidney. The most characteristic presentation is a patient with a nonproductive cough with bilateral hilar adenopathy on chest x-ray. Treatment with prednisone is usually reserved for patients with diminishing pulmonary function, evidenced by reduced diffusing capacity or reduced lung volumes; 70 to 80 percent of untreated, stable patients will spontaneously remit.

176–179. The answers are 176-D, 177-A, 178-C, 179-B. *(Murray, pp 1462–1474.)* Connective tissue disorders frequently have pulmonary manifestations. There may be significant overlap in the pulmonary involvement seen among the connective tissue disorders. In addition, the spectrum of disease seen in any of these disorders may make it hard to accurately classify a particular patient. SLE, perhaps the most common of these disorders, can exhibit many different pulmonary manifestations. Pleuritis and pericarditis are the most common. Other types of pulmonary involvement include vasculitis, interstitial fibrosis, pulmonary hemorrhage, elevation of the diaphragm and loss of lung volume ("vanishing lung syndrome"), and rarely pulmonary hypertension.

Rheumatoid arthritis, another common disorder, can cause pleuritis and pleural effusion as in SLE; however, pericarditis is rare. Pulmonary nodules are seen frequently in this disorder, and they are usually asymptomatic.

In scleroderma, interstitial fibrosis is the most common pulmonary complication. Pulmonary hypertension, although relatively uncommon, is more likely to occur in scleroderma than in other connective tissue disorders.

The most common clinical feature of Sjögren's syndrome is keratoconjunctivitis sicca in which patients have diminished salivary gland production and present with dry mouth and eyes. The most common pulmonary manifestation of this disorder is dry cough, although airway obstruction may be seen in about 10 percent of cases. An interesting association with this disorder is lymphoma, as patients with Sjögren's syndrome are at a fortyfold greater risk of developing lymphoma when compared with the general population. Occasionally, these lymphomas will primarily involve the lung.

Cardiology

Each question below contains five suggested responses. Select the **one best** response to each question.

180. In differentiating ventricular tachyarrhythmias from supraventricular tachyarrhythmias with aberrant ventricular conduction, findings that favor ventricular origin of the beats include all the following EXCEPT

(A) QRS duration exceeding 140 ms on scalar electrocardiogram
(B) fusion (Dressler) beats on rhythm strip
(C) AV dissociation on esophageal electrographic recording
(D) 2:1 AV block on cardiac monitor during carotid massage
(E) capture beats on cardiac rhythm strip

181. All the following statements regarding atrial fibrillation are correct EXCEPT

(A) atrial fibrillatory activity on the electrocardiogram (f waves) occurs at rates of 350 to 600 beats per minute
(B) symptoms from atrial fibrillation are, for the most part, due to reduced left ventricular filling as a result of rapid ventricular rates and loss of atrial contraction
(C) stroke risk is 5 to 7 times higher in persons with atrial fibrillation compared with those in normal sinus rhythm
(D) antiarrhythmic drugs from classes IA, IC, and III are useful in the prevention of recurrences of atrial fibrillation
(E) modalities for the acute termination of rapid atrial fibrillation include rapid atrial pacing

182. The development of states of high cardiac output in the presence of underlying heart disease may result in heart failure. All the following statements regarding high-output heart failure are correct EXCEPT

(A) elevation of cardiac output and physical findings of anemia occur in patients with sickle cell anemia and hemoglobin SC disease at hemoglobin levels that are higher than those in patients with other anemias

(B) the rapid atrial fibrillation associated with hyperthyroidism is exquisitely sensitive to the rate-slowing effect of digitalis glycosides

(C) oxygenated blood in the inferior vena cava and right atrium seen with arteriovenous fistulas in syndromes such as hereditary hemorrhagic telangiectasia (Osler-Weber-Rendu disease) may lead to misdiagnosis of atrial septal defect

(D) beriberi heart disease results from severe thiamine deficiency of at least 3 months' duration and fulminant forms of the disease may result in death within 48 h of the onset of symptoms

(E) the state of high cardiac output associated with Paget's disease of bone requires involvement of at least 15 percent of the skeleton

183. Cardiac auscultatory findings during normal pregnancy include all the following EXCEPT

(A) increase in intensity of the first heart sound

(B) persistent expiratory splitting of the second heart sound

(C) presence of a third heart sound

(D) presence of a fourth heart sound

(E) presence of a mammary souffle

184. All the following indications for implantation of permanent cardiac pacemakers are correct EXCEPT

(A) asymptomatic complete heart block with a documented escape rate of less than 40 beats per minute

(B) asymptomatic sinus bradycardia with heart rates below 40 beats per minute

(C) symptomatic chronic bifascicular block with intermittent type II second-degree AV block

(D) persistent advanced second-degree or complete AV block after acute myocardial infarction

(E) intermittent second-degree AV block with symptomatic bradycardia

185. Hypertension is widely regarded as a major risk factor in the development of coronary heart disease. All the following statements regarding the association of hypertension and coronary heart disease are correct EXCEPT

(A) patients with mild hypertension account for approximately 60 percent of the premature deaths attributable to this risk factor

(B) a 10-mmHg rise in mean arterial pressure results in approximately a 30 percent rise in risk of coronary heart disease

(C) for all age groups and races in both sexes, a graded, incremental risk of fatal or nonfatal myocardial infarction has been demonstrated at diastolic blood pressures below the conventional 90-mmHg cutoff

(D) hypertension medications may have unfavorable effects on other coronary heart disease risk factors such as blood lipids and glucose and on cardiac rhythm disturbances

(E) the pharmacotherapeutic treatment of diastolic hypertension in the range of 90 to 105 mmHg has been shown to favorably influence morbidity and mortality of coronary heart disease

186. All the following statements regarding hypersensitive carotid sinus syndrome are correct EXCEPT

(A) ventricular asystole lasting 3 s or longer during carotid sinus stimulation characterizes cardioinhibitory carotid sinus hypersensitivity

(B) a drop in systolic blood pressure equal to or greater than 50 mmHg, or greater than 30 mmHg in association with reproducible symptoms, characterizes vasodepressor carotid sinus hypersensitivity

(C) intrinsic sinus nodal dysfunction is generally recognized as the major culprit in asystole in the hypersensitive carotid sinus syndrome

(D) mixed vasodepressor and cardioinhibitory carotid sinus hypersensitivity may account for recurrent episodes of syncope following pacemaker implantation for ventricular asystole in this syndrome

(E) pharmacotherapeutic agents such as beta-adrenergic blocking drugs, digitalis glycosides, α-methyldopa, and clonidine may accentuate cardioinhibitory and vasodepressor responses

187. The rhythm strip displayed below reveals

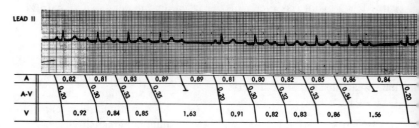

(A) atrial premature contractions
(B) junctional premature contractions
(C) AV dissociation
(D) type I second-degree AV block
(E) type II second-degree AV block

188. The electrocardiogram displayed below reveals which of the following patterns?

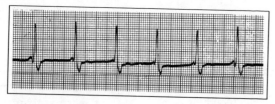

(A) Normal sinus rhythm
(B) Ventricular preexcitation
(C) Idioventricular rhythm
(D) Complete heart block
(E) Atrioventricular dissociation

189. A 43-year-old woman with a 1-year history of episodic leg edema and dyspnea is noted to have clubbing of the fingers. Her ECG is shown below. The correct diagnosis is

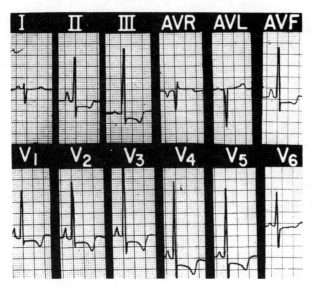

(A) inferior wall myocardial infarction
(B) right bundle branch block
(C) anterior wall myocardial infarction
(D) Wolff-Parkinson-White syndrome
(E) cor pulmonale

190. All the following statements regarding cardiac effects of human immunodeficiency virus (HIV) are correct EXCEPT

(A) HIV affects the heart in approximately one-quarter to one-half of patients with acquired immunodeficiency syndrome (AIDS)
(B) congestive heart failure is the most common clinical manifestation of cardiac involvement by HIV
(C) although opportunistic infections account for a portion of the cases of myocarditis, the majority are suspected to be caused by the HIV virus
(D) malignant complications of AIDS may result in infiltrative cardio-myopathy
(E) cardiac involvement by HIV results in clinically apparent heart disease in 1 percent of AIDS patients

191. All the following statements regarding peripartum cardiomyopathy are correct EXCEPT

(A) the vast majority of patients with this condition experience clinical deterioration and death within the first 6 to 12 months; a small percentage demonstrates chronic, stable left ventricular dysfunction or recovery

(B) in the majority of cases, symptoms of left ventricular dysfunction appear during the last month of gestation or immediately post partum

(C) peripartum cardiomyopathy is more frequent in women who are multiparous, have twin pregnancies, are over 30 years of age, or are black

(D) possible etiologies of peripartum cardiomyopathy include myocarditis, nutritional deficiencies, and maternal immunological response to fetal antigen

(E) treatment includes oxygen, diuretics, inotropic and vasodilator therapy, anticoagulation, and occasionally intraaortic balloon counterpulsation, left ventricular assist devices, or cardiac transplantation

192. Which of the following statements correctly describes the most common primary cardiac tumor?

(A) The majority are located in the left ventricle

(B) It occurs more commonly in men than in women

(C) Clinical presentation usually mimics mitral valve disease

(D) It is histologically malignant

(E) Peak incidence occurs in the second decade of life

193. Warfarin (Coumadin) anticoagulation is used for a variety of cardiac conditions. Each of the following medications increases the anticoagulant effect of warfarin EXCEPT

(A) cimetidine

(B) rifampin

(C) quinidine

(D) α-methyldopa

(E) phenylbutazone

194. All the following statements concerning the rhythm strip displayed below are true EXCEPT

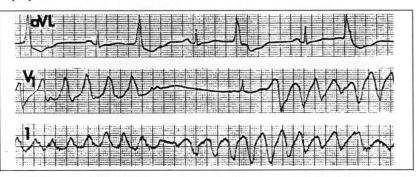

(A) it is usually initiated by a premature ventricular contraction in the presence of a long QT interval
(B) it most frequently results from drug administration
(C) once the arrhythmia is terminated by ventricular pacing, prophylaxis with quinidine is appropriate therapy
(D) it is associated with bradycardia, particularly when caused by AV block
(E) it may degenerate into ventricular fibrillation

195. The rhythm strip displayed below demonstrates

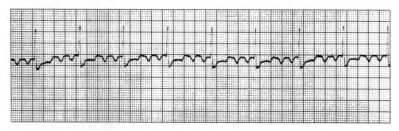

(A) normal sinus rhythm
(B) junctional rhythm
(C) atrial flutter with 4:1 atrioventricular block
(D) paroxysmal atrial tachycardia with 2:1 atrioventricular block
(E) complete heart block with 2:1 atrioventricular block

196. Mitral valve prolapse, the most common abnormality of human heart valves, is characterized by all the following statements EXCEPT

(A) migration of the systolic click and systolic murmur toward the first heart sound occurs during squatting
(B) echocardiography demonstrates systolic posterior motion of one or both mitral valve leaflets
(C) propranolol has been found to be helpful in those patients with palpitations and chest pain
(D) the syndrome appears to be inherited as an autosomal dominant condition with variable penetrance
(E) progression of the valvular defect to severe mitral regurgitation that necessitates surgical repair may occur

197. Digitalis glycosides are widely used in the treatment of heart failure and arrhythmias. Digoxin has a narrow therapeutic window, and in order to avoid digitalis intoxication, downward adjustment of digoxin dosage should be effected when it is given in conjunction with each of the following medications EXCEPT

(A) verapamil
(B) quinidine
(C) amiodarone
(D) erythromycin
(E) metoclopramide

198. Each of the following cardiac conditions creates a relatively high risk of development of infective endocarditis EXCEPT

(A) coarctation of the aorta
(B) ventricular septal defect
(C) atrial septal defect
(D) prosthetic heart valve
(E) patent ductus arteriosus

199. Each of the following statements pertaining to the coronary arterial circulation is correct EXCEPT

(A) the right coronary artery supplies the sinoatrial node in greater than 75 percent of patients
(B) the right coronary artery supplies the atrioventricular node in greater than 75 percent of patients
(C) the left circumflex coronary artery gives rise to obtuse marginal branches
(D) the left anterior descending artery gives rise to septal and diagonal branches
(E) the left anterior descending coronary artery arises from the left main coronary artery and courses along the anterior intraventricular groove

200. All the following statements regarding coarctation of the aorta are true EXCEPT that

(A) affected patients may complain of leg pain or fatigue
(B) it rarely produces symptoms of congestive heart failure in infancy
(C) it has a higher risk than normal of occurring in patients with Turner's syndrome
(D) it is commonly associated with aortic stenosis due to a bicuspid valve
(E) the lesion usually appears just distal to the left subclavian artery

201. Paradoxical splitting of the second heart sound may occur in association with each of the following cardiovascular disorders EXCEPT

(A) aortic stenosis
(B) right bundle branch block
(C) left bundle branch block
(D) left ventricular ischemia
(E) hypertension

202. A syphilitic aneurysm of the aorta is most likely to occur at which of the following sites?

(A) Ascending aorta
(B) Aortic arch
(C) Descending thoracic aorta
(D) Abdominal aorta
(E) Bifurcation of the iliac arteries

203. All the following statements regarding ventricular aneurysms are true EXCEPT

(A) they should be suspected in the presence of a persistent ST-segment elevation following a myocardial infarction
(B) they are more common with anterior than inferior wall myocardial infarctions
(C) risk of cardiac rupture is usually unrelated to reinfarction in the region
(D) recurrent arterial emboli may be the presenting sign
(E) the diagnosis may be suggested by the x-ray finding of calcium in the cardiac border

204. The rhythm strip displayed below reveals normal sinus rhythm with

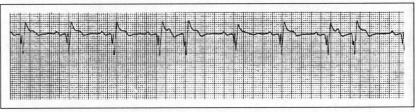

(A) periods of atrioventricular dissociation
(B) periods of Wenckebach atrioventricular block
(C) atrial premature contractions
(D) periods of complete heart block
(E) ventricular premature contractions

205. Hypertrophic cardiomyopathy is characterized by all the following statements EXCEPT that

(A) the carotid pulse of affected patients reveals a slow upstroke
(B) the associated murmur increases in the standing position
(C) a prominent fourth heart sound frequently occurs
(D) mitral regurgitation is present in 50 percent of affected patients
(E) beta blockers or calcium antagonists are useful for treating affected patients who have dyspnea or light-headedness

DIRECTIONS: Each question below contains four suggested responses of which **one or more** is correct. Select

A	if	**1, 2, and 3**	are correct
B	if	**1 and 3**	are correct
C	if	**2 and 4**	are correct
D	if	**4**	is correct
E	if	**1, 2, 3, and 4**	are correct

206. True statements about toxic damage to the heart include which of the following?

(1) Cardiac histopathological findings in cocaine users include myocarditis, contraction band necrosis, and thickening of the intramural coronary arteries

(2) Coronary arterial lesions in young patients who have undergone radiotherapy demonstrate fibrosis and loss of smooth muscle cells in the media

(3) Cumulative doses of doxorubicin, the glycoside antibiotic and potent antineoplastic agent, greater than 450 to 500 mg/m² are associated with a severe form of dilated cardiomyopathy

(4) Myocardial ischemia, vaso-occlusion, and myocarditis have been associated with the antineoplastic agent 5-fluorouracil

207. Hemodynamic derangements in heart failure include reduction in cardiac output and atrial hypertension. Neurohormonal alterations that occur as a result of these changes include

(1) elevation of circulating norepinephrine concentration

(2) activation of the renin-angiotensin-aldosterone axis

(3) elevation of circulating arginine vasopressin concentrations

(4) elevation of circulating atrial natriuretic peptide concentrations

208. Indications for cardiac surgical intervention in infectious endocarditis include

(1) congestive heart failure as a result of valvular dysfunction

(2) abscesses of the myocardium or valve ring

(3) instability or dysfunction of a prosthetic valve

(4) inability to eradicate the infection

DIRECTIONS: Each group of questions below consists of lettered headings followed by a set of numbered items. For each numbered item select the **one** lettered heading with which it is **most** closely associated. Each lettered heading may be used **once, more than once, or not at all.**

Questions 209–211

For each cardiac disorder below, select the clinical finding with which it is most closely associated.

(A) Sharp y descent in jugular pulse tracing
(B) Middiastolic rumble at apex
(C) Large v waves in jugular pulse tracing
(D) Slow y descent in jugular pulse tracing
(E) Prominent c waves in jugular pulse tracing

209. Tricuspid stenosis

210. Aortic regurgitation

211. Constrictive pericarditis

Questions 212–215

Match the agents below with associated side effects.

(A) Increased triglyceride levels
(B) Volume retention
(C) Lupuslike syndrome
(D) Nephrotic syndrome
(E) Gynecomastia

212. Captopril

213. Hydralazine

214. Propranolol

215. Minoxidil

Questions 216–219

For each electrolyte abnormality below, select the electrocardiographic picture with which it is most commonly associated.

(A) No known electrocardiographic abnormalities
(B) Prolonged QT interval
(C) Short QT interval
(D) Widened QRS complex
(E) Prominent U waves

216. Hypokalemia

217. Hyperkalemia

218. Hypocalcemia

219. Hyponatremia

Questions 220–222

Match the following.

(A) Bronchiectasis
(B) Coarctation of the aorta
(C) Ventricular septal defect
(D) Homocystinuria
(E) None of the above

220. Dextrocardia

221. Dilatation of aortic and pulmonary arteries

222. Hyperextensible joints

Questions 223–227

A normal jugular venous pulse wave in relation to first and second heart sounds is displayed below. For each cardiac phenomenon described, select the segment of the venous pulse wave with which it is most likely to be associated.

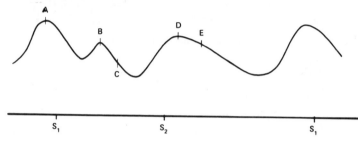

223. Atrial contraction

224. Filling of right atrium while tricuspid valve is closed

225. Opening of tricuspid valve

226. Bulging of tricuspid valve into right atrium

227. S_4 gallop

Questions 228–231

Match the definitions below with the appropriate terms related to probability analysis.

(A) Sensitivity
(B) Specificity
(C) Positive predictive value
(D) Negative predictive value
(E) None of the above

228. True positives divided by true positives plus false positives

229. True positives divided by true positives plus false negatives

230. True negatives divided by true negatives plus false negatives

231. True negatives divided by true negatives plus false positives

Questions 232–235

Match each pulse pattern with the correct disorder.

(A) Hypertrophic obstructive cardiomyopathy
(B) Dilated cardiomyopathy
(C) Cardiac tamponade
(D) Aortic stenosis
(E) None of the above

232. Pulsus parvus et tardus

233. Pulsus alternans

234. Pulsus paradoxus

235. Pulsus bisferiens

DIRECTIONS: The group of questions below consists of four lettered headings followed by a set of numbered items. For each numbered item select

A	if the item is associated with	(A) **only**
B	if the item is associated with	(B) **only**
C	if the item is associated with	**both** (A) and (B)
D	if the item is associated with	**neither** (A) nor (B)

Each lettered heading may be used **once, more than once, or not at all.**

Questions 236–240

    (A) Cardiac tamponade
    (B) Constrictive pericarditis
    (C) Both
    (D) Neither

236. Marked pulsus paradoxus

237. Inspiratory increase in right atrial pressure

238. Elevation of intrapericardial pressure

239. Predominant x descent and absence of or attenuated y descent on right atrial pressure tracing

240. Prominent dip-and-plateau pattern in the right and left ventricular pressure pulses

Cardiology

Answers

180. The answer is D. *(Schlant, 8/e, pp 731–736. Wellens, Am J Med 64:27, 1978.)* While QRS duration less than 120 ms strongly favors supraventricular origin of cardiac rhythm, no similar feature as accurately predicts ventricular origin. Although QRS duration of greater than 140 ms strongly supports the diagnosis of ventricular origin, aberrant conduction of supraventricular beats may exceed this duration as well. AV dissociation similarly favors ventricular origin; however, AV junctional tachycardias without retrograde conduction (allowing independent atrial activity) may occur. Fusion and capture beats strongly favor ventricular origin, although varying degrees of fusion of two supraventricular impulses may also occur. AV block induced by carotid massage suggests that ventricular activation is dependent on atrial discharge and supports supraventricular origin of the rhythm.

181. The answer is E. *(Braunwald, 4/e, pp 682–684.)* Electrical cardioversion reestablishes normal sinus rhythm in more than 90 percent of patients. Rapid atrial pacing, however, is not effective in terminating atrial fibrillation. Although amiodarone is the most effective of all classes IA, IC, and III antiarrhythmic agents in preventing recurrences of atrial fibrillation, its use is limited by a serious adverse effect profile. Irregular atrial activity on the electrocardiogram (f waves) at rates of 350 to 600 beats per minute represents only a portion of total atrial activity that summates into large vectors and is recorded. The ventricular response of atrial fibrillation is dependent upon the refractory period and conductivity of the AV node. Reduction in cardiac output from rapid ventricular rates and loss of atrial contraction during atrial fibrillation may result in symptoms of fatigue and lightheadedness. Additionally, the rapid ventricular response of atrial fibrillation may be perceived as fast, irregular palpitations. Cerebral embolization is more frequently seen with nonvalvular atrial fibrillation than with any other cardiac disease. Nonvalvular atrial fibrillation confers a five- to sevenfold increase in stroke risk over normal sinus rhythm. The coexistence of mitral stenosis with atrial fibrillation confers an even greater risk of embolization.

182. The answer is B. *(Braunwald, 4/e, pp 458–462.)* Heart failure with high cardiac output is associated with conditions of reduced afterload or hypermetabolism or both. The abnormally large volume load needed to satisfy tissue metabolic oxygen requirements affects the myocardium in a fashion similar to that of valvular regurgitation or left-to-right shunt. The rapid atrial fibrillation associated with hyperthyroidism, with ventricular rates about 200 beats per minute, is relatively resistant to the slowing effects of digitalis glycosides. Beta-adrenergic blocking agents are effective in achieving ventricular rate control by prolonging the refractory period of the AV node. Small doses of beta blockers should be cautiously administered, since depression of myocardial contractility may worsen the heart failure. Patients with sickle cell anemia and hemoglobin SC disease demonstrate high cardiac output and physical findings of anemia at higher hemoglobin levels than patients with other forms of anemia. Congenital or acquired systemic arteriovenous fistulas may result in states of high cardiac output. Congestive heart failure and cardiac outputs as high as 10 L/min/m^2 have been demonstrated in patients with hemangioendotheliomia of the liver or with surgical arteriovenous shunts for vascular access in hemodialysis. Severe thiamine (vitamin B$_1$) deficiency of greater than 3 months' duration may result in beriberi heart disease, in which the high cardiac output, which follows reduced systemic vascular resistance and augmented venous return, results in biventricular heart failure. Administration of thiamine results in diuresis, decreased cardiac rate and size, and improvement in congestive heart failure. Digitalis and diuretic therapy should be coadministered with thiamine to prevent the low-output failure that may accompany resolution of vasodilatation. A state of high cardiac output is seen in active Paget's disease of bone when greater than 15 percent of the skeleton is involved. The augmentation in blood flow is believed to occur in cutaneous tissue that overlies affected bone and to be due to increased heat from enhanced metabolic activity.

183. The answer is D. *(Braunwald, 4/e, pp 1791–1792.)* Cardiac auscultatory findings of pregnancy begin in the first trimester and generally disappear within the first few days after parturition. Increase in heart rate and ventricular contractility result in increased amplitude of the first heart sound. The second heart sound demonstrates persistent expiratory splitting, especially during the third trimester. Third heart sounds, which are common in the young, increase in intensity during pregnancy as a result of increased rate and flow. Healthy young women do not have fourth heart sounds during normal pregnancy. Innocent midsystolic murmurs, which originate from flow in pulmonary and brachiocephalic arteries, increase in intensity owing to increased cardiac output and stroke volume during gestation. The mammary souffle is a systolic or continuous murmur heard over the breasts in late pregnancy and in the postpartum lactating woman. The murmurs of mitral, aortic, or pulmonic stenosis increase in intensity because of increased blood flow and shortening of diastolic filling time. Murmurs of mitral and aortic regurgitation may decrease in intensity as the systemic vascular resistance falls during pregnancy. The systolic murmurs of mitral valve prolapse and hypertrophic cardiomyopathy may decrease in amplitude because of increasing left ventricular volume during pregnancy.

184. The answer is B. *(Braunwald, 4/e, pp 728–730.)* A joint committee of the American College of Cardiology and the American Heart Association established indications for implantation of permanent cardiac pacemakers. Class I indications (conditions for which there is general agreement that permanent pacemakers should be implanted) include the following: permanent or intermittent complete heart block associated with symptomatic bradycardia, congestive heart failure, conditions that require drug therapy that may suppress escape focus automaticity, asystole of greater than or equal to 3 s or an escape rate of less than 40 beats per minute; symptomatic permanent or intermittent second-degree AV block; atrial fibrillation, atrial flutter, or supraventricular tachycardia with complete or advanced AV block, bradycardia, and conditions as described under complete heart block; persistent advanced second-degree or complete AV block after acute myocardial infarction; symptomatic chronic bifascicular block with intermittent complete heart block; symptomatic bifascicular block with intermittent type II second-degree AV block; symptomatic sinus bradycardia; and recurrent episodes of syncope associated with spontaneous events provoked by stimulation of the carotid sinus in patients who manifest greater than or equal to 3 s of asystole in response to minimal carotid sinus pressure. There is general agreement that implantation of a permanent cardiac pacemaker is unnecessary for asymptomatic patients with sinus bradycardia.

185. The answer is E. *(Houston, Am Heart J 117:911, 1989.)* There has been a decline in age-adjusted death rates from cerebrovascular accident, coronary heart disease (CHD), and all cardiovascular diseases since 1968 in the United States. It is believed that the reduction in CHD mortality is mainly due to reduction in the risk factors of CHD and out-of-hospital as well as in-hospital survival of patients with acute myocardial infarction. Antihypertensive drug therapy of patients with diastolic pressures equal to or greater than 110 mmHg has been shown to reduce the incidence of CHD. However, pharmacotherapeutic treatment of mild hypertension (diastolic blood pressure 90 to 105 mmHg) has not demonstrated favorable effects on the morbidity and mortality of CHD, possibly as a result of unfavorable effects of antihypertensive medications on other CHD risk factors, such as lipids and glucose.

186. The answer is C. *(Braunwald, 4/e, pp 676–677, 878. Schlant, 8/e, p 818.)* Hypersensitive carotid sinus syndrome is a condition in which stimulation of the carotid sinus results in ventricular asystole caused by sinus arrest or sinoatrial block, or hypotension caused by vasodilatation, or both. The absence of atrial activity probably masks transient coexistent atrioventricular (AV) block. The absence of junctional or ventricular escape rhythms in some patients suggests the influence of enhanced vagal tone on these subsidiary pacemakers as well. The postulated mechanism for the carotid sinus reflex involves pressure-sensitive receptors in the adventitia of the carotid artery, afferent neural traffic via the glossopharyngeal nerve or other routes through cervical sympathetics through the twelfth cranial nerve, and efferent innervation via the vagus nerve and sympathetics. It is believed that the vagus nerve is responsible for the cardioinhibitory component, while sympathetic fibers mediate inhibition of arterial vasoconstriction and possible cholinergic vasodilator activity. Although atropine transiently blocks cardioinhibitory carotid sinus hypersensitivity, permanent pacemaker implantation is often necessary for recurrent episodes. Because of the likelihood of coexistent AV block during episodes, a ventricular or AV sequential pacemaker should be used. The vasodepressor form, as well as the mixed vasodepressor and cardioinhibitory form of this syndrome, is especially difficult to treat. Patients should be instructed to avoid any activities that may exert pressure on the carotid sinus. Medications that may accentuate carotid sinus hypersensitivity (including beta-adrenergic blocking agents, digitalis glycosides, α-methyldopa, and clonidine) should be withdrawn. Pharmacotherapy with anticholinergic and sympathomimetic agents may be effective in controlling symptoms when avoidance of carotid sinus stimulation and administration of medications is unsuccessful in preventing episodes of syncope. Additional measures, including surgical denervation or radiotherapy ablation of the carotid sinus nerve, may be undertaken. Since mixed cardioinhibitory and vasodepressor carotid sinus hypersensitivity will often coexist, a pronounced vasodepressor component with recurrent syncope may manifest itself despite permanent pacemaker implantation.

187. The answer is D. *(Schlant, 8/e, pp 749, 886.)* Type I second-degree AV block, the more common of the two forms of second-degree

AV block, is characterized by the following: (1) after progressive lengthening of the PR interval, the final P wave is not followed by a QRS complex, (2) the increment by which the PR interval increases progressively decreases, and (3) the RR interval that contains the dropped beat is less than two times the shortest preceding RR interval. Type I second-degree AV block is usually due to a conduction delay within the AV node.

188. The answer is E. *(Braunwald, 4/e, pp 715–717. Mandel, 2/e, pp 241–253.)* The rhythm strip exhibited both in the question and below reveals a P wave before the first QRS complex, with a short PR interval. The P waves then move into the QRS complexes until the end of the strip, where a P wave is again seen preceding a QRS complex. This strip reveals atrioventricular (AV) dissociation in which the atria are being depolarized by the sinus node and the ventricles are being depolarized by a junctional or AV nodal focus. This particular example of AV dissociation is termed *isorhythmic dissociation* since the rates of atria and ventricles are almost equal. The preferred meaning of AV dissociation implies two separate pacemakers, with the lower focus faster in rate than the higher focus. This situation differs from complete heart block, in which the rate of the lower focus (an escape rhythm) is slower than the higher. In AV dissociation, the lower focus is firing faster than the higher because of increased automaticity and thus controls the ventricles. AV dissociation is commonly associated with digitalis toxicity and inferior wall myocardial infarction.

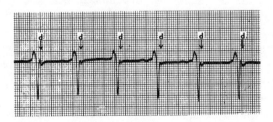

189. The answer is E. *(Schlant, 8/e, pp 1895–1904.)* Cor pulmonale is characterized by the presence of pulmonary hypertension and consequent right ventricular dysfunction. Its causes include diseases leading to hypoxic vasoconstriction, as in cystic fibrosis; occlusion of the pulmonary vasculature, as in pulmonary thromboembolism; and parenchymal destruction, as in sarcoidosis. The right ventricle, in the presence of a chronic increase in afterload, becomes hypertrophic, dilates, and fails. The electrocardiographic findings, as illustrated in the question, include tall, peaked P waves in leads II, III, and aVF, which indicate right atrial enlargement; tall R waves in leads V_1 to V_3 and a deep S wave in V_6 with associated ST-T wave changes, which indicate right ventricular hypertrophy; and right axis deviation. Right bundle branch block occurs in 15 percent of patients.

190. The answer is E. *(Braunwald, 4/e, pp 1427–1428.)* Although cardiac involvement by HIV in patients with AIDS has been demonstrated by echocardiography, endomyocardial biopsy, and autopsy in 25 to 50 percent of patients, clinically overt heart disease occurs in only about 10 percent of patients. Congestive heart failure, with dilated cardiomyopathy picture of left ventricular dilatation and dysfunction, is the most frequent clinical finding. The HIV virus is suspected to be a major culprit in the development of myocarditis, with lesser involvement of viral, fungal, parasitic, and bacterial opportunistic infections. In addition to myocarditis, endocarditis (bacterial, fungal, and marantic), pericarditis (infectious, noninfectious, with and without effusions), arteriopathic lesions, drug-induced toxic lesions, and metastatic involvement from Kaposi's sarcoma and malignant lymphoma have been demonstrated in the hearts of AIDS patients.

191. The answer is A. *(Braunwald, 4/e, pp 1798–1799.)* Peripartum cardiomyopathy is a type of dilated cardiomyopathy that occurs predominantly in the last month of gestation or immediately post partum with an incidence of 1 in 1,300 to 1 in 15,000 in the United States. It is more frequently seen in women who are multiparous, have twin pregnancies, are over 30 years of age, or are black. Although the cause is unknown, suspected culprits include myocarditis, nutritional deficiency, and the maternal immunological response to fetal antigen, as well as possible hormonal effects, toxemia, and small vessel coronary arteriopathy. Congestive heart failure (with four-chamber enlargement and marked reduction in left ventricular systolic function), chest discomfort, ventricular and supraventricular arrhythmias, pericardial effusions, mitral and tricuspid regurgitation, and cardiogenic emboli characterize the clinical picture. About half of patients with peripartum cardiomyopathy demonstrate total or nearly total recovery within 6 months after delivery. The other half of patients have chronic heart failure or continued deterioration and death. Treatment includes oxygen, diuretics, inotropic and vasodilator therapy, anticoagulation, and, if necessary, intraaortic balloon counterpulsation, left ventricular assist devices, or cardiac transplantation.

192. The answer is C. *(Braunwald, 4/e, pp 1451–1457.)* Myxomas are histologically benign and account for up to one-half of all cases of primary cardiac tumors. Because they are most commonly located in the left atrium and are pedunculated, they are particularly prone to mimicking mitral stenosis as a result of a ball-valve effect and causing mitral regurgitation due to trauma to the mitral leaflets. Noncardiac manifestations of myxomas include fever, weight loss, arthralgia, and anemia. Surgical excision is curative. Cardiac sarcomas are the most common malignant primary cardiac tumor and are uniformly rapidly fatal.

193. The answer is B. *(Braunwald, 4/e, pp 1782–1783.)* A variety of pharmacotherapeutic agents alter the anticoagulant effect of warfarin. Some compete for albumin binding, which displaces warfarin from the blood and increases its delivery to the liver for excretion. Other drugs increase microsomal enzyme activity and thereby enhance drug metabolism. Finally, others impair intestinal absorption of the drug. Drugs that increase the anticoagulant effect of warfarin include certain antibiotics, α-methyldopa, cimetidine, quinidine, anabolic steroids, phenylbutazone, thyroxine, sulfinpyrazone, and clofibrate. Drugs that decrease the anticoagulant effect of warfarin include vitamin K, antihistamines, certain antacids, rifampin, cholestyramine, barbiturates, and griseofulvin. In addition, metabolic and dietary influences that change the disposition of albumin and vitamin K alter the anticoagulant effect of warfarin as well.

194. The answer is C. *(Braunwald, 4/e, pp 707–709. Somberg, Am Heart J 111:1162–1176, 1986.)* Torsades de pointes is a rapid ventricular tachycardia characterized by unusual QRS complexes whose axes shift back and forth around the baseline. It occurs most commonly in patients who have prolonged QT intervals. Indeed, any influence that prolongs the QT interval—such as quinidine, procainamide, tricyclic antidepressants, phenothiazines, hypokalemia, or hypocalcemia—or congenital QT prolongation may cause torsades. This rhythm is clinically important because it may degenerate to ventricular fibrillation, and it should not be treated with QT-lengthening antiarrhythmics. Emergent therapy may include either ventricular pacing or isoproterenol infusion along with correction of the underlying abnormality in the acquired forms or with the addition of drugs that shorten the QT interval (such as phenytoin and beta blockers) in the congenital varieties. For patients with recurrent symptomatic torsades despite maximal medical therapy, left-sided cervicothoracic sympathetic ganglionectomy may be effective. If this surgery is also ineffective in preventing symptomatic arrhythmias, implantation of an automatic cardioverter-defibrillator should be considered.

195. The answer is C. *(Braunwald, 4/e, pp 679–682. Mandel, 2/e, pp 228–230.)* The rhythm strip exhibited in the question reveals atrial flutter with 4:1 atrioventricular (AV) block. Atrial flutter is characterized by an atrial rate of 280 to 320 per minute; the electrocardiogram typically reveals a sawtooth baseline configuration due to the flutter waves. In the strip presented, every fourth atrial depolarization is conducted through the AV node, resulting in a ventricular rate of 75 per minute.

196. The answer is A. *(Braunwald, 4/e, pp 1029–1035.)* The fundamental defect in mitral valve prolapse is an abnormality of the valve's connective tissue with secondary proliferation of myxomatous tissue. The redundant leaflet or leaflets prolapse toward the left atrium in systole, which results in the auscultated click and murmur and characteristic echocardiographic findings. Any maneuver that reduces left ventricular size, such as standing or Valsalva, allows the click and murmur to occur earlier in systole; conversely, those maneuvers that increase left ventricular size, such as squatting and propranolol administration, delay the onset of the click and murmur. While most patients with mitral valve prolapse have a benign prognosis, a small percentage die suddenly. Antibiotic prophylaxis to prevent endocarditis is recommended for those with typical auscultatory findings, including a systolic murmur.

197. The answer is E. *(Braunwald, 4/e, pp 484–486. Schlant, 8/e, pp 573–588.)* Drugs interact with digoxin by a variety of mechanisms. Verapamil decreases renal and total body clearance of digoxin and results in approximately a 70 to 100 percent increase in steady-state serum digoxin levels; verapamil thus requires a decrease in digoxin dose by approximately one-half. Quinidine increases absorption, decreases volume of distribution, and decreases renal and total body clearance of digoxin. The result is approximately a 100 percent increase in steady-state serum digoxin level, which requires a decrease in digoxin dosage by approximately one-half. Amiodarone decreases renal and total body clearance of digoxin and increases steady-state serum digoxin levels by 70 to 100 percent; it likewise requires a decrease in digoxin dosage by one-half. Erythromycin increases the bioavailability of digoxin by decreasing intestinal metabolism of digoxin by certain gut flora; the result is a 43 to 150 percent increase in steady-state digoxin levels. Metoclopramide decreases bioavailability of digoxin by increasing intestinal motility, which results in a 25 to 36 percent drop in steady-state digitalis levels. Other medications that decrease serum digoxin levels include cholestyramine, certain antacids, neomycin, and sulfasalazine.

198. The answer is C. *(Schlant, 8/e, pp 1682–1683.)* The list of conditions at relatively high risk of development of infective endocarditis includes Marfan's syndrome, prosthetic heart valves, coarctation of the aorta, aortic valve disease, ventricular septal defect, mitral insufficiency, and patent ductus arteriosus. Mitral valve prolapse, pure mitral stenosis, and tricuspid and pulmonary valve disease are among the conditions at intermediate risk. Among the conditions considered to be at very low risk are atrial septal defect, syphilitic aortitis, and cardiac pacemakers.

199. The answer is A. *(Braunwald, 4/e, pp 239–242.)* The right coronary artery supplies the sinoatrial node in approximately 50 to 60 percent of cases and the atrioventricular node in approximately 77 to 90 percent of cases. The left anterior descending coronary artery arises from the left main coronary artery and courses along the anterior interventricular sulcus toward the cardiac apex. Along its course it gives rise to septal branches, which perfuse the interventricular septum, and diagonal branches, which perfuse the anterolateral aspect of the heart. The left circumflex coronary artery arises from the left main coronary artery and courses along the left atrioventricular sulcus; it gives rise to obtuse marginal branches, which perfuse the lateral aspect of the left ventricle. The right coronary artery arises from the right aortic sinus and courses along the right atrioventricular sulcus; it gives rise to acute marginal branches and posterior left ventricular branches. The dominant coronary artery (the right coronary artery in 77 to 90 percent of cases and the left circumflex in the remainder) supplies the diaphragmatic portion of the left ventricle and the inferior portion of the interventricular septum.

200. The answer is B. *(Braunwald, 4/e, pp 967–968.)* Coarctation of the aorta is a congenital abnormality characterized by a region of narrowed aorta; 95 percent of these lesions occur just distal to the left subclavian artery. Because of decreased blood flow to the lower extremities, affected patients may complain of leg fatigue or pain on exertion. A congenital bicuspid aortic valve occurs concomitantly with coarctation in approximately 50 percent of such people. Symptoms of congestive heart failure are common in infants who have coarctation and usually appear in the first months of life. Patients afflicted with Turner's syndrome have a high incidence of aortic coarctation.

201. The answer is B. *(Schlant, 8/e, pp 269–273.)* Normally, the second heart sound (S_2) is composed of aortic closure followed by pulmonic closure. Because inspiration increases blood return to the right side of the heart, pulmonic closure is delayed, which results in normal splitting of S_2 during inspiration. Paradoxical splitting of S_2, however, refers to a splitting of S_2 that is narrowed instead of widened with inspiration consequent to a delayed aortic closure. Paradoxical splitting can result from any electrical or mechanical event that delays left ventricular systole. Thus, aortic stenosis and hypertension, which increase resistance to systolic ejection of blood, delay closure of the aortic valve. Acute ischemia from angina or acute myocardial infarction also can delay ejection of blood from the left ventricle. The most common cause of paradoxical splitting—left bundle branch block—delays electrical activation of the left ventricle. Right bundle branch block results in a wide splitting of S_2 that widens further during inspiration.

202. The answer is A. *(Braunwald, 4/e, pp 1548–1549.)* Aneurysms of the aorta from syphilis occur most commonly in the ascending aorta and least commonly in the descending thoracic or abdominal aorta. Calcification in the wall of the ascending aorta is frequently present. Aneurysm formation occurs 15 to 30 years following infection with syphilis. Aortic valvular insufficiency is the most common complication of syphilitic aortitis. In addition, the coronary ostia may be involved, resulting in angina or myocardial infarction.

203. The answer is C. *(Schlant, 8/e, pp 1153, 1369, 1387.)* The formation of a ventricular aneurysm is a late complication of myocardial infarction and the diagnosis is suggested by the presence of persistent ST-segment elevation several months after the infarction. Patients who have an aneurysm may present with arterial emboli, recurrent ventricular arrhythmias, or intractable congestive heart failure. Rupture is extremely unlikely unless there is a reinfarction over the same involved area of the ventricle. The chest x-ray occasionally reveals calcium in the wall of the aneurysm or in a mural thrombus within the aneurysm.

204. The answer is C. *(Braunwald, 4/e, pp 679–680. Mandel, 2/e, pp 187, 199.)* The rhythm strip shown below and in the question demonstrates normal sinus rhythm with two atrial premature contractions (beats numbered 5 and 9). P waves of atrial premature contractions appear earlier than expected and differ in morphology from the P waves of the sinus beats. They may be conducted to the ventricles and result in relatively normal-appearing QRS complexes or, if they occur during the refractory period of the atrioventricular node or the ventricles, they may be blocked. In that situation, premature P waves would differ in morphology from the P waves of the sinus beats and no QRS complex would follow the premature P wave.

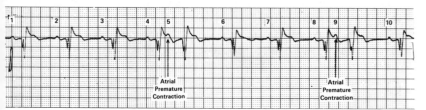

205. The answer is A. *(Braunwald, 4/e, pp 1404–1415.)* Hypertrophic cardiomyopathy is characterized by thickening of the muscular interventricular septum, which results in obstruction to left ventricular ejection of blood during ventricular systole and impairment of left ventricular filling during diastole. The typical murmur is a systolic ejection murmur along the left sternal border. Any maneuver that increases left ventricular volume will decrease the obstruction and murmur. Conversely, standing, which causes venous pooling in the lower extremities, will decrease ventricular volume and thus cause the obstruction and murmur to increase. The arterial pulse has a typical brisk upstroke and may display two palpable peaks in the pulse wave. A loud fourth heart sound is common and results from the encounter of the blood from atrial systole with a thick, noncompliant ventricle. Associated systolic anterior motion of the anterior leaflet of the mitral valve causes mitral regurgitation in 50 percent of patients. Beta blockers or calcium antagonists, by affecting hypercontractile systolic function and abnormal diastolic filling, may relieve symptoms like dyspnea on exertion, chest pain, or light-headedness.

206. The answer is E (all). *(Braunwald, 4/e, pp 1434–1446, 1754–1760.)* The use of cocaine has been associated with myocardial ischemia or infarction as a result of increased myocardial oxygen demand, decreased myocardial oxygen supply (coronary vasoconstriction), accelerated atherosclerosis, or coronary artery thrombosis. Histopathology has demonstrated myocarditis, contraction band necrosis, and thickening of intramural coronary arteries. It is unclear whether vasoconstrictor, sympathomimetic, hypersensitivity, thrombogenic, or direct toxic effects are responsible. Pericarditis is the most frequent acute radiation-induced cardiac abnormality, with an incidence of 10 to 15 percent in patients who receive over 4000 rads to the mediastinum. The peak incidence is 5 to 9 months following radiotherapy. The vast majority of patients with clinical radiation pericarditis demonstrate pericardial effusion on echocardiography. Radiation-induced myocarditis may result in mild transient depression of left ventricular systolic function, nonspecific electrocardiographic abnormalities, papillary muscle dysfunction with mitral regurgitation, interstitial myocardial fibrosis that affects the right ventricle more than the left, or endocardial fibrosis that manifests as a restrictive cardiomyopathy. Coronary arterial occlusive disease follows radiation exposure by approximately a decade. Findings include severe medial, adventitial, and epicardial fibrosis, a decrease in smooth muscle cells in the media, and a paucity of lipid in intimal lesions. The proximal coronary arteries are involved more than distal vessels. The antineoplastic agent doxorubicin has been associated with early cardiotoxicity including dysrhythmias and electrocardiographic changes, as well as the rare complications of pericarditis-myocarditis syndrome, left ventricular dysfunction, myocardial infarction, and sudden death. Late doxorubicin cardiotoxicity involves the development of a dose-dependent dilated cardiomyopathy, which is fatal in over 50 percent of cases. Because the incidence of cardiomyopathy increases progressively with cumulative doses of doxorubicin above 500 mg/m^2, it is recommended that the cumulative dose be limited to under 450 to 500 mg/m^2. The use of the chemotherapeutic agent 5-fluorouracil has been associated with chest pain, electrocardiographic abnormalities, and arrhythmias (suggestive of myocardial ischemia due to coronary vasospasm), as well as vasoocclusive phenomena (including acute myocardial infarction) and a myocarditis characterized by swelling of myocardial fibers without inflammatory infiltrate.

207. The answer is E (all). *(Braunwald, 4/e, pp 408–413.)* In acute systolic heart failure, neurohumoral changes function to expand intraarterial blood volume and assure perfusion of vital organs. In chronic heart failure, excessive volume retention and increased afterload exacerbate the condition. Circulating norepinephrine concentrations at rest are approximately two to three times higher in patients with heart failure than in normal subjects. The extent of this elevation correlates directly with the degree of left ventricular dysfunction. Adrenergic stimulation of beta$_1$ adrenoceptors in the juxtaglomerular apparatus of the kidney and activation of baroreceptors in the renal vasculature in response to decreased renal blood flow result in an increase in renin release with subsequent elevations in angiotensin II and aldosterone. Patients with heart failure demonstrate levels of circulating arginine vasopressin approximately twice those of normal subjects. The counterregulatory hormone atrial natriuretic peptide (ANP) produces vasodilatation and salt and water excretion in response to increases in atrial distending pressure.

ANP may prevent volume overload by decreasing renin production, counteracting the effects of angiotensin II on vascular tone and secretion of aldosterone and vasopressin, and increasing renal salt and water excretion. Additionally, atrial natriuretic peptide may modify baroreceptor function and blunt increases in heart rate.

208. The answer is E (all). *(Braunwald, 4/e, pp 1095–1096.)* Bacterial endocarditis that results in aortic insufficiency with congestive heart failure is associated with extremely high mortality and warrants urgent valve replacement. Surgical drainage is required for myocardial or valve ring abscesses. Prosthetic valve endocarditis is commonly associated with myocardial invasion and may result in instability of the prosthesis. Uncontrolled infection (persistent bacteremia or fungal infection) is also an indication for operative intervention. The occurrence of multiple embolic episodes is considered by many a major indication for surgery as well.

209–211. The answers are 209-D, 210-B, 211-A. *(Schlant, 8/e, pp 1471–1472, 1519–1521, 1662.)* Tricuspid stenosis is characterized by a slow y descent of the jugular pulse and a diastolic rumble at the lower left sternal border.

Aortic regurgitation, in addition to generating the characteristic decrescendo diastolic murmur along the left sternal border, may also cause a diastolic rumble at the apex. Termed an Austin Flint murmur, this diastolic rumble is thought to result from the effect of the regurgitant jet of blood on the anterior leaflet of the mitral valve. Although distinguishing this murmur from that of mitral stenosis may be difficult, the absence of both an opening snap and loud first heart sound should suggest an Austin Flint murmur.

Constrictive pericarditis is characterized by a sharp y descent. This diagnosis should be considered in any patient who has unexplained edema or ascites.

212–215. The answers are 212-D, 213-C, 214-A, 215-B. *(Braunwald, 4/e, pp 858–870. Schlant, 8/e, pp 1429–1437.)* Captopril, by inhibiting the angiotensin converting enzyme, is a potent antihypertensive agent because it prevents the generation of angiotensin II, a vasoconstrictor, and inhibits the degradation of bradykinin, a vasodilator. While especially useful in renovascular hypertension, it may cause membranous glomerulopathy, the nephrotic syndrome, and leukopenia.

Hydralazine is an arterial vasodilator generally used in conjunction with drugs that prevent reflex sympathetic stimulation of the heart, such as beta blockers and methyldopa. A lupuslike syndrome has been associated with the use of hydralazine.

Propranolol is a nonselective beta blocker and may therefore cause bronchospasm in susceptible patients. Beta blockers, as a class, may reduce HDL cholesterol and increase serum triglyceride levels.

Minoxidil is a more potent vasodilator than hydralazine but its use is limited by a high incidence of hirsutism. Marked fluid retention may also occur.

Gynecomastia is not a side effect of the drugs listed, although spironolactone, a potassium-sparing diuretic, and methyldopa, a centrally acting antiadrenergic agent, are two antihypertensives that may cause this problem.

216–219. The answers are 216-E, 217-D, 218-B, 219-A. *(Braunwald, 4/e, pp 149–151. Schlant, 8/e, pp 342–346, 761–770.)* Hypokalemia typically increases automaticity of myocardial fibers, which results in ectopic beats or arrhythmias. Electrocardiography in hypokalemia reveals flattening of the T wave and prominent U waves.

Hyperkalemia decreases the rate of spontaneous diastolic depolarization in all pacemaker cells. It also results in slowing of conduction. One of the earliest electrocardiographic signs of hyperkalemia is the appearance of tall, peaked T waves. More severe elevations of the serum potassium result in widening of the QRS complex.

Hypocalcemia results in prolongation of the QT interval. Low serum calcium levels may also be associated with a decrease in myocardial contractility.

At serum sodium levels compatible with life, neither hyponatremia nor hypernatremia results in any characteristic electrocardiographic abnormalities.

220–222. The answers are 220-A, 221-D, 222-C. *(Braunwald, 4/e, pp 889–890, 1644–1645.)* Dextrocardia is a prominent feature of Kartagener's syndrome, an inherited condition that features situs inversus, chronic sinusitis, and bronchiectasis.

Dilatation of the aortic and pulmonary arteries commonly occurs with homocystinuria, an inborn error of metabolism. This condition, which is caused by a deficiency of the enzyme cystathionine synthetase, is characterized by the presence of intravascular thrombosis, lens subluxation, and osteoporosis, as well as large-vessel dilatation.

Hyperextensible joints, one of the common defects in Down's syndrome (trisomy 21), are frequently associated with cardiac abnormalities, including an endocardial cushion defect, atrial and ventricular septal defects, and the tetralogy of Fallot. Hypotonia often accompanies the hyperextensible joints.

223–227. The answers are 223-A, 224-D, 225-E, 226-B, 227-A. *(Braunwald, 4/e, p 19. Schlant, 8/e, pp 238–241.)* The normal jugular venous pulse wave consists of three positive waves and two troughs. Normally, the *a* wave is the largest wave and is due to right atrial contraction. The *c* wave that follows is probably related to bulging of the tricuspid valve into the atrium. Relaxation of the atrium and downward displacement of the tricuspid valve toward the apex during ventricular systole result in the *x* descent. The *v* wave results from the filling of the right atrium with blood while the tricuspid valve is still closed. The *y* descent is the result of opening of the tricuspid valve and ventricular filling. An S_4 gallop is produced by atrial contraction and thus would occur at approximately the same time as the *a* wave.

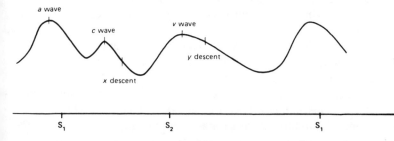

228–231. The answers are 228-C, 229-A, 230-D, 231-B. *(Braunwald, 4/e, pp 168–169, 1697.)* Probability analysis is useful in clinical decision making. Frequently used terms are defined below. A true positive (TP) test is one that gives a positive result in a patient with disease. A true negative (TN) test is one that gives a negative result in a patient without disease. A false positive (FP) test is one that gives a positive result in a patient without disease. A false negative (FN) test is one that gives a negative result in a patient with disease.

The term *sensitivity* refers to the percentage of patients who will test positive out of all patients who have disease. The term *specificity* refers to the percentage of patients who will test negative out of all patients who are free of disease. The predictive value of a positive test refers to the percentage of true positives out of all positive tests. The predictive value of a negative test refers to the percentage of true negatives out of all negative tests. The sensitivity and specificity of a test cannot alone assess the probability of presence of disease. Bayes' theorem, which includes prevalence of disease in the population under study as well as the sensitivity and specificity of the testing method, is a useful tool in assessing the probability of presence of disease in an individual. For example, an exercise stress test demonstrating a 1-mm horizontal ST-segment depression is likely to represent a false positive test for ischemia in a 6-year-old girl and is likely to represent a true positive test for ischemia in a 60-year-old male smoker with hyperlipidemia and hypertension.

232–235. The answers are 232-D, 233-B, 234-C, 235-A. *(Braunwald, 4/e, pp 22–24. Schlant, 8/e, pp 235–237.)* Pulsus parvus et tardus is the small-amplitude pulse with slow rate of rise and delayed systolic peak that is characteristic of severe aortic stenosis.

Pulsus alternans is an alternation of the amplitude of the pulse that can be detected when systolic blood pressure varies by more than 20 mmHg from beat to beat. This is a sign of severe depression of myocardial function during regular rhythm and can be confused with pulsus bigeminus, in which alternation of the pulse amplitude occurs as a result of bigeminal rhythm.

Pulsus paradoxus is a decrease in the amplitude of the arterial pulse during inspiration by greater than 10 mmHg and is palpable when an inspiratory drop in systolic pressure of greater than 20 mmHg occurs. Lesser degrees of pulsus paradoxus can be detected by sphygmomanometry and auscultation. Pulsus paradoxus is an exaggerated form of the normal inspiratory decrease in systolic pressure and is due to increased right ventricular stroke volume, decreased left ventricular stroke volume, and the effect of negative intrathoracic pressure on the aorta.

Pulsus bisferiens is a pulse with two systolic peaks that occurs in hypertrophic obstructive cardiomyopathy and in other conditions in which a large stroke volume is rapidly ejected from the left ventricle. In hypertrophic obstructive cardiomyopathy, rapid ejection of blood during early systole results in a prominent percussion wave, followed by a rapid decline in pulse as outflow obstruction occurs, and then followed by the tidal (reflected) wave. In hypertrophic obstructive cardiomyopathy, the magnitude of the bisferiens pulse is related to the degree of obstruction to left ventricular outflow. In patients with minor degrees of obstruction, the bisferiens pulse may be elicited by hemodynamic maneuvers such as Valsalva or inhalation of amyl nitrite.

236–240. The answers are 236-A, 237-B, 238-A, 239-A, 240-B. *(Braunwald, 4/e, pp 1473–1489.)* Accumulation of fluid in the pericardial space results in an increase in intrapericardial pressure. When this pressure rises to the level of right atrial and right ventricular diastolic pressures, cardiac tamponade occurs. As fluid continues to accumulate, intrapericardial and cardiac diastolic pressures continue to rise with an associated fall in cardiac output and systemic arterial pressure. In cardiac tamponade, intracardiac pressures are elevated, which leads to impaired diastolic ventricular filling and a consequent drop in stroke volume and cardiac output. Compensatory increases in adrenergic tone result in tachycardia and increased ejection fraction, as well as increased systemic vascular resistance, which attempts to preserve systemic arterial pressure while sacrificing a degree of cardiac output. Compensatory mechanisms are unable to maintain systemic arterial pressure when cardiac outputs are very low and severe hypoperfusion and ischemia supervene. Under normal conditions, cardiac filling occurs twice during the cardiac cycle: once during ventricular ejection (systolic x descent of the right atrial and jugular venous pressure pulse) and again during right atrial emptying through the tricuspid valve in diastole (the diastolic y descent of the right atrial and jugular venous pressure pulse). In cardiac tamponade, because of cardiac compression throughout the cardiac cycle, only when intracardiac volume decreases during ejection does venous blood enter the right atrium. Intrapericardial pressure elevations that equal or exceed right atrial pressure prevent cardiac filling during diastole. The prominent systolic x descent and attenuated-or-absent early diastolic y descent in right atrial or systemic venous waveforms reflect cardiac tamponade physiology. With normal cardiac physiology, inspiration causes a decrease in intrathoracic and intrapericardial pressure with augmentation of venous return. This causes a small increase in right ventricular size and a small decrease in left ventricular size due to leftward shifting of the interventricular septum. In cardiac tamponade, inspiration decreases the elevated intrapericardial and right atrial pressure and increases venous return, which results in a relatively large increase in right ventricular dimensions and reduction in left ventricular dimensions due to leftward bulging of the interventricular septum. Left atrial and left ventricular diastolic pressures decline, which results in a decrease in aortic flow and systolic arterial pressure. The inspiratory decrease in aortic systolic pressure greater than 10 mmHg is termed *pulsus paradoxus*.

Constrictive pericarditis occurs when fibrosis and calcification of the pericardium restrict (usually symmetrically) the diastolic filling of all chambers of the heart. Early diastolic filling is rapid and not impaired because venous pressure is elevated and intracardiac volume is below that of the constricting pericardium. When intracardiac volume reaches that of the noncompliant pericardium, rapid early diastolic filling ceases abruptly. Ventricular diastolic pressure waveforms exhibit the characteristic dip-and-plateau pattern. Unlike cardiac tamponade, in constrictive pericarditis intrapericardial pressure is not increased and diastolic filling is unimpeded until the volume limit of the noncompliant pericardium is reached. The symmetrical stiff scarring of the pericardium results in equalization of elevated diastolic pressures in all four cardiac chambers. Right and left atrial and jugular venous waveforms demonstrate prominent deep diastolic y descents and less prominent systolic x descents, which reflects right atrial filling during ventricular systolic ejection and early diastolic periods. In normal physiology, venous return is predominantly during systole, but in constrictive pericarditis, it is predominantly during diastole. As a result of the fibrotic, thickened pericardium, intrathoracic pressure changes during respiration are not transmitted to the pericardium and intracardiac chambers. Significant pulsus paradoxus does not occur because systemic venous and right atrial pressures do not decline during inspiration and there is no augmentation of venous return to the right atrium. Constrictive pericarditis may be associated with an inspiratory increase in systemic venous pressure (Kussmaul's sign), which does not occur in cardiac tamponade because the drop in intrathoracic pressure is transmitted to the pericardium and right atrium.

I - 21 β Hydroxyplase - (cortisol)

II 21 β - Hyd 2 — (salt Loovi)

III

Endocrinology and Metabolic Disease

DIRECTIONS: Each question below contains five suggested responses. Select the **one best** response to each question.

241. You are asked to see a 20-year-old Asian woman for hirsutism and irregular menstrual periods. The hair growth began about 5 years ago and is mainly over her lower abdomen, outer upper lip, chin, and sideburns. Menarche was at age 14 and the menstrual periods have been irregular and unpredictable. Average number of periods are five to seven per year. Initial laboratory findings are listed.

Testosterone	1.8 nmol/L (N<2.5)
DHEAS	12.3 nmol/L (N<10)
Androstenedione	9.6 nmol/L (N<10)
Prolactin	14 μg/L (N<16)
LH	4.8 IU/L (N<15 during follicular phase)
FSH	6.3 IU/L (N<10 during follicular phase)
17 α-hydroxyprogesterone	2.3 nmol/L (N<4 during follicular phase)

Demonstration of diagnosis can be done by

(A) LH/FSH ratio
(B) free testosterone
(C) ACTH-stimulated 17-hydroxyprogesterone level
(D) ultrasound of ovaries
(E) CT of adrenals

242. A 15-year-old boy and his parents are concerned about the absence of any signs of puberty. His friends have all entered puberty and he feels embarrassed. He is nervous but well and his growth curves for height and weight are adequate. The physician asks the boy if his ability to smell is impaired. He thinks it is but as he did not volunteer the information his physician is uncertain of the significance of the answer. Physical examination is unrevealing except for prepubertal testes. His physician should consider all the following tests and recommendations EXCEPT

(A) basal serum levels of follicle-stimulating hormone (FSH), luteinizing hormone (LH), and testosterone
(B) serum prolactin
(C) a provocative test for growth hormone secretion, such as insulin tolerance test
(D) thyroid function tests
(E) evaluation of olfactory nerve function by smell testing

243. A 42-year-old woman is evaluated for hypoglycemia. She has experienced recurrent episodes of inappropriate behavior and dizziness for the past year, and she had syncope on one occasion after mowing her lawn. She denies hunger or palpitations and only occasionally has noted sweating. The patient has gained 15 pounds during the last year. Laboratory plasma studies reveal a glucose level of 65 mg/dL, insulin level of 18 μU/mL (normal: 10 to 20) after an overnight fast, and a diabetic glucose tolerance test (2-h value: 225 mg/dL) without reactive hypoglycemia. After 48 h of fasting, the patient became confused. At this time her plasma glucose and insulin levels are 34 mg/dL and 20 μU/mL, respectively. The most likely diagnosis is

(A) Addison's disease
(B) reactive hypoglycemia
(C) diabetes mellitus
(D) insulinoma
(E) hepatoma

244. The patient pictured below complains of the sudden onset of a painful "lump" in her neck following an upper respiratory infection. Physical examination reveals a soft, round, tender, midline mass at the level of the hyoid bone. The most likely diagnosis is

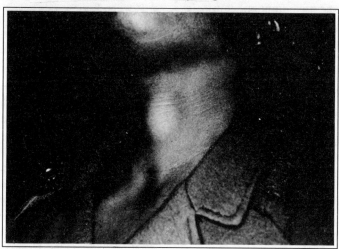

(A) acute suppurative thyroiditis
(B) subacute thyroiditis
(C) thyroglossal duct cyst
(D) toxic nodular goiter
(E) thyroid adenoma

245. A 52-year-old man complains of impotence. On physical examination he has an elevated jugular venous pulse, S_3 gallop, and hepatomegaly. He also appears tanned, with pigmentation along joint folds. His left knee is swollen and tender. The plasma glucose is 250 mg/dL, and liver enzymes are elevated. Your next study to establish the diagnosis should be

(A) detection of nocturnal penile tumescence
(B) determination of serum ferritin
(C) determination of serum copper
(D) detection of hepatitis B surface antigen
(E) echocardiography

246. A 25-year-old woman who has insulin-dependent diabetes develops recurrent hypoglycemia. Her history reveals amenorrhea of 2 months' duration. A urinalysis is negative for glucose and protein; a vaginal smear shows no evidence of estrogen deficiency. The most likely diagnosis is

(A) pregnancy
(B) renal failure
(C) hypopituitarism
(D) insulinoma
(E) hyperthyroidism

247. A patient develops severe hypotension immediately after removal of a pheochromocytoma. The most appropriate management would be the administration of which of the following?

(A) Corticosteroids
(B) Mineralocorticoids
(C) Alpha-stimulating agents
(D) Beta-stimulating agents
(E) Blood or plasma

248. A 35-year-old woman has a 6-month history of amenorrhea. She had regular periods since menarche at age 12 until 3 years ago, when her periods became irregular. She also complains of fatigue, hot flashes, and dry skin. On physical examination she has a goiter and pigmentation of the gums and skin. Family history is significant for diabetes and thyroid disease. Laboratory studies reveal macrocytic anemia. A 5-day course of medroxyprogesterone acetate (Provera) 10 mg fails to induce withdrawal bleeding, while vaginal bleeding occurs following 20 days of conjugated estrogen and progesterone administration. Her amenorrhea is a result of

(A) primary ovarian failure
(B) polycystic ovary syndrome
(C) endometrial failure (Asherman's syndrome)
(D) pituitary failure
(E) thyroid disorder

249. A 30-year-old man is evaluated for a thyroid nodule. The patient reports that his father died from "thyroid cancer" and that a brother had a history of recurrent renal stones. Blood calcitonin concentration is 2000 pg/mL (normal: less than 100); serum calcium and phosphate levels are normal. Before referring the patient to a surgeon, the physician should

(A) obtain a liver scan
(B) perform a calcium infusion test
(C) measure urinary catecholamines
(D) administer suppressive doses of thyroxine and measure levels of thyroid-stimulating hormone
(E) treat the patient with radioactive iodine

250. A 32-year-old woman has a 3-year history of oligomenorrhea that has progressed to amenorrhea during the past year. She has observed loss of breast fullness, reduced hip measurements, acne, increased body hair, and deepening of her voice. Physical examination reveals frontal balding, clitoral hypertrophy, and a male escutcheon. Urinary free cortisol and dehydroepiandrosterone sulfate (DHEAS) are normal. Her plasma testosterone level is 6 ng/mL (normal: 0.2 to 0.8). The most likely diagnosis of this patient's disorder is

(A) hilar cell tumor
(B) Cushing's syndrome
(C) arrhenoblastoma
(D) polycystic ovary syndrome
(E) granulosa-theca cell tumor

251. A 35-year-old woman presents with weakness, weight loss, and a skin rash of 8 months' duration. There is no previous history except for mild diabetes mellitus. Physical examination shows a widely scattered, necrolytic, erythematous rash with few bullae; the perineum is particularly severely affected. There is angular stomatitis and glossitis, the fingernails are brittle, and muscle wasting is evident. The results of laboratory tests are:

Hemoglobin	9.3 g/dL
Mean corpuscular volume	90 μm³
Reticulocyte count	1%
Serum iron	38 μg/dL
Plasma glucose	225 mg/dL

The results of all other screening hematology and chemistry studies are normal. Which of the following should be the next diagnostic study?

(A) CT of the abdomen
(B) Measurement of plasma glucagon
(C) Radionuclide thyroid scan
(D) Renal ultrasound examination
(E) Measurement of plasma somatostatin

252. An otherwise healthy 60-year-old man is noted on routine examination to have a firm thyroid nodule. Serum thyroxine is 8.0 μg/dL (normal: 4 to 11). Thyroid scan demonstrates a "cold" nodule. The most appropriate management would be which of the following procedures?

(A) Complete lobectomy
(B) Fine-needle aspiration cytology
(C) Levothyroxine
(D) Radioactive iodine therapy
(E) External irradiation

253. A 60-year-old woman presents with generalized muscle weakness, loss of appetite, palpitations, and a small diffuse nodular goiter. An electrocardiogram reveals rapid atrial fibrillation. Despite adequate digitalization, there is little slowing of her ventricular rate. Thyroid function studies reveal a serum thyroxine level of 12 μg/dL (normal: 5 to 12), with a triiodothyronine (T_3) level of 200 ng/dL (normal: 80 to 160), as measured by radioimmunoassay and a highly sensitive thyroid-stimulating hormone (TSH) of 0.05 μIU/mL (normal 0.3 to 3.0). The most likely diagnosis and appropriate treatment would be

(A) typical Graves' disease; therapy with antithyroid drugs
(B) mild Graves' disease; initiation of therapy with low dose of ^{131}I
(C) toxic multinodular goiter; therapy with antithyroid drugs followed by surgery
(D) toxic multinodular goiter; initiation of therapy with antithyroid agents followed by high dose of ^{131}I when euthyroid
(E) sick euthyroid syndrome; continuation of treatment of heart disease with digoxin and propranolol

254. A 54-year-old man who has had a Billroth II procedure for peptic ulcer disease now presents with abdominal pain and is found to have recurrent ulcer disease. The physician is considering this patient's illness to be secondary either to a retained antrum or to a gastrinoma. Which of the following tests would best differentiate the two conditions?

(A) Random gastrin level
(B) Determination of 24-h acid production
(C) Serum calcium level
(D) Secretin infusion
(E) Insulin-induced hypoglycemia

255. A 55-year-old woman who has a history of severe depression and who had radical mastectomy for carcinoma of the breast 1 year previously develops polyuria, nocturia, and excessive thirst. Laboratory values are as follows:

Serum electrolytes (meq/L):
  Na$^+$ 149; K$^+$ 3.6
Serum calcium: 9.5 mg/dL
Blood glucose: 110 mg/dL
Blood urea nitrogen: 30 mg/dL
Urine osmolality: 150 mOsm/kg

The most likely diagnosis is

(A) psychogenic polydipsia
(B) renal glycosuria
(C) hypercalciuria
(D) diabetes insipidus
(E) inappropriate antidiuretic hormone syndrome

DIRECTIONS: Each question below contains four suggested responses of which **one or more** is correct. Select

A	if	**1, 2, and 3**	are correct
B	if	**1 and 3**	are correct
C	if	**2 and 4**	are correct
D	if	**4**	is correct
E	if	**1, 2, 3, and 4**	are correct

256. A 45-year-old man is noted on physical examination to have coarse facial features, oily skin, and an enlarged tongue. Initial laboratory studies reveal a fasting glucose of 190 mg/dL. Which of the following would support the physician's presumptive diagnosis of acromegaly?

(1) An increase in growth hormone with oral glucose administration
(2) Thyromegaly
(3) Signs consistent with carpal tunnel syndrome
(4) Normal basal growth hormone levels with elevated somatomedin C

257. A 42-year-old man complains of impotence. His physician discovers that he is taking a drug that is known to interfere with the hormonal control of erection. Drugs having such an effect include

(1) chlorpheniramine
(2) spironolactone
(3) azathioprine
(4) cimetidine

258. Correct statements regarding the adrenal pathology and function in patients who have acquired immunodeficiency syndrome (AIDS) include which of the following?

(1) The adrenal gland is almost always involved by cytomegalovirus (CMV)
(2) Rifampin, a medication used in treatment of many AIDS patients, might cause adrenal failure
(3) Clinical adrenal failure as a complication of AIDS is uncommon
(4) Normal baseline and ACTH-stimulated aldosterone levels are seen in patients with hyporeninemic hypoaldosteronism

259. A 52-year-old man complains of breast enlargement, which was noticed about 2 months ago. He denies any other significant problems and claims to have normal libido and potency. He has two children from his last marriage. He uses marijuana frequently and alcohol occasionally. Results of physical examination are normal except for gynecomastia. Estradiol, testosterone, hCG, and LH levels are all elevated. Appropriate management will include

(1) testicular ultrasound
(2) CT scan of the pituitary
(3) CT scan of the chest
(4) advice to discontinue marijuana and be retested in 8 weeks

260. Correct statements concerning the management of impending thyroid storm include that

(1) antithyroid drugs should be given prior to saturated solution of potassium iodine
(2) propranolol may help to control marked sinus tachycardia
(3) dexamethasone inhibits the generation of T_3 from T_4
(4) methimazole is as efficacious as propylthiouracil

261. A thin, 30-year-old woman complains of nervousness, mild sweating, palpitations, scanty menses, and weight loss. Her blood pressure is 150/80 mmHg and pulse rate 96 beats per minute. She displays mild hyperpigmentation and telangiectasis on the face. A small thyroid nodule is palpable. Serum thyroxine is 9.0 µg/dL (normal: 4.5 to 10); resin T_3 uptake is normal; radioactive iodine uptake is 30 percent (normal: 5 to 35); and thyroid scan shows uptake by a solitary left-sided thyroid nodule (no uptake by the right lobe). The diagnosis of hyperthyroidism in this patient may be established by

(1) thyrotropin-releasing hormone test
(2) serum triiodothyronine radioimmunoassay
(3) highly sensitive serum thyroid-stimulating hormone assay
(4) thyroid-stimulating immunoglobulin (TSI) assay

262. A 32-year-old woman presents with a serum calcium of 11.8 mg/dL and a mildly elevated parathyroid hormone (PTH) concentration. There is a family history of hypercalcemia but no history of kidney stones or bone diseases. Indicated studies include

(1) urinary cyclic adenosine monophosphate (cAMP)
(2) cortisone suppression test
(3) serum calcitonin
(4) calcium/creatinine clearance ratio

263. A 21-year-old woman who is 12 weeks pregnant is noted to have hypertension. History is negative for any problems except tonsillectomy at age 8 for recurrent infections. Physical examination does not reveal postural hypotension. Blood pressure is comparable in all four extremities. Skin examination reveals café au lait spots. Probable causes of increased blood pressure in this patient include

(1) pheochromocytoma
(2) gestational hypertension
(3) renal artery dysplasia
(4) aldosterone-producing adenoma

264. A 20-year-old man who has a history of polyuria and hypotonic urine is placed on restricted water intake. After a period of dehydration his urine osmolality stabilizes at 450 mOsm/kg. Following injection of vasopressin (Pitressin) his urine osmolality rises to 600 mOsm/kg. This patient's symptoms are likely to improve if he is treated with

(1) chlorpropamide
(2) thiazide diuretics
(3) deamino-D-arginine vasopressin (dDAVP, desmopressin)
(4) glyburide

265. A 25-year-old woman complains of a recent onset of nervousness, palpitations, and increased sweating. Her serum thyroxine is 15 μg/dL (normal: 4 to 11), and radioactive iodine uptake is 1 percent. Hyperthyroidism in this patient may have been induced by

(1) thyroxine
(2) thyroiditis
(3) cholecystography
(4) oat cell carcinoma of the lungs

266. True statements regarding management of ocular complications of diabetes include which of the following?

(1) Patients with type 1 diabetes should be screened annually for retinopathy beginning 10 years after the onset of diabetes

(2) Photocoagulation therapy reduces the rate of developing visual loss by about 50 percent in patients with macular edema

(3) Ophthalmoscopic screening is indicated in gestational diabetes, as there is risk of worsening proliferative retinopathy

(4) Screening ophthalmic examination with stereoscopic photographs can be repeated after a 4-year interval if the baseline does not reveal retinopathy

267. Endocrinologic effects seen in patients treated with lithium include

(1) hypothyroidism
(2) hypercalcemia
(3) diabetes insipidus
(4) hyperglycemia

268. A 30-year-old man complains of symptoms of sinusitis. Sinus x-rays incidentally show enlargement of the sella turcica. These findings are consistent with a diagnosis of

(1) pituitary adenoma
(2) craniopharyngioma
(3) empty-sella syndrome
(4) internal carotid artery aneurysm

269. Cushing's syndrome is characterized by which of the following statements?

(1) The cause is most likely to be a pituitary microadenoma

(2) Although truncal obesity is generally present, a redistribution of weight is characteristic and approximately half the affected patients exhibit no weight gain

(3) Adrenal hyperplasia secondary to either pituitary or nonendocrine ACTH production can often be differentiated by a high-dosage dexamethasone suppression test

(4) The dexamethasone suppression test is less useful in screening for this syndrome than the now generally available radioimmunoassay for ACTH

270. Long-acting gonadotropin-releasing hormone (GnRH) agonists are used in the management of

(1) true precocious puberty
(2) polycystic ovarian syndrome
(3) prostatic carcinoma
(4) endometriosis

271. Thyroglobulin levels are elevated

(1) in pregnancy severalfold
(2) in endemic nontoxic goiters
(3) following thyroid trauma
(4) in thyrotoxicosis factitia

272. Gynecomastia is associated with which of the following situations?

(1) Cirrhosis
(2) Digitalis administration
(3) Puberty
(4) Hyperthyroidism

273. Hyperaldosteronism is often associated with

(1) diuretic therapy
(2) Cushing's syndrome
(3) malignant hypertension
(4) licorice ingestion

274. Hypercalcemia in sarcoidosis is associated with

(1) seasonal changes in serum calcium
(2) improvement following corticosteroid therapy
(3) reduced parathormone concentration
(4) brown tumors

275. Toxic nodular goiter (Plummer's disease) is associated with

(1) exophthalmos
(2) thyroid acropathy
(3) thyroid dermopathy
(4) onycholysis

276. Active patients afflicted with Paget's disease (osteitis deformans) generally demonstrate elevated levels of which of the following substances?

(1) Serum alkaline phosphatase
(2) Serum calcium
(3) Urine hydroxyproline
(4) Urine calcium

277. A 24-year-old woman complains of chronic fatigue. She tires easily and at times feels almost as if she is going to pass out, especially when she overexerts herself. She has lost about 10 pounds over the last 3 months because she does not "feel like eating." She was told she was suffering from multiple allergies because of the presence of allergic cells in her blood. At midafternoon her blood sugar was 62 mg/dL. Her blood pressure is 90/60 mmHg, pulse 90 beats per minute, weight 105 pounds, and height 64 inches. Which of the following clinical and laboratory procedures should be conducted immediately?

(1) Determination of blood pressure in supine and standing positions
(2) Careful inspection of the skin and oral cavity
(3) Screening cosyntropin stimulation test
(4) Determination of glucose and insulin levels after 72-h fast

278. A 26-year-old woman consults her gynecologist for amenorrhea. She has been on oral contraceptives for 5 years but these were discontinued 6 months ago when she had a serious accident that required her to remain in traction in the hospital for 4 weeks. During this time she became extremely anxious and agitated and she was treated with haloperidol. The drug was gradually withdrawn but she had no further menstrual periods. Her amenorrhea is consistent with which of the following endocrinologic or radiologic findings?

(1) Serum prolactin 75 ng/ml; negative magnetic resonance imaging (MRI) of hypothalamus and pituitary gland
(2) Serum prolactin 300 ng/mL; 10-mm pituitary defect detected by coronal CT with contrast
(3) Suprasellar mass containing calcifications and a cystic compartment seen on MRI
(4) TSH 20 μU/mL (normal 0.3 to 3 μU/mL) with T_4 1.0 μg/dL (normal 4 to 12 μg/dL)

SUMMARY OF DIRECTIONS

A	B	C	D	E
1, 2, 3 only	1, 3 only	2, 4 only	4 only	All are correct

279. Osteoporosis has been associated with which of the following?

(1) Thyroxine treatment that suppresses TSH to zero
(2) Renal tubular acidosis
(3) Rheumatoid arthritis
(4) Polycystic ovarian syndrome

280. A 22-year-old woman was referred by an orthopedic surgeon who treated her for a stress fracture of the femur. Which of the following aspects of the history and physical examination would be consistent with the development of osteoporosis?

(1) She experiences amenorrhea when she increases her jogging to greater than 60 miles a week
(2) She jogs and diets to keep her weight below 115 pounds, which is 90 percent of her ideal body weight
(3) She develops bloating, flatulence, and abdominal discomfort when she drinks milk or eats milk products
(4) She had childhood obesity and developed large bones

DIRECTIONS: Each group of questions below consists of lettered headings followed by a set of numbered items. For each numbered item select the **one** lettered heading with which it is **most** closely associated. Each lettered heading may be used **once, more than once, or not at all.**

Questions 281–284

For each case presentation below, select the most likely alteration in lipoprotein metabolism

(A) Familial lipoprotein lipase dysfunction
(B) Low-density lipoprotein (LDL) receptor disorder
(C) Inborn error of apolipoprotein E
(D) Increased production of very low-density lipoproteins (VLDL)
(E) Increased transfer of apolipoprotein C from VLDL to high-density lipoproteins (HDL)

281. A 45-year-old diabetic patient complains of intermittent claudication. Physical examination reveals xanthomas of the palmar and digital creases and tuberoeruptive xanthomas of the elbows. Serum cholesterol and triglycerides are 320 and 280 mg/dL, respectively

282. A 12-year-old girl complains of acute abdominal pain. Physical examination reveals eruptive xanthomas, hepatosplenomegaly, and lipemia retinalis. Blood drawn on hospital admission looks like "cream of tomato soup" with serum cholesterol and triglycerides of 840 and 4000 mg/dL, respectively

283. A 32-year-old man has chest pain on exertion and a strong family history of coronary artery disease. Xanthomas are present on his Achilles tendon. Serum cholesterol and triglycerides are 380 and 150 mg/dL, respectively

284. A 72-year-old man who is an active jogger has a normal cardiac exercise stress test

Questions 285-288

For each case presentation below, select the most appropriate diagnosis. (Laboratory values appear in the table below.)

(A) Adrenal carcinoma
(B) Congenital adrenal hyperplasia
(C) Cushing's disease
(D) Oat cell carcinoma of the lung
(E) Nelson's syndrome

	Laboratory Values					
	Serum		Plasma		Urine	
Patient Number	K⁺ (meq/L)	HCO₃ (meq/L)	Cortisol at 8 A.M. (μg/100 mL)*	ACTH 40-100 (pg/100 mL)†	17-OHCS (mg/24h)★	17-KS (mg/24h)‡
285.	3.0	35	40	1000	35	40
286.	3.9	25	20	90	15	15
287.	3.2	32	80	5	35	70
288.	3.8	25	13	250	4	65

*Normal: 10 to 24.   ★Normal: 3 to 12.
†Normal: 40 to 100.   ‡Normal: 5 to 20.

285. A 45-year-old man complains of severe weakness. He appears chronically wasted and is mildly hyperpigmented. His blood pressure is 160/100 mmHg. A high-dose dexamethasone suppression test (2 mg every 6 h) causes no suppression of urinary free cortisol, 17-hydroxy-corticosteroids (17-OHCS), or 17-ketosteroids (17-KS)

286. A 26-year-old woman complains of irregular menses, obesity, and low back pain. She has mild hypertension, central obesity, broad striae, acne, and mild hirsutism. A low-dose dexamethasone suppression test (0.5 mg every 6 h) causes no suppression of urinary free cortisol and 17-OHCS. A high-dose dexamethasone suppression test causes greater than 50 percent suppression of urinary free cortisol and 17-OHCS

287. A 20-year-old woman complains of weakness, easy bruising, hirsutism, and irregular menses. She exhibits a moon face, central obesity, and severe hirsutism involving the face and trunk, but no virilism. A high-dose dexamethasone suppression test causes no suppression of free cortisol, 17-OHCS, or 17-KS. Plasma dehydroepiandrosterone (DHEA) sulfate is fourfold normal

288. A 15-year-old boy complains of short stature. He has a history of early sexual development and accelerated growth that ceased 5 years ago. He displays hyperpigmentation. A high-dose dexamethasone suppression test causes greater than 50 percent suppression of urinary 17-KS

DIRECTIONS: Each group of questions below consists of four lettered headings followed by a set of numbered items. For each numbered item select

A	if the item is associated with	(A) **only**
B	if the item is associated with	(B) **only**
C	if the item is associated with	**both** (A) and (B)
D	if the item is associated with	**neither** (A) nor (B)

Each lettered heading may be used **once, more than once, or not at all.**

Questions 289–293

(A) Multiple endocrine neo-
    plasia, type I (MEN I)
(B) Multiple endocrine neo-
    plasia, type II (MEN II)
(C) Both
(D) Neither

289. Medullary thyroid carcinoma

290. Multicentric parathyroid involvement

291. Increased ratio of urinary
epinephrine to norepinephrine

292. Peptic ulcer disease as the
major cause of morbidity and
mortality

293. Carcinoid tumors

Questions 294–298

(A) Propylthiouracil (PTU)
(B) Methimazole
(C) Both
(D) Neither

294. Decrease in the peripheral
conversion of T_4 to T_3

295. Inhibition of the incorporation of iodide into thyroglobulin

296. Leukopenia

297. Interference with the release of previously formed thyroid hormone

298. Intrathyroidal concentrations reflected by serum levels

Endocrinology and Metabolic Disease

Answers

241.   The answer is C.   *(White N Engl J Med 316:1519–1524, 1580–1586, 1987. Wilson, 8/e, pp 565–567.)* Some persons with P-450 C-21 deficiency do not manifest any developmental abnormalities or salt-wasting tendencies but present in childhood or at the time of puberty with evidence of androgen excess (males are usually asymptomatic). This clinical syndrome (usually referred to as *nonclassic form* or *late-onset congenital adrenal hyperplasia*) may be indistinguishable from polycystic ovary disease. The diagnosis is usually considered because of androgen excess. Adrenal androgens (DHEAS and androstenedione) are elevated. Current diagnosis depends on demonstrating increased basal or ACTH-stimulated plasma 17α-hydroxyprogesterone concentrations. Nomograms have been developed for classic and nonclassic forms of P-450 C-21 deficiency and their carrier states. LH/FSH ratio and ultrasound of ovaries are useful tests in the diagnosis of polycystic ovarian syndrome (PCOS). As baseline DHEAS is elevated and LH/FSH levels are normal, congenital adrenal hyperplasia is the more likely diagnosis in this patient. CT scan of the adrenals is indicated only when diagnosis of an adrenal neoplasm is a consideration. Such a patient usually presents with rapidly progressive hirsutism, severe menstrual disorder, and signs of virilization. The levels of adrenal androgens and testosterone are very high.

242.   The answer is C.   *(Wilson, 12/e, pp 1769–1773.)* A delay in the onset of puberty is much more common in boys than in girls and is usually a psychological hazard that can be handled with appropriate counseling. Genetic factors are important, and a history of delayed puberty in a father or an older brother would strongly suggest that no further investigations are needed. A physician would obviously look for signs of malnutrition from primary or secondary causes, such as a catabolic illness like regional ileitis. Such systemic illnesses can inhibit growth and consequently lead to delay in puberty. Since the patient appears to be well with normal weight and growth, systemic disorders as well as defects in growth hormone secretory dynamics are unlikely. Thus, provocative testing of growth hormone secretion is not indicated in this patient. Common endocrinopathies must then be excluded, such as hyperthyroidism, hypothyroidism, and prolactin-secreting pituitary adenomas. Measurement of the serum prolactin will detect the last, but levels will also be elevated in hypothyroidism and other central nervous system tumors such as craniopharyngioma, which interferes with normal hypothalamic inhibitory regulation of prolactin secretion. Elevation of prolactin from any cause will interfere with sexual function and must be pursued by pituitary imaging studies. In the absence of prolactin abnormalities, defects in the hypothalamic-pituitary-testicular axis—such as genetic errors in the testes and idiopathic gonadotropin deficiencies—must be excluded. Elevation of FSH and LH indicates a primary testicular disorder such as Klinefelter's syndrome. Low gonadotropins are consistent with normal physiological delay in puberty but also with a defect in the hypothalamus or pituitary. The most common defect is a lack of hypothalamic secretion of luteinizing hormone releasing factor (LHRF). Such a defect can occur in association with other symptoms and signs such as anosmia, color blindness, and midline skeletal deformities that cluster together as Kallman's syndrome. Thus, defects in olfaction are strongly suggestive of the syndrome. Diagnosis is confirmed by testing with gonadorelin, a synthetic form of LHRF.

243. The answer is D. *(Felig, 2/e, pp 1184–1187. Wilson, 12/e, pp 1759–1765.)* The case history presented in the question is classic for insulinoma. The predominance of exercise-induced hypoglycemia and weight gain is characteristic of this disorder. Affected patients may have plasma insulin levels within normal limits after an overnight fast, but the ratio of serum insulin to serum glucose concentration is greater than 0.4. These patients frequently have glucose intolerance after glucose ingestion. The failure of insulin to fall when fasting hypoglycemia develops establishes the diagnosis of hyperinsulinism. In contrast, patients having reactive hypoglycemia do not develop hypoglycemia with fasting. Although hepatoma and Addison's disease may be associated with fasting hypoglycemia, insulin values fall appropriately during a fast in these disorders.

244. The answer is C. *(Wilson, 12/e, pp 1709–1712.)* Thyroglossal duct cyst is the most important anomaly of thyroid development. Excision of the cyst is generally indicated because of the cyst's propensity for infection. Infection may enter the duct if a communication persists with the pharynx through the foramen cecum at the base of the tongue. After an acute upper respiratory infection, the duct may become obstructed.

The obstruction can lead to cystic dilatation, thereby making the lesion clinically apparent.

245. The answer is B. *(Wyngaarden, 19/e, pp 1133–1136.)* Iron overload should be considered among patients who present with any one or a combination of the following: hepatomegaly, weakness, pigmentation, atypical arthritis, diabetes, impotence, unexplained chronic abdominal pain, or cardiomyopathy. Excessive alcohol intake increases the diagnostic probability. Diagnostic suspicions should be particularly high when the family history is positive for similar clinical findings. The most frequent cause of iron overload is a common genetic disorder known as ("idiopathic") hemochromatosis. Secondary iron storage problems can occur in a variety of anemias. The most practical screening test is the determination of serum iron, transferrin saturation, and plasma ferritin. Plasma ferritin values above 300 ng/mL in males and 200 ng/mL in females suggest increased iron stores, and definitive diagnosis can be done by liver biopsy. Determination of serum copper is needed when Wilson's disease is the probable cause of hepatic abnormalities. The clinical picture here is inconsistent with that diagnosis. Nocturnal penile tumescence and echocardiogram can confirm clinical findings but will not help to establish the diagnosis.

246. The answer is A. *(Felig, 2/e, pp 1155–1162. Wilson, 12/e, p 1785.)* Insulin-dependent diabetic women who desire pregnancy are advised to normalize their glucose control with frequent home glucose monitoring and multiple insulin injections prior to conception. This itself increases the risk of hypoglycemia. When pregnancy occurs, the risk is greater because of fetal utilization of glucose and gluconeogenic substrates. Later in pregnancy, insulin resistance occurs secondary to a rise in placental contrainsular hormones. In the patient presented in the question, diabetic nephropathy is highly unlikely because of the absence of proteinuria. Evidence of estrogen effect on vaginal smear makes hypopituitarism unlikely. Hyperthyroidism causes oligomenorrhea and generally produces an insulin-resistant state.

247. The answer is E. *(Felig, 2/e, pp 667–672. Wilson, 8/e, pp 678–679. Wilson, 12/e, pp 1735–1739.)* Patients who have pheochromocytoma frequently demonstrate reduced circulating plasma volume, probably as a consequence of chronic, excessive alpha-adrenergic stimulation. Reduced plasma volume is suggested clinically by orthostatic hypotension or by elevated hematocrit. If plasma volume is reduced preoperatively and not corrected by treatment with phenoxybenzamine and administration of copious amounts of fluid, severe hypotension may occur during surgery immediately after removal of the tumor. Hypotension under such circumstances is best treated with volume expansion (e.g., blood replacement) rather than with a vasoconstrictive agent.

248. The answer is A. *(Wyngaarden, 19/e, p 1368.)* The patient's history suggests that she had a normal hypothalamic pituitary gonadal axis until recently. Presence of hot flashes suggests primary rather than secondary ovarian failure. Absence of responses to Provera suggests estrogen deficiency (ruling out polycystic ovaries). Response to combination pills suggests normal endometrium and outlet, which excludes Asherman's syndrome. Estrogen deficiency can occur as a result of pituitary failure or primary ovarian failure. Although there are signs of other endocrine deficiencies in this patient (dry skin and goiter indicating hypothyroidism, fatigue and increased pigmentation indicating adrenal insufficiency), these are not from pituitary failure. Hypothyroidism from pituitary failure is not associated with goiter, and hyperpigmentation is seen only in primary adrenal failure. Polyendocrine autoimmune failure type II is the most common of the immunoendocrinopathy syndromes and is usually defined by the occurrence in the same patient of two or more of the following: primary adrenal insufficiency, hyperthyroidism or primary hypothyroidism, type I diabetes mellitus, or primary hypogonadism. Myasthenia gravis, vitiligo, alopecia, serositis, Parkinson's disease, and pernicious anemia occur with increased frequency in these persons.

249. The answer is C. *(Felig, 2/e, pp 1670–1675. Wilson, 8/e, pp 1542–1548. Wilson, 12/e, pp 1811–1812.)* For the patient described in the question, the markedly increased calcitonin levels indicate the diagnosis of medullary carcinoma of the thyroid. In view of the family history, the patient most likely has multiple endocrine neoplasia (MEN) type II, which includes medullary carcinoma of the thyroid gland, pheochromocytoma, and parathyroid hyperplasia. Pheochromocytoma may exist without sustained hypertension as indicated by excessive urinary catecholamines. Before thyroid surgery is performed on this patient, a pheochromocytoma must be ruled out through urinary catecholamine determinations; the presence of such a tumor might expose him to a hypertensive crisis during surgery. The entire thyroid gland must be removed because foci of parafollicular cell hyperplasia, a premalignant lesion, may be scattered throughout the gland. Successful removal of the medullary carcinoma can be monitored with serum calcitonin levels. Hyperparathyroidism, while unlikely in this patient, is probably present in his brother.

250. The answer is C. *(Felig, 2/e, pp 964–966. Wilson, 12/e, pp 1727–1729.)* The symptoms of masculinization (e.g., alopecia, deepening of voice, clitoral hypertrophy) in the patient presented in the question are characteristic of active androgen-producing tumors. Such extreme virilization is very rarely observed in polycystic ovary syndrome or in Cushing's syndrome; moreover, the presence of normal cortisol and markedly elevated plasma testosterone levels indicates an ovarian rather than adrenal cause of her findings. Although hilar cell tumors are capable of producing the picture seen in this patient, they are very rare and usually arise in postmenopausal women. Arrhenoblastomas are the most common androgen-producing ovarian tumors. Their incidence is highest during the reproductive years. Composed of varying proportions of Leydig's and Sertoli's cells, they are generally benign. In contrast to arrhenoblastomas, granulosa-theca cell tumors produce feminization, not virilization.

251. The answer is B. *(Wyngaarden, 19/e, 1319.)* The glucagonoma syndrome is characterized by a waxing and waning skin rash (necrolytic migratory erythema), diabetes, hypoaminoacidemia, weight loss, and anemia. The rash consists of blisters with an erythematous base, most prominently on the perineum, along intertriginous folds, and around the mouth and nose. Glossitis, stomatitis, cheilitis, and onycholysis are common. Frank diabetes occurs in 60 percent of patients and an additional 30 percent have glucose intolerance, but diabetic ketoacidosis is rare. The diagnosis is made by elevated levels of glucagon and by excluding other conditions associated with hyperglucagonemia. Most patients with glucagonoma have levels in excess of 500 pg/mL. Although renal and other abdominal malignancies are considerations in patients with weakness, wasting, weight loss, and anemia, the description of the typical skin rash and diabetes mellitus should alert to the possibility of a glucagon-producing pancreatic tumor. CT scan of the abdomen is not a good study for localizing such tumors. Patients with somatostatinoma will have mild diabetes mellitus but none of the other features described in this patient.

252. The answer is B. *(Wilson, 12/e, pp 1709–1711.)* The most serious diagnostic possibilities—i.e., anaplastic tumor, lymphoma, or metastatic disease—will either be readily confirmed or highly suggested by thyroid cytology. The more indolent tumors such as papillary or follicular carcinomas may also be diagnosed if the specimen is highly cellular or there are neoplastic features in the cytology. Otherwise a benign cytology would permit a cautious trial of exogenous levothyroxine suppression to determine if the nodule regresses in size over 6 to 12 months. Radioactive iodine therapy and external irradiation are used to treat thyroid carcinoma postoperatively.

253. The answer is D. *(Wilson, 12/e, pp 1702–1706.)* The clinical description is typical of apathetic hyperthyroidism, which may be caused by subtle Graves' disease or toxic multinodular goiter. The signs of hyperthyroidism are attenuated in the later decades of life and women are affected much more frequently than men. The clinical presentation differs from that of Graves' disease because of the absence of exophthalmos. Thyrotoxic cardiac disease is extremely common. Goiter may not be palpable. Resistance to the usual therapeutic dosages of digitalis is common. The syndrome of sick euthyroidism is more commonly associated with low serum thyroxine and triiodothyronine values in debilitated elderly patients. The treatment of choice for this patient is radioactive iodine, and large doses are required. In order to prevent an exacerbation of thyrotoxic symptoms caused by the destruction of the thyroid gland and the release of thyroxine as a result of a radiation-induced thyroiditis, it is prudent to initiate therapy with antithyroid agents and administer the radioactive iodine as a definitive treatment only when the affected patient has become euthyroid.

254. The answer is D. *(Wilson, 12/e, pp 1239–1243, 1811.)* The diagnosis of gastrinoma should be considered in all patients with either recurrent ulcers after surgical correction for peptic ulcer disease, ulcers in the distal duodenum or jejunum, ulcer disease associated with diarrhea, or evidence suggestive of the multiple endocrine neoplasia (MEN) type I (familial association of pituitary, parathyroid, and pancreatic tumors) in ulcer patients. Because basal serum gastrin and basal acid production may both be normal or only slightly elevated in patients with gastrinomas, provocative tests may need to be employed for diagnosis. Both the secretin and calcium infusion tests are used; a paradoxical increase in serum gastrin concentration is seen in response to both infusions in patients with gastrinomas. In contrast, other conditions associated with hypergastrinemia such as duodenal ulcers, retained antrum, gastric outlet obstruction, antral G-cell hyperplasia, and pernicious anemia will respond with either no change or a decrease in serum gastrin.

255. The answer is D. *(Felig, 2/e, pp 357–368. Wilson, 12/e, pp 1684–1689. Wyngaarden, 19/e, p 1242.)* Metastatic tumors rarely cause diabetes insipidus but of the tumors that may cause it, carcinoma of the breast is by far the most common. In the patient discussed in the question, the diagnosis of diabetes insipidus is suggested by hypernatremia and a low urine osmolality. Psychogenic polydipsia is an unlikely diagnosis since serum sodium is usually mildly reduced in this condition. Renal glycosuria would be expected to induce a higher urine osmolality than this patient has because of the osmotic effect of glucose. While nephrocalcinosis secondary to hypercalcemia may produce polyuria, hypercalciuria does not. Finally, the findings of inappropriate antidiuretic hormone syndrome are the opposite of those observed in diabetes insipidus and thus incompatible with the clinical picture in this patient.

256. The answer is E (all). *(Wilson, 12/e, pp 1660–1664.)* Hypersecretion of growth hormone is usually secondary to a somatotropic pituitary cell adenoma. Prior to epiphyseal closure, an increase in growth rate with minimal bony deformity is the common presentation; in adults, coarsening of facial features, soft tissue swelling of hands and feet, and bony proliferation are typical manifestations. Diagnosis rests on characteristics of growth hormone secretion that are unique to acromegalics. Random serum determinations range from normal to grossly elevated but an oral glucose tolerance test fails to suppress serum growth hormone levels. In contrast, 70 to 80 percent of patients with acromegaly actually increase growth hormone in response to glucose. Acromegaly may be caused by micropituitary tumors (less than 10 mm) that maintain normal growth hormone levels, but the absence of physiological regulation causes increased levels of somatomedin C produced in the liver in response to growth hormone. Thyromegaly, frequently seen in acromegaly, is indicative of growth hormone's effect in stimulating generalized organomegaly. Similarly, carpal tunnel syndrome indicates bony overgrowth.

257. The answer is C (2, 4). *(Wilson, 12/e, pp 296–299.)* Although psychological causes of impotence are responsible for the majority of cases, there are many drugs that have impotence as a side effect. Diuretics, methyldopa, clonidine, and beta blockers can produce complete or incomplete impotence. Recently it has been discovered that the widely used drugs cimetidine and spironolactone act as antiandrogens; in antagonizing the effects of androgen on the target tissue, they can affect the hormonal control of erection. While it is important to stress that the majority of patients taking these drugs do not suffer from impotence, physicians need to be aware of this possibility as these drugs have not been traditionally thought of in this context. Although clinical skills remain the best tools for sorting out the different causes of impotence, there are disturbances in endocrine function that may be responsible. Usually the measurement of plasma testosterone and prolactin in patients who have been consistently impotent for a period of more than 3 months will allow physicians to decide which patients have abnormalities of the endocrine system that require a more detailed evaluation. In one recent study of 105 patients presenting with impotence, 37 were found to have organic hypogonadism. Twenty of these patients had a hypothalamic pituitary deficiency. The incidence of impotence associated with antihypertensive treatment is as high as 17 percent.

258. The answer is E (all). *(Dobs, Am J Med 84:611–616, 1988. Am J Med 82:1035–1038, 1987.)* The nonspecific signs and symptoms of chronic adrenal insufficiency may mimic those of AIDS. As the adrenal gland is almost always involved by CMV, clinical suspicion should be high. Although subclinical disease and abnormal tests of adrenal reserve are common, clinical adrenal failure as a complication of AIDS is uncommon. Hyperkalemia in these patients can also be related to isolated hyporeninemic hypoaldosteronism. Fludrocortisone normalizes the serum potassium levels, even though baseline and ACTH-stimulated cortisol and aldosterone are within normal limits. Rifampin, ketoconazole, phenytoin, and opiates might potentiate or cause adrenal failure.

259. The answer is B (1, 3). *(Wilson, 8/e, pp 965–966.)* Rapid onset of gynecomastia should alert for the risk of malignancy even though there are no other associated clinical findings. Although marijuana is associated with development of gynecomastia, an elevated β-hCG level is always abnormal in men and indicates the presence of choriocarcinoma. The search should include ultrasound of testes, and the imaging of chest and abdomen to evaluate for tumor. An elevated LH level is probably spurious because of cross reaction of the antibody with β-hCG. Assay of FSH is not affected by the presence of β-hCG in serum. Therefore, pituitary CT scan is not needed.

260. The answer is A (1, 2, 3). *(Wilson, 12/e, pp 1708–1709.)* Thyroid storm is an acute exacerbation of partially treated or untreated thyrotoxicosis evoked by a precipitating factor such as infection, trauma, surgery, diabetic ketoacidosis, or pregnancy. The patient usually presents with fever, restlessness, nausea and vomiting, abdominal pain, tachycardia, diaphoresis, and, rarely, delirium. Treatment involves antagonizing all facets of thyroid hormone synthesis. Propylthiouracil is a first-line agent in the treatment of storm because it inhibits the iodination of tyrosine and monoiodotyrosine and prevents the coupling of iodotyrosines to form T_3 and T_4. As it also prevents the conversion of T_4 to T_3, it is preferred over methimazole, which does not affect this final step. Once iodination is inhibited, large doses of iodine are then administered in order to prevent the release of thyroid hormones. Dexamethasone, in addition to assuring adequate glucocorticoid stores, supports the actions of both prophylthiouracil and iodine by inhibiting glandular release of hormone and preventing the conversion of T_4 to T_3. Propranolol is also given in order to reduce the effects of the increased sympathetic state.

261. The answer is A (1, 2, 3). *(Felig, 2/e, p 418. Wilson, 12/e, pp 1702–1705.)* The clinical and laboratory findings in the patient presented in the question are most consistent with "T_3 toxicosis." This hyperthyroid state is a result of overproduction of triiodothyronine in the presence of normal or slightly elevated thyroxine. Radioactive iodine uptake may be normal or increased. "T_3 toxicosis" is observed most commonly in patients who have autonomous nodules or who have been treated for Graves' disease. The diagnosis is established either by the presence of elevated serum triiodothyronine (radioimmunoassay) or suppression of the highly sensitive thyroid-stimulating hormone (HS-TSH) assay. If HS-TSH assay is not available, then the failure to stimulate TSH release by injection of thyrotropin-releasing hormone is consistent with hyperthyroidism. In the patient presented, serum thyroid-stimulating immunoglobulin (TSI) would not be present. TSI is observed in Graves' disease but not in the presence of an autonomous nodule.

262. The answer is D (4). *(Marx, N Engl J Med 307:416–426, 1982.)* Primary considerations in PTH-mediated familial hypercalcemic syndromes are multiple endocrine neoplasia (MEN) types I and II, familial hypocalciuric hypercalcemia, and rarely familial pheochromocytoma. Ninety to ninety-five percent of gene carriers in MEN I will develop clinical evidence of hyperparathyroidism. Associated neoplasms usually include pituitary and pancreatic tumors. Hyperparathyroidism occurs only in 10 to 20 percent of known gene carriers in MEN II. Most cases have been described in older patients with palpable medullary thyroid carcinoma. An occasional patient will develop hypercalcemia in association with pheochromocytoma, which is probably related to PTH-linked peptide production. As there are no evident features of MEN, familial hypocalciuric hypercalcemia is the primary consideration, especially because of the benign family history. It is characterized by a generally mild clinical course, a low urine calcium excretion, and a low calcium/creatinine clearance ratio. Hypercalcemia persists after standard subtotal parathyroidectomy, and it is imperative that this diagnosis is considered in PTH-mediated hypercalcemia before surgery is attempted. A cortisone suppression test is helpful when hypercalcemia is related to vitamin D excess. In these patients measured PTH should be low.

263. The answer is B (1, 3). *Wyngaarden, 19/e, p 2143.*) Neurofibromatosis type 1 (von Recklinghausen's disease) is characterized by multiple café au lait spots on the skin, multiple peripheral nerve tumors, and a variety of other dysplastic abnormalities of the skin, nervous system, bones, endocrine organs, and blood vessels. One of the most common genetic diseases, neurofibromatosis type 1 occurs once in every 3000 births and is inherited as an autosomal dominant trait. Pheochromocytoma occurs in about 5 percent of these patients, usually in adult life. Hypertension in young patients may result from renal artery dysplasia. Gestational hypertension by definition is hypertension that occurs in the last trimester or immediately post partum and for which no other underlying cause can be demonstrated. There is no relation between aldosteronoma and neurofibroma. Moreover there are no clinical features such as weakness or hypokalemia suggestive of hyperaldosteronism.

264. The answer is A (1, 2, 3). *(Felig, 2/e, pp 357–368. Wilson, 8/e, p 337. Wilson, 12/e, pp 1684–1688. Wyngaarden, 19/e, p 1245.)* The ability of the patient presented in the question to concentrate urine clearly is impaired. His response to vasopressin (Pitressin) establishes the diagnosis of partial diabetes insipidus and thus rules out psychogenic or nephrogenic causes for his urinary findings. Patients who have some antidiuretic hormone (ADH) secretion generally respond to chlorpropamide, thiazide diuretics, or dDAVP. Chlorpropamide enhances the action of ADH in the kidney. The negative salt balance induced by the diuretic leads to a reduction in glomerular filtration rate and to enhanced proximal tubular water reabsorption. This results in the delivery of less water to water-impermeable distal segments and so to reduced water excretion. dDAVP is a potent analogue of ADH. In contrast to chlorpropamide, the second-generation sulfonylureas glyburide and glipizide have no ADH-like effects.

265. The answer is A (1, 2, 3). *(Wilson, 12/e, p 1708.)* Thyrotoxicosis associated with decreased radioactive iodine (RAI) uptake has been observed in (1) patients who are surreptitiously taking thyroxine; (2) Graves' disease with iodine loading; (3) iodine-induced thyrotoxicosis (jodbasedow phenomenon); (4) acute phase of thyroiditis; (5) struma ovarii; and (6) metastatic follicular carcinoma. While a few rare cases of pituitary adenomas that produce thyroid-stimulating hormone (TSH) have been reported, in this condition RAI uptake would be increased. Oat cell carcinoma is associated with several ectopic hormone syndromes, including ectopic ACTH production and the syndrome of inappropriate antidiuretic hormone, but not with thyroid overproduction.

266. The answer is C (2, 4). *(Singer, Ann Intern Med 116:660–671, 1992.)* The essential findings of randomized clinical trials (Diabetic Retinopathy Study and Early Treatment Diabetic Retinopathy Study) show that photocoagulation therapy reduces the rate of developing visual loss in patients with proliferative retinopathy and macular edema by about 50 percent, that this effect is long-lasting, and that it is particularly impressive in certain high-risk groups. The effect of photocoagulation is primarily preventive. It generally does not reverse visual loss. Patients with vision-threatening retinopathy may not have symptoms. As a result, ongoing evaluation for retinopathy is a valuable strategy. The most sensitive screening technique is stereo-fundus photography. Yearly dilated ophthalmoscopic examination seems the most available approach at present. The following guidelines are suggested:

1. Patients with type 1 diabetes should be screened annually for retinopathy beginning 5 years after the onset of diabetes. In general, screening is not indicated before the start of puberty.

2. Patients with type 2 diabetes should have an initial examination for retinopathy shortly after the diagnosis of diabetes is made. If dilated ophthalmoscopy is used, then examination should be repeated annually. If skilled reading of seven-field stereoscopic photographs is available and reveals no retinopathy at the initial screen, then the next screening examination does not need to be done for 4 years. Care should be taken not to lose those patients to follow-up. After this 4-year examination, subsequent screening with stereoscopic photographs or dilated ophthalmoscopy should be done annually. Patients with persistently elevated glucose levels (for example, mean plasma glucose above 280 mg/dL) or with proteinuria should have yearly examinations regardless of screening technique.

3. When planning pregnancy, women with preexisting diabetes should be counseled on the risk for the development or progression of diabetic retinopathy. Women with diabetes who become pregnant should have a comprehensive eye examination in the first trimester and close follow-up throughout pregnancy. This

does not apply to women who develop gestational diabetes because such persons are not at increased risk for diabetic retinopathy.

4. Patients with macular edema, moderate to severe nonprolif-
erative retinopathy, or any proliferative retinopathy require the
prompt care of an ophthalmologist knowledgeable and experienced in the management of diabetic retinopathy.

267. The answer is E (all). *(Mallete, Arch Intern Med 146:770, 1986.
Wilson, 12/e, pp 2141–2143.)* Lithium, often referred to as an "anti-
manic" drug, is a mood-stabilizing agent used mainly in the treatment
of bipolar affective disorder. Many endocrine effects have been described, although the mechanisms of action are not completely eluci-
dated. Lithium causes evident hypothyroidism in 1 to 4 percent of patients who receive the drug. In addition, about 5 percent of patients
develop goiters, which are usually diffuse and nontender. Many patients
have only laboratory evidence of hypothyroidism including decreased
thyroxine and triiodothyronine and increased radioactive iodine uptake.
Long-term lithium therapy may alter calcium, magnesium, and parathyroid hormone homeostasis; these alterations result in mild asymptomatic primary hyperparathyroidism. Abnormal glucose tolerance and decreased sensitivity to insulin with resultant hyperglycemia have been
observed. Nephrogenic diabetes insipidus manifested as polyuria and
polydipsia occurs in about 30 to 50 percent of treated patients after 1 to
2 years of therapy. Lithium-induced diabetes insipidus is resistant to
vasopressin but responds to amiloride.

268. The answer is E (all). *(Wilson, 12/e, pp 1675–1678.)* Enlargement
of the sella turcica is characteristic, but not diagnostic, of pituitary tumors. Suprasellar lesions like craniopharyngiomas and aneurysms may
extend into the sella, producing enlargement of the sella and erosion of
its walls. In addition, cerebrospinal fluid pressure can force the subarachnoid space into the sella, which results in enlargement of the sella
and compression of the normal pituitary (empty-sella syndrome). The
differential diagnosis can be readily made by cross-sectional imaging of
the hypothalamus and pituitary by computed tomography (CT) with
contrast injection or magnetic resonance imaging (MRI) with gadolin-
ium enhancement.

269. The answer is B (1, 3). *(Felig, 2/e, p 608. Wilson, 12/e, pp 1720–
1723.)* Regardless of pathogenesis, Cushing's syndrome is characterized by excess production of cortisol. Most cases are due to bilateral

adrenal hyperplasia secondary to overproduction of ACTH by a pituitary microadenoma. Harvey Cushing originally suggested (1932) that the excess ACTH was produced by pituitary basophil adenomas, a condition that was designated Cushing's disease before it was recognized that pituitary basophilism was only one of the causes of the syndrome that would bear his name. Tumors may be very small and difficult to detect or not present at all. Petrosal sinus vein catheterization for ACTH levels is being more commonly used to localize these microtumors. The 48-h dexamethasone suppression test is still an important screening test, since the failure of suppression of urinary 17-hydroxysteroid levels to less than 3 mg/24 h or of plasma cortisol levels to less than 5 µg/dL by this test is virtually diagnostic of the syndrome. The most common nonendocrine tumor that secretes ACTH is a small cell (oat cell) carcinoma of the lung. Some carcinoid tumors also produce ACTH but because of their indolent, slowly progressive course, they are difficult to discriminate from ACTH-producing pituitary microtumors. In these patients or in others with adrenal neoplasms, no suppression occurs after dexamethasone administration, since pituitary ACTH secretion is already suppressed by the elevated cortisol levels. While routine laboratory examinations are rarely of major diagnostic utility in the diagnosis of Cushing's syndrome, certain abnormalities are suggestive: high normal values of hemoglobin, hematocrit, and red-cell count; a total lymphocyte count below normal in 35 percent of patients, and an eosinophil count usually below 100/mm³, and fasting hyperglycemia in 10 to 15 percent of patients.

270. The answer is E (all). *(Wilson, 12/e, pp 1839, 1902–1903, 2016–2017.)* The elucidation of the structure of GnRH in 1971 opened many avenues of investigation and treatment. It led to the finding that GnRH must be administered in a pulsatile manner to activate gonadotropin secretion. If given continuously, it will desensitize pituitary GnRH receptors and inhibit secretion of LH and FSH. Many potent and long-acting agonistic analogues have been synthesized that are capable of inhibiting pituitary gonadotropin secretion. In conditions such as isosexual precocity, endometriosis, leiomyomata, and hirsutism secondary to polycystic ovarian syndrome where gonadal suppression is desired, the long-acting GnRH analogues are very effective. Side effects are few, toxicity appears to be low, and gonadal function returns quickly after discontinuation of the drug. The GnRH analogues have proved highly successful in the treatment of gonadotropin-dependent precocious puberty (constitutional or secondary to organic disease) and in the medical treatment of metastatic carcinoma of the prostate.

271. The answer is A (1, 2, 3). *(Wilson, 8/e, p 405.)* Thyroglobulin is present in the sera of virtually all normal persons. Concentrations are somewhat higher in women, but are increased severalfold during pregnancy. Distinctly elevated values are present mainly in three types of thyroid disorders: goiter and thyroid hyperfunction, inflammatory and traumatic conditions of the thyroid, and differentiated thyroid tumor. Subnormal or undetectable concentrations are found in patients with thyrotoxicosis factitia and aid in differentiating this disorder from other causes of thyrotoxicosis associated with a low radioactive iodine uptake. The major clinical value of measurements of the serum thyroglobulin concentration is in the management, but not the diagnosis, of differentiated thyroid carcinoma. Elevations of the serum thyroglobulin level while thyroxine suppressive therapy is being taken suggests the presence of residual local or metastatic cancer.

272. The answer is E (all). *(Felig, 2/e, pp 886–889. Wilson, 12/e, pp 1796–1798.)* Cirrhosis and uremia are among the most common causes of gynecomastia. Estrogen- and gonadotropin-secreting tumors and hypogonadism must also be considered as causes. In addition, exogenous estrogens, spironolactone, and digitalis may produce this abnormality. Gynecomastia occurs commonly during puberty, occasionally in association with hyperthyroidism, and after recovery from severe malnutrition.

273. The answer is B (1, 3). *(Felig, 2/e, pp 751–764. Wilson, 12/e, pp 1716, 1725–1727.)* Diuretic therapy and malignant hypertension often induce excessive secretion of renin, which leads to secondary hyperaldosteronism, a condition that may be distinguished from primary hyperaldosteronism by elevated levels of renin. Renin is characteristically suppressed in primary hyperaldosteronism. Aldosterone levels are normal or low in Cushing's syndrome; hypokalemia in this disorder results from excessive cortisol and deoxycorticosterone production. Excessive licorice ingestion may produce hypokalemia and hypertension because of glycyrrhizic acid in the licorice. This mineralocorticoid-like substance expands plasma volume and reduces aldosterone secretion.

274. The answer is A (1, 2, 3). *(Felig, 2/e, pp 1415–1416. Wilson, 12/e, pp 1908–1909.)* The association of hypercalcemia with sarcoidosis is often most striking in summer and, in fact, may disappear in winter. This fluctuation probably is mediated by the effects of sunlight on vitamin D synthesis in skin. Characteristically, patients who have sarcoidosis, vitamin D intoxication, or certain malignancies demonstrate a fall in serum calcium after prednisone treatment (40 to 80 mg/day). Para-thormone levels in hypercalcemic disorders not associated with hyper-parathyroidism characteristically are low. Brown tumors are associated with hyperparathyroidism and represent areas of increased osteoclastic activity; they are not observed in sarcoidosis.

275. The answer is D (4). *(Felig, 2/e, pp 422–423. Wilson, 12/e, pp 1703–1707.)* Onycholysis, or distal separation of the nail bed, is ob-served in over 10 percent of patients who have hyperthyroidism from either Graves' disease or toxic nodular goiter; it usually begins in the nail of the fourth finger. In contrast, thyroid dermopathy (formerly called pretibial myxedema) and exophthalmos are virtually pathogno-monic of Graves' disease and are not observed in patients who have toxic nodular goiter. Thyroid acropathy, almost always associated with a history of exophthalmos and Graves' disease, is characterized by clubbing of the fingers and toes, swelling of the subcutaneous tissues of the extremities, and subperiosteal bone changes without new bone for-mation.

276. The answer is B (1, 3). *(Felig, 2/e, pp 1483–1491. Wilson, 12/e, pp 1938–1941.)* Paget's disease is characterized by excessive and abnormal remodeling of bone. The markedly increased bone turnover leads to el-evations in serum alkaline phosphatase level and in urine hydroxypro-line excretion. Serum and urinary calcium levels are normal; however, during periods of immobilization, patients afflicted with Paget's disease can develop severe hypercalcemia and hypercalciuria.

277. The answer is A (1, 2, 3). *(Wilson, 12/e, pp 1729–1732.)* The pa-tient has nonspecific symptoms consistent with the diagnosis of primary adrenal insufficiency, or Addison's disease. In contrast to patients with weakness secondary to functional causes, this patient has weight loss, eosinophilia, and low blood glucose and blood pressure. Orthostatic hy-potension is found in 50 percent of the patients with Addison's disease. Evidence of subtle hyperpigmentation in the creases of the hand, the rough surface of the knees and elbows, or the mucosal membranes, such as gingiva or vagina, is found in 95 percent of the cases. Since Addison's disease can quickly decompensate into acute adrenal crisis, a cosyntropin test should be done as soon as possible. A normal re-sponse to this synthetic ACTH derivative is an increment in serum cor-tisol of at least 7 μg/dL and a peak value over 18 μg/dL. This would exclude further consideration of the diagnosis. When the index of suspicion is high, patients are treated with glucocorticoid pending the test results. The 72-h fast is ordered to confirm the diagnosis of fasting hypoglycemia, which is usually caused by an insulinoma.

278. The answer is E (all). *(Wilson, 12/e, pp 1657–1660, 1675–1677.)* Serum prolactin is an essential test in her evaluation since hyperprolactinemia of any cause is associated with amenorrhea. Causes of hyperprolactinemia include prolactin-secreting pituitary microadenomas (usually defined as less than 10 mm diameter with serum prolactin less than 200 ng/mL) or macroadenomas; hypothalamic or pituitary disorders, such as tumors or sarcoidosis, that interfere with hypothalamic secretion of prolactin inhibitory factor; and functional disorders, including hypothyroidism and idiopathic hyperprolactinemia. Since changes in serum prolactin in response to stimulatory or inhibitory agents will not consistently differentiate a functional from an anatomical etiology for hyperprolactinemia, the diagnosis of functional hyperprolactinemia is made by exclusion of anatomical processes by MRI or CT. Thus, this patient may have functional hyperprolactinemia caused by estrogen's direct stimulatory effect on prolactin secretion, but this diagnosis can only be made following a negative MRI (choice 1). She may have a prolactin-secreting macroadenoma (choice 2) or a craniopharyngioma (choice 3), both of which are easily detected by CT or MRI. Hypothyroidism (choice 4) should always be excluded and treated prior to directly treating the hyperprolactinemia with bromocriptine or other dopamine agonists.

279. The answer is B (1, 3). *(Wilson, 12/e, pp 1922–1930.)* Osteoporosis is a complication of many systemic disorders. Hyperthyroidism increases calcium turnover of bone, which can result in a reversible form of osteoporosis. This has recently been recognized as an iatrogenic phenomenon in the treatment of nodular thyroid glands with thyroxine, which may suppress TSH into the hyperthyroid range. Rheumatoid arthritis is a systemic catabolic illness with symmetrical arthritis. The resulting pain and stiffness in joints is associated with limited bone use and disuse osteoporosis. Renal tubular acidosis causes phosphaturia and hypophosphatemia, which results in the decreased mineralization of normal bone matrix known as osteomalacia. Polycystic ovarian syndrome is associated with obesity and usually mild androgenic abnormalities. Despite the lack of cyclic ovulatory menses, these women have steady-state estrogen secretion. These factors result in decreased risk of osteoporosis.

280. The answer is A (1, 2, 3). *(Wilson, 12/e, pp 1921–1926.)* Intensive exercise does not protect women from developing osteoporosis if the exercise results in amenorrhea. Cyclic release of estrogens during a normal menstrual cycle, as well as adequate protein and mineral intake, is necessary for bones to develop normally and mature. Women who excessively exercise or assiduously maintain lean weights associated with amenorrhea are at risk of fractures from osteoporosis. Another risk factor for osteoporosis is reduced dietary calcium intake secondary to lactase deficiency or alcoholism. In contrast, women with early onset of obesity develop a large bone frame, which is considered to be secondary to increased nutrient intake and protects them to some extent from osteoporosis.

281–284. The answers are 281-C, 282-A, 283-B, 284-E. *(Felig, 2/e, pp 1245–1280. Wilson, 12/e, pp 1814–1823.)* Lipoprotein disorders are now being described as specific apolipoprotein abnormalities that define the clinical entity. "Broad beta" disease, or type III hyperlipoproteinemia, is caused by critical changes in the amino acid sequence of apolipoprotein E. The result is accumulation of remnants of abnormal, very low-density lipoproteins (VLDL). These remnants, displaying a mobility on lipoprotein electrophoresis between prebeta- and betalipoproteins, present as a broad smear ("broad-beta band") between those two lipoprotein zones. On ultracentrifugation, however, the remnants sediment with VLDL. Plasma triglycerides and cholesterol are present in an approximate 1:1 ratio. The disorder is familial and associated with premature vascular disease. Planar xanthomas and tuberoeruptive xanthomas (confluent, eruptive lesions) of the elbows are virtually pathognomonic of broad-beta disease.

Familial defect in lipoprotein lipase can occur because of a genetic error in the enzyme or in apolipoprotein CII, which along with insulin activates lipoprotein lipase. The result is a failure to delipidate chylomicrons at the endothelial surface. The disorder usually appears in childhood, producing recurrent abdominal pain, pancreatitis, and signs of extreme elevations of triglycerides. The plasma will show a thick creamy layer on top and clear plasma below indicative of hyperchylomicronemia.

Disorders of the LDL receptors are inherited as a dominant trait. Afflicted heterozygous persons generally develop ischemic heart disease before the fifth decade of life. Clinical features include tendinous and tuberous xanthomas, arcus cornea, and occasionally xanthelasma. The disorder is a result of decreased receptor-mediated clearance of LDL. Increased production of VLDL can be induced by excessive caloric intake of alcohol, fat, or carbohydrates, or by conditions or agents that increase peripheral insulin resistance, such as diabetes mellitus, uremia, hydrochlorothiazides, glucocorticoids, or estrogens.

Increased levels of HDL are associated with reduced risk for atherosclerosis. HDL cholesterol levels are usually inversely related to triglyceride levels. The enhanced uptake of triglycerides from VLDL associated with exercise results in relative abundance of apolipoprotein C in the VLDL particle. This condition causes the apolipoprotein C to break off and transfer in the plasma to nascent HDL particles synthesized in the liver. The insertion of apolipoprotein C into nascent HDL results in a mature HDL, which has the capacity to pick up cholesterol in the periphery and transport the sterol to the liver for excretion or recycling.

285–288. The answers are 285-D, 286-C, 287-A, 288-B. *(Felig, 2/e, pp 599–620, 1692–1698. Wilson, 12/e, pp 1718–1725, 1727–1729.)* Ectopic adrenocorticotropic hormone (ACTH) syndrome, as may be caused by oat cell carcinoma, is characterized by hypokalemic alkalosis, hyperpigmentation associated with elevated levels of ACTH, and myopathy. The characteristic clinical features of Cushing's syndrome are generally absent, probably because of the rapid development of the disorder. Urinary free cortisol, 17-hydroxycorticosteroids (OHCS), and 17-ketosteroids (KS), as well as plasma cortisol, are markedly elevated; dexamethasone fails to suppress 17-OHCS even when high doses are given.

Cushing's disease (pituitary-dependent bilateral adrenal hyperplasia) is characterized by the loss of diurnal variation in plasma cortisol, elevated urinary glucocorticoids and androgens, and the failure to suppress urinary free cortisol or 17-OHCS with the low-dose dexamethasone test. Plasma ACTH concentration is normal and mildly elevated and hypokalemic alkalosis is rarely present. Urinary 17-KS levels representing adrenal androgen production are increased in proportion to 17-OHCS since the glucocorticoid and the androgen producing zones of the adrenal gland are equally responsive to ACTH.

Patients who have adrenal carcinoma often display signs of excess adrenal androgen production that sometimes overshadow the signs of Cushing's syndrome. Plasma cortisol and DHEA sulfate and urinary 17-KS may be dramatically increased; there is no 17-OHCS or 17-KS suppression even with the high-dose dexamethasone test. Characteristically, in adrenal carcinoma plasma ACTH is very low; in contrast, in Cushing's syndrome and ectopic ACTH syndrome, the ACTH levels are normal or increased.

Congenital adrenal hyperplasia results from a deficiency of one of several possible cortisol synthetic enzymes, the most common being

21-hydroxylase. Adrenal androgen production often is dramatically increased, while adrenal cortisol production may be normal or decreased. As a consequence of the excess androgen production, virilism occurs in the female and short stature is frequent in the male because of early closure of bony epiphyses. Urinary 17-KS levels are increased in congenital adrenal hyperplasia but are suppressed by dexamethasone. This feature distinguishes the disorder from adrenal tumors. Hyperpigmentation results from the compensatory increase in ACTH secretion.

Nelson's syndrome, which features marked hyperpigmentation and is caused by a pituitary macrotumor that appears after bilateral adrenalectomy for Cushing's disease, is disappearing as a clinical entity since transsphenoidal hypophysectomy is now the treatment of choice for the primary pituitary tumor.

289–293. The answers are 289-B, 290-C, 291-B, 292-A, 293-A. *(Wilson, 12/e, pp 1811–1812.)* The components of MEN I are hyperparathyroidism, pancreatic islet cell tumors, and anterior pituitary tumors; tumors of the adrenal cortex and thyroid are less frequent features. The syndrome is inherited in an autosomal dominant fashion and presentations occur at any age. While asymptomatic hypercalcemia is common, 50 percent of patients have renal stones and 25 percent have osteitis fibrosa as manifestations of hyperparathyroidism. Most pancreatic islet cell tumors secrete gastrin or insulin and 10 percent of patients have complications of both. The diagnosis of gastrinomas rests on the demonstration of increased gastrin levels after secretin infusion, while insulinomas are characterized by fasting hypoglycemia coexistent with an elevated plasma insulin level. Islet cell tumors have the histological appearance of carcinoid tumors. Pituitary tumors present either because of their size or because of their secretory capabilities; prolactinomas are the most common tumor type.

MEN II, in contrast, is characterized by medullary thyroid carcinoma, pheochromocytoma, and hyperparathyroidism; it is also transmitted in autosomal dominant fashion. Glandular involvement is typically multicentric as it is in MEN I. Medullary thyroid carcinoma is associated with early metastatic disease and multiple secretory products, the most common of which is calcitonin. Pheochromocytoma, the major cause of morbidity and mortality in patients with MEN II, typically develops at an older age and occurs as bilateral adrenal tumors in 60 to 70 percent of cases. These tumors manifest as hypertension and paroxysms of flushing, sweating, and headaches, or they may be asymptomatic. They are diagnosed by finding increased levels of catecholamines or catecholamine metabolites in a 24-h urine collection. Unlike patients with MEN I, most patients with MEN II and parathyroid hyperplasia are normocalcemic.

294–298. The answers are 294-A, 295-C, 296-C, 297-D, 298-D. *(Felig, 2/e, pp 432–435. Wilson, 12/e, p 1705.)* Hyperthyroidism results from the excessive secretion of thyroid hormones and is most commonly due to Graves' disease, thyroiditis, multinodular goiter, or thyroid adenoma. The choice of therapy, whether with antithyroid drugs, radiation, or surgery, is influenced by the patient's age and sex, status of the hyperthyroidism and cardiovascular system, and history of previous management of the disease.

The thionamide drugs used in the United States are propylthiouracil (PTU) and methimazole. Both drugs inhibit the incorporation of iodide into thyroglobulin by blocking iodine oxidation and organification and iodotyrosine coupling. They do not, however, block the release of previously formed and stored thyroid hormone. PTU has the advantage of inhibiting the extrathyroidal conversion of T_4 to T_3. Both drugs also have immunosuppressive activity: thyroid antibody production is inhibited, as are lymphocyte function and viability.

While the plasma half-life of PTU is 1 to 2 h and that of methimazole is 4 to 6 h, because the drugs are concentrated in the thyroid gland, serum levels do not reflect intrathyroidal concentrations.

Toxic reactions to these drugs occur in 5 to 10 percent of patients and most commonly consist of pruritus and urticaria and other rashes; more serious side effects include fever, arthritis, vasculitis, hepatitis, anemia, and thrombocytopenia. In less than 0.5 percent of patients, a rapidly developing agranulocytosis occurs.

Gastroenterology

DIRECTIONS: Each question below contains five suggested responses. Select the **one best** response to each question.

299. All the following abnormalities are poor prognostic factors in pancreatitis (Ranson criteria) EXCEPT

(A) significant decrease in hematocrit level
(B) hypocalcemia
(C) leukocytosis
(D) hyperglycemia
(E) steatorrhea

300. Primary biliary cirrhosis may produce all the following laboratory test results EXCEPT

(A) elevated serum immunoglobulin M (IgM)
(B) absent alpha₁ spike on serum protein electrophoresis (SPEP)
(C) elevated antimitochondrial antibody (AMA) titers
(D) hyperbilirubinemia
(E) elevated serum alkaline phosphatase level

301. All the following are indications for colonoscopy EXCEPT

(A) history of prior colonic adenomas
(B) age over 50 years and history of colon cancer in one biological parent
(C) ulcerative colitis for more than 10 years
(D) adenoma found on flexible sigmoidoscopy
(E) fulminant, acute, nonbloody diarrhea that began after recent antibiotic therapy

302. Which one of the following clinical or laboratory findings is LEAST likely to occur in chronic pancreatitis?

(A) Steatorrhea
(B) Diabetes mellitus
(C) Pancreatic calcifications
(D) Bronzing of the skin
(E) Vitamin B₁₂ malabsorption

303. In a patient who is seropositive for human immunodeficiency virus (HIV), all the following *intestinal* infections or tumors would be diagnostic of AIDS EXCEPT

(A) *Cryptosporidium* infection
(B) cytomegalovirus (CMV) infection
(C) tuberculosis
(D) *Mycobacterium avium-intracellulare* infection
(E) lymphoma

304. All the following statements about achalasia are correct EXCEPT

(A) the lower esophageal sphincter (LES) functions abnormally in achalasia
(B) the upper esophageal sphincter (UES) usually functions normally in achalasia
(C) achalasia may result from severe chronic reflux esophagitis
(D) achalasia can be due to *Trypanosoma cruzi* infection
(E) the clinical and radiographic findings in achalasia may be mimicked by cancer of the esophagogastric junction (gastric cardia)

305. All the following ulcer characteristics or laboratory abnormalities would support the diagnosis of the Zollinger-Ellison syndrome EXCEPT

(A) elevated serum gastrin level
(B) multiple gastrointestinal ulcers
(C) gastrointestinal ulcers at unusual locations
(D) positive urease breath test
(E) positive (abnormal) secretin stimulation test

306. Which of the following serological patterns is most consistent with chronic active hepatitis due to hepatitis B?

(A) Hepatitis B surface antigen (HBsAg) positive, hepatitis B surface antibody (HBsAb) negative
(B) HBsAg negative, hepatitis B core antibody (HBcAb) positive, HBsAb negative
(C) Hepatitis B e antigen (HBeAg) negative
(D) HBsAg negative, HBcAb negative, hepatitis BsAb positive
(E) Hepatitis BsAg negative, HBcAb positive, hepatitis BsAb positive

DIRECTIONS: Each question below contains four suggested responses of which **one or more** is correct. Select

A	if	**1, 2, and 3**	are correct
B	if	**1 and 3**	are correct
C	if	**2 and 4**	are correct
D	if	**4**	is correct
E	if	**1, 2, 3, and 4**	are correct

307. Which of the following laboratory tests would typically be abnormal (positive) in a patient with celiac (nontropical) sprue?

(1) Small-bowel biopsy
(2) Fat content in 72-h stool collection
(3) D-Xylose test
(4) Secretin stimulation test

308. Vitamin B$_{12}$ (cyanocobalamin) deficiency may be produced by

(1) pernicious anemia
(2) Crohn's disease
(3) ileal resection
(4) chronic pancreatitis

309. Correct statements about pancreatic neuroendocrine tumors include

(1) pancreatic VIPoma (tumor that secretes vasoactive intestinal polypeptide) is not associated with diarrhea
(2) patients with an insulinoma often present with brittle diabetes
(3) pancreatic cholera is caused by *Vibrio cholerae* infection of the pancreas
(4) a glucagonoma may be associated with a skin rash

310. Chronic pancreatitis frequently produces

(1) diabetes mellitus
(2) malabsorption of fat-soluble vitamins D and K
(3) steatorrhea
(4) Courvoisier's sign

311. Risk factors for colon cancer include

(1) prior colonic adenomatous polyps
(2) Crohn's disease
(3) ulcerative colitis
(4) a large colonic lipoma

312. *Clostridium difficile* infection is reliably diagnosed by

(1) identification of *Clostridium difficile* toxin in the stool
(2) isolation of *Clostridium difficile* in a stool culture
(3) detection of typical pseudomembranes on sigmoidoscopy in a patient who had diarrhea after administration of antibiotics
(4) detection of IgG antibodies against *Clostridium difficile* in the serum

313. Features more characteristic of ulcerative colitis than Crohn's disease include

(1) skip lesions
(2) crypt abscesses
(3) granulomas
(4) superficial mucosal involvement

314. Diseases correctly matched with geographic regions with a high disease incidence include which of the following?

(1) Gastric cancer: Japan
(2) Giardiasis: St. Petersburg (formerly Leningrad)
(3) Histoplasmosis: Mississippi River Valley
(4) Ulcerative colitis: Africa

315. Gastrointestinal lymphoma in a patient with known infection by human immunodeficiency virus (HIV)

(1) is diagnostic of acquired immunodeficiency syndrome (AIDS)
(2) responds poorly to conventional chemotherapy
(3) is associated with rapid demise
(4) usually presents as isolated gastric involvement

316. Common causes of colonic pseudoobstruction include

(1) medications such as analgesics or phenothiazines
(2) electrolyte abnormalities such as hypokalemia or hypercalcemia
(3) parkinsonism
(4) colon cancer

317. Esophageal adenocarcinoma is accurately characterized by which of the following statements?

(1) It usually occurs with prior Barrett's mucosa
(2) It is frequently related to prior reflux disease
(3) It may cause dysphagia
(4) It is associated with ingestion of lye

318. Risk factors for hepatocellular cancer include

(1) hemochromatosis
(2) hepatitis B
(3) hepatitis C
(4) aflatoxin

319. Warning signs that a gastric ulcer may be malignant include

(1) location of the ulcer in the distal antrum (near the pylorus)
(2) an ulcer associated with atrophic gastritis
(3) gastric folds that are seen to radiate to the margin of the ulcer on an upper gastrointestinal series
(4) lack of healing after 6 weeks of appropriate antiulcer therapy

320. The differential diagnosis of a lesion of the terminal ileum includes

(1) Crohn's disease
(2) tuberculosis
(3) lymphoma
(4) periappendiceal abscess

321. Patients with familial polyposis coli

(1) inevitably develop colon cancer without colectomy
(2) develop numerous colonic adenomatous polyps
(3) should undergo colectomy after they reach puberty
(4) have a disease believed to be caused by a slow growing virus

322. In patients with the acquired immunodeficiency syndrome (AIDS), reported causes of secondary sclerosing cholangitis include infection with

(1) cryptospporidium
(2) *Mycobacterium tuberculosis*
(3) cytomegalovirus
(4) *Salmonella enteritidis*

323. Cytomegalovirus in patients with the acquired immunodeficiency syndrome (AIDS) can cause

(1) colitis with colonic ulceration
(2) pancreatitis
(3) acalculous cholecystitis
(4) colonic pseudoobstruction

DIRECTIONS: Each group of questions below consists of lettered headings followed by a set of numbered items. For each numbered item select the **one** lettered heading with which it is **most** closely associated. Each lettered heading may be used **once, more than once, or not at all.**

Questions 324–327

For each histological abnormality found on liver biopsy, select the liver disease with which it is associated.

(A) Schistosomiasis
(B) Primary biliary cirrhosis
(C) Alpha₁-antitrypsin deficiency
(D) Hemochromatosis
(E) Alcoholic hepatitis

324. Steatosis

325. Pipe-stem fibrosis

326. Paucity of bile ducts

327. PAS (periodic acid–Schiff)–positive granules

Questions 328–331

For each laboratory test or set of tests, choose the hepatobiliary disease in which it is most likely to be abnormal.

(A) Sclerosing cholangitis
(B) Primary biliary cirrhosis
(C) Autoimmune (lupoid) hepatitis
(D) Wilson's disease
(E) Hemochromatosis

328. Antinuclear antibodies (ANA)

329. Ceruloplasmin

330. Serum iron, total iron-binding capacity (TIBC), ferritin

331. Antimitochondrial antibodies (AMA)

Questions 332–335

For each of the listed forms of hepatic injury, select the medicinal agent most likely to cause this injury.

(A) Thorotrast (20% solution of thorium dioxide)
(B) Estrogens
(C) Methyldopa (Aldomet)
(D) 6-Mercaptopurine
(E) Chlorpromazine

332. Cholestasis *E*

333. Hepatitis *C*

334. Hepatic adenoma *B*

335. Hepatic angiosarcoma *A*

Questions 336–339

For each disease choose the laboratory test that would be most helpful in making the diagnosis.

(A) Bentiromide test
(B) Small-bowel series
(C) Small-bowel biopsy
(D) Endoscopic retrograde cholangiopancreatography (ERCP)
(E) Serum folate level

336. Sclerosing cholangitis *D*

337. Blind loop syndrome *B*

338. Celiac disease (nontropical sprue) *C*

339. Chronic pancreatitis (pancreatic insufficiency)

Questions 340–343

For each of the following physical findings, select the liver disease with which it is most closely associated.

(A) Wilson's disease
(B) Alpha$_1$-antitrypsin disease
(C) Primary biliary cirrhosis
(D) Dubin-Johnson syndrome
(E) Hemochromatosis

340. Xanthomas *C*

341. Sunflower cataracts *A*

342. Bronzing of the skin *E*

343. Kayser-Fleischer rings *A*

Questions 344–347

For each clinical finding, select the appropriate gastrointestinal disease.

(A) Cholera
(B) Pancreatic cholera
(C) Salmonellosis
(D) Gastrinoma
(E) Shigellosis

344. Dysentery *E*

345. Watery diarrhea and hypochlorhydria *B*

346. Watery diarrhea without hypochlorhydria *A*

347. Acidic diarrhea *D*

Gastroenterology
Answers

299. The answer is E. *(Eastwood, pp 231–239.)* The Ranson criteria are used to gauge the severity of pancreatitis. The following abnormalities on admission, or within 2 days of admission, are associated with a worse prognosis: old age; leukocytosis; hyperglycemia; elevations of the serum LDH (lactate dehydrogenase), SGOT, or SGPT levels; hypoxemia; hypocalcemia; a declining hematocrit level; a significant base deficit; significant fluid sequestration; and hypoalbuminemia. Pancreatic insufficiency from chronic pancreatitis leads to steatorrhea.

300. The answer is B. *(Schiff, 6/e, pp 979–999.)* Primary biliary cirrhosis is a disease that primarily affects middle-aged women. Clinical findings include pruritus and elevated serum alkaline phosphatase and bilirubin levels. Patients with this disease characteristically develop antimitochondrial antibodies. Immunoelectrophoresis usually demonstrates an increase in the serum immunoglobulin M (IgM) levels. An absent alpha$_1$ spike on serum protein electrophoresis (SPEP) occurs in alpha$_1$-antitrypsin disease.

301. The answer is E. *(Sivak, pp 868–880.)* Colonoscopy is indicated for members of high-risk groups for colon cancer. Most colon cancers arise from adenomatous polyps. The finding of an adenoma on flexible sigmoidoscopy requires colonoscopy to exclude synchronous polyps in the unexamined colon. A history of prior adenomas is an indication for colonoscopy to detect and remove metachronous (subsequent) polyps. Patients with prior colon cancer should undergo surveillance colonoscopy to detect recurrent or new cancer. Patients with a strong family history of colon cancer have an increased risk of developing colon cancer and should undergo surveillance colonoscopy that begins about age 50. The risk of colon cancer increases with the duration of ulcerative colitis. Colonoscopy is recommended for patients who have had ulcerative colitis for about 8 or more years. During colonoscopy for ulcerative colitis, random biopsies are taken throughout the colon to detect colonic dysplasia, a potentially premalignant lesion.

The differential diagnosis of severe, acute diarrhea after antibiotic administration includes *Clostridium difficile* infection, acute bacterial infection, and other enteric infections. Less likely etiologies include inflammatory bowel disease and colon cancer. The evaluation of acute diarrhea includes bacterial culture of stool, histological examination of multiple fresh stool specimens for ova and parasites, stool assay for *Clostridium difficile* toxin, and histological examination for fecal leukocytes. The evaluation may also include sigmoidoscopy. Sigmoidoscopic identification of classic pseudomembranes in the setting of recent antibiotic administration is generally diagnostic of *Clostridium difficile* colitis. Colonoscopy is not indicated in the evaluation of acute nonbloody diarrhea, but may be required later for persistent diarrhea if the initial tests are nondiagnostic.

302. The answer is D. *(Eastwood, pp 240–247.)* Chronic pancreatitis results from chronic pancreatic damage. Because of inadequate production of pancreatic lipase, triglycerides are not enzymatically cleaved into free fatty acids and are malabsorbed. This results in steatorrhea, an elevated concentration of stool fat. The damaged pancreas may also produce insufficient insulin. Normally, R factors bind to ingested vitamin B_{12} in the stomach; trypsin present in the duodenal lumen cleaves the R factors and permits intrinsic factor to bind to vitamin B_{12} so that the vitamin can be absorbed in the terminal ileum. With pancreatic insufficiency, trypsin is not available, so that vitamin B_{12} does not complex with intrinsic factor and is not absorbed. In contrast to other triglycerides, vitamin D is absorbed from the gastrointestinal tract intact without digestion by lipase. It is absorbed normally in patients with chronic pancreatitis. The scarred and fibrosed pancreas in chronic pancreatitis may develop calcifications.

303. The answer is A. *(Wilson, 12/e, pp 1402–1410.)* Patients with HIV infection are at increased risk of developing severe infection with cytomegalovirus, tuberculosis, *Mycobacterium avium-intracellulare,* and *Cryptosporidium.* They are also at greatly increased risk of developing non-Hodgkin's lymphoma. Healthy patients may also develop an acute infection with *Cryptosporidium.* However, cryptosporidiosis for more than 1 month is diagnostic of AIDS. The other four diseases, when they involve the intestine, are diagnostic of AIDS.

304. The answer is C. *(Reynolds, Gastroenterol Clin North Am 18:223–255, 1989.)* Achalasia is a neuromuscular disease of the esophagus characterized by abnormal function of the esophageal body and lower esophageal sphincter (LES). The characteristic manometric esophageal abnormalities in achalasia are a high resting pressure of the lower esophageal sphincter, failure of the lower esophageal sphincter to relax with swallowing, and abnormal esophageal peristalsis. The upper esophageal sphincter (UES) functions normally in achalasia. The cause of achalasia is usually idiopathic. *Trypanosoma cruzi* infection can cause secondary achalasia. The clinical and radiographic findings of achalasia can be mimicked by cancer of the gastric cardia. Endoscopy is recommended to exclude cancer in patients presenting with apparent achalasia. Severe chronic reflex esophagitis can cause an esophageal ulcer or stricture, but not achalasia.

305. The answer is D. *(Sleisenger, 4/e, pp 909–925.)* The Zollinger-Ellison syndrome is characterized by a severe ulcer diathesis due to excessive gastrin production by a neurosecretory tumor that stimulates gastrin hyperacidity. Multiple gastrointestinal ulcers frequently occur. Ulcers may occur at unusual locations, such as the esophagus and descending duodenum. The screening test for this disorder is a serum gastrin level obtained after an overnight fast. Pernicious anemia with atrophic gastritis or antral G cell hyperplasia can also produce an elevated gastrin level. A secretin test is used to differentiate between an elevated gastrin level due to a gastrinoma and one due to these other conditions. Elevation of the serum gastrin level by more than 200 pg/mL after intravenous administration of secretin is characteristic of a gastrinoma. The urease breath test is used to detect *Helicobacter* (previously *Campylobacter*) *pyloris* infection of the stomach. *Helicobacter pyloris* has been implicated as a cause of acute and chronic gastritis and may be associated with peptic ulcers.

306. The answer is A. *(Schiff, 6/e, pp 466–475.)* HBsAg appears in the circulation a few weeks before the onset of symptoms or abnormalities of serum biochemical parameters of liver function from acute hepatitis B infection. This antigen persists for a variable period during the acute illness and is usually cleared following formation of immune aggregates of HBsAg with HBsAb (the specific antibody). About 5 to 10 percent of patients do not develop surface antibody and fail to clear surface antigen. These patients are chronic carriers of hepatitis B and can develop chronic persistent hepatitis or chronic active hepatitis (serological pattern of choice A).

HBcAb develops during acute infection at about the time that serum aminotransferase (AST, ALT) levels become elevated. It usually persists for years. HBcAb is not a neutralizing antibody, and detection of this antibody does not signal recovery from hepatitis B infection. HBcAb is useful to diagnose acute infection during the "window" period after surface antigen has disappeared and before surface antibody has appeared (serological pattern of choice B).

HBeAg is a marker for active viral replication and infectivity. It is useful in assessing the risk of viral transmission from an accidental needle stick (serological pattern of choice C).

HBsAb is usually detected during the late convalescent phase, 4 or more months after the onset of acute illness and weeks to months after the disappearance of surface antigen. HBsAb is a neutralizing and protective antibody. Development of this antibody signals recovery from acute infection and immunity from reinfection (serological pattern of choices D and E).

307. The answer is A (1, 2, 3). *(Stein, 3/e, pp 295–296, 360–362.)* Celiac disease is caused by a reaction to gluten present in cereals. Pathological examination of a small-bowel mucosal biopsy reveals flattened villi and intense mucosal inflammation. D-Xylose is absorbed by the enterocyte with no intraluminal digestion. It is inadequately absorbed in celiac disease because of mucosal damage. In contrast, the D-xylose test is normal in pancreatic insufficiency. Celiac disease causes fat malabsorption and steatorrhea, which is proved by analysis of the total fat content in a 72-h collection of stool. Intravenous administration of secretin is used to analyze pancreatic function in suspected chronic pancreatitis and to determine whether a gastrinoma is present in a patient with a mildly elevated gastrin level.

308. The answer is E (all). *(Eastwood, pp 161–162.)* Ingested vitamin B_{12} is first bound in the stomach to R factor proteins. In the duodenum, pancreatic enzymes cleave the R factors from vitamin B_{12}, which permits intrinsic factor to bind to the vitamin. Vitamin B_{12} bound to intrinsic factor is absorbed in the terminal ileum. The vitamin will not be absorbed in pernicious anemia because of an absence of intrinsic factor, after ileal resection or in Crohn's disease because of loss of the absorptive site, and in chronic pancreatitis because of a lack of pancreatic enzyme cleavage of the R factor.

309. The answer is D (4). *(Sleisenger, 4/e, pp 1884–1900.)* Pancreatic neuroendocrine tumors include insulinoma, pancreatic cholera (Verner-Morrison syndrome), glucagonoma, and somatostatinoma. These tumors generally produce symptoms due to hormonal secretion. Insulinomas are the most common symptomatic pancreatic neuroendocrine tumors. Insulinomas produce hypoglycemia due to increased insulin release. The characteristic laboratory finding is fasting hypoglycemia with elevated plasma insulin levels. Other laboratory findings include elevated plasma proinsulin and C-peptide levels. About 90 percent of insulinomas are benign.

A pancreatic VIPoma produces the WDHA (watery diarrhea, hypokalemia, achlorhydria) syndrome, which is clinically characterized by profound watery diarrhea associated with hypokalemia, achlorhydria, and dehydration. Other metabolic disturbances such as hypercalcemia and hyperglycemia commonly occur. This syndrome is believed to be due to VIP secretion by a neuroendocrine tumor, usually within the pancreas. The syndrome is diagnosed by finding an elevated plasma VIP level. Surgical removal of the tumor is recommended after rehydration and correction of electrolyte abnormalities. Cholera is an enteric infection due to *Vibrio cholerae*. The microorganism produces a severe, secretory watery diarrhea due to elaboration of an enterotoxin. *Pancreatic cholera* is an older name for a pancreatic VIPoma. This name refers to the similarity of the profuse diarrhea in a VIPoma to that in infectious cholera. The term *pancreatic cholera* is currently disfavored because about 20 percent of VIPomas are extrapancreatic.

Patients with a glucagonoma develop a characteristic eczematous dermatitis called *migratory necrolytic erythema*. Other clinical findings include hyperglycemia, a normocytic normochromic anemia, involuntary weight loss, and hypolipemia. The symptoms are due to pancreatic tumor production of glucagon. The plasma glucagon level is characteristically elevated.

310. The answer is B (1, 3). *(Eastwood, pp 240–247.)* Chronic pancreatitis is due to pancreatic damage from recurrent attacks of acute pancreatitis. Pancreatic damage leads to deficient secretion of lipase and to steatorrhea. Insulin deficiency may result in diabetes mellitus. Vitamins D and K are absorbed intact from the intestines without digestion by lipase and are therefore absorbed normally in pancreatic insufficiency. Courvoisier's sign is a palpable, nontender gallbladder in a jaundiced patient. This finding suggests the presence of a malignancy, especially pancreatic cancer.

311. The answer is A (1, 2, 3). *(Sleisenger, 4/e, pp 1419–1477, 1483–1518. Yamada, pp 1768–1813.)* Colon cancer is the second most common cause of internal malignancy in males and the third most common cause of internal malignancy in females. Risk factors for colon cancer include old age, prior colon cancer, Crohn's disease, and a family history of colon cancer. Most colon cancers are believed to evolve from adenomatous colonic polyps, and a history of prior or current adenomatous colonic polyps is a risk factor for colon cancer. Adenomas are characterized as tubular or villous according to whether the glands are arranged in a tubular or villous (frondlike) pattern. Among the adenomas, the villous type carries the greatest risk of developing colon cancer. In the genetic disease familial polyposis coli, the entire colon becomes carpeted with colonic adenomas; these patients inevitably develop colon cancer. Chronic ulcerative colitis is associated with a significant risk of developing colon cancer. Patients with ulcerative colitis for about 8 or more years should undergo surveillance colonoscopy. At colonoscopy random biopsies should be taken throughout the colon. The pathological finding of colonic dysplasia, a potentially premalignant lesion, demands close patient follow-up.

Colonic lipomas are benign polyps that contain fatty tissue and are typically found on the ileocecal valve. They are not associated with colon cancer.

312. The answer is B (1, 3). *(Bartlett, Rev Infect Dis 12 (suppl 2):243–251, 1990.)* *Clostridium difficile* is an important cause of diarrhea in patients who receive antibiotic therapy. *Clostridium difficile* proliferates in the gastrointestinal tract when the normal enteric flora is altered by antibiotics. Commonly implicated antibiotics include ampicillin, penicillin, clindamycin, cephalosporins, and trimethoprim-sulfamethoxazole. The diarrhea is usually mild to moderate but can occasionally be profound. Other clinical findings include pyrexia, abdominal pain, abdominal tenderness, leukocytosis, and serum electrolyte abnormalities. The diagnosis is made by demonstration at sigmoidoscopy of yellowish plaques of pseudomembranes that cover the colonic mucosa or by detection of *Clostridium difficile* toxin in the stool. The pseudomembranes consist of a tenacious fibrinopurulent mucosal exudate that contains extruded leukocytes, mucin, and sloughed mucosa. Isolation of *Clostridium difficile* from stool cultures is not very specific because of asymptomatic carriage, particularly in infants. Serological tests are not clinically useful for diagnosing this infection. Pseudomembranous colitis demands discontinuance of the offending antibiotic. Antibiotic therapy for moderate or severe disease includes oral vancomycin, metronidazole, or bacitracin. Cholestyramine and colestipol are also used therapeutically to bind the diarrheogenic toxin.

313. The answer is C (2, 4). *(Yamada, pp 1588–1645.)* Ulcerative colitis and Crohn's disease are inflammatory bowel diseases. Both diseases are idiopathic and related to autoimmune phenomena. Symptoms of both diseases include diarrhea, fever, abdominal pain, and gastrointestinal bleeding. Ulcerative colitis tends to involve only the superficial mucosa of the colon while Crohn's disease tends to involve deeper tissue of the colon or terminal ileum. The rectum is usually grossly involved in ulcerative colitis but not Crohn's disease. Crypt abscesses are characteristic of ulcerative colitis. In a crypt abscess colonic crypts are distorted by neutrophilic invasion. Other colonic diseases such as infectious colitis can sometimes produce crypt abscesses. Granulomas are common in Crohn's disease but not ulcerative colitis. A granuloma consists of a rim of lymphocytes surrounding a patch of histiocytes. Crohn's disease may involve different bowel segments between relatively normal segments of bowel (skip lesions). In ulcerative colitis, skip lesions do not occur.

314. The answer is A (1, 2, 3). *(Sleisenger, 4/e, pp 745–772, 1153–1155, 1435–1438. Wyngaarden, 19/e, pp 1887–1890.)* The Japanese have a very high incidence of gastric cancer and have established screening programs for this disease. Descendants of Japanese immigrants to America have a lower incidence of gastric cancer than native Japanese, which suggests that an environmental factor may be important in the development of this cancer. Although the etiology of gastric cancer is unknown, the disease has been associated with dietary consumption of nitrates and nitrites.

There is a high incidence of giardiasis in St. Petersburg, Russia. *Giardia lamblia,* a protozoan, colonizes the proximal small bowel and produces diarrhea, abdominal discomfort, and bloating. The diagnosis may be missed by examination of the stool for ova and parasites; examination of a duodenal aspirate obtained at esophagogastroduodenoscopy (EGD) is the most sensitive test. Giardiasis is frequently transmitted by contaminated water.

Histoplasmosis is a common cause of a mild respiratory illness in the midwestern river valleys of the United States. Cave explorers or bird handlers are at high risk of developing the infection from infected birds. AIDS patients develop severe, extrapulmonic histoplasmosis.

Blacks appear to have a *lower* incidence of ulcerative colitis than whites. One ethnic group with a high incidence of ulcerative colitis is American Jews.

315. The answer is A (1, 2, 3). *(Levine, Med Clin North Am 76:253–268, 1992.)* The incidence of non-Hodgkin's lymphoma is markedly increased in HIV-seropositive patients. This malignancy in an HIV-seropositive patient establishes the diagnosis of AIDS. The lymphomas typically are of B-cell origin and are high grade. AIDS patients usually develop extranodal involvement at such unusual sites as the central nervous system or rectum. These patients typically respond less well to chemotherapy than do immunocompetent patients, and they usually have rapid dissemination and early demise. About 5 percent of lymphomas in patients *without* AIDS present as primary gastric lymphoma. In patients with AIDS, however, isolated gastric involvement is rare.

316. The answer is A (1, 2, 3). *(Yamada, pp 715–731.)* It is important to differentiate colonic pseudoobstruction from colonic obstruction because the two diseases have a different therapy. Colonic pseudoobstruction and colonic obstruction frequently present similarly. Symptoms and signs in both diseases may include recent constipation; inability to pass flatus; nausea; vomiting; anorexia; abdominal distention, pain, tenderness, and tympany; and high-pitched, "tinkling" bowel sounds. In both cases abdominal radiographs may show dilated loops of colon that contain multiple air-fluid levels. Colonic obstruction rather than pseudoobstruction is suggested by rapid clinical decompensation, signs of systemic toxicity or sepsis (including leukocytosis and fever), and severe abdominal signs.

Colonic pseudoobstruction is due to failure of the normal propulsive colonic mechanisms to expel stool. Important causes include electrolyte abnormalities (such as hypokalemia, hypercalcemia, and hypomagnesemia), hypothyroidism, parkinsonism, scleroderma, and other collagen vascular diseases. Medications that can affect colonic motility and cause pseudoobstruction include analgesics, phenothiazines, narcotics, atropine and other anticholinergics, barbiturates, tricyclic antidepressants, and vincristine. Enteric neuropathies or myopathies may alter colonic motility and cause chronic pseudoobstruction. Colonic pseudoobstruction is usually treated medically by correction of electrolyte abnormalities or other etiological factors, cessation of oral alimentation, enteric decompression with a nasogastric or rectal tube, and careful monitoring of abdominal signs for decompensation that requires surgery. Colonic obstruction is due to mechanical blockage of stool passage. It is usually treated surgically. Causes include colonic cancer, colonic polyps, intestinal volvulus, intussusception, intestinal adhesions, and gallstone ileus.

317. The answer is A (1, 2, 3). *(Yamada, pp 1165–1169.)* Esophageal adenocarcinoma, which represents about 5 percent of esophageal cancers, is related to gastroesophageal reflux. When damaged by acid from gastroesophageal reflux, the normal squamous mucosa of the esophagus is replaced by abnormal, metaplastic, adenomatous mucosa, which is called Barrett's mucosa.

Patients experience dysphagia, or difficulty swallowing, when the esophageal lumen becomes narrowed because of an esophageal mass, esophageal stricture, or extrinsic compression. Causes of these lesions include esophageal cancer, benign tumors, and other conditions such as esophagitis or ingestion of lye.

318. The answer is E (all). *(Schiff, 6/e, pp 1118–1133.)* Chronic hepatitis B, particularly when associated with chronic active hepatitis and cirrhosis, is an important risk factor for hepatocellular carcinoma (hepatoma). Other risk factors include alcoholic cirrhosis, hemochromatosis, and aflatoxins. Aflatoxins are products of the mold *Aspergillus flavus,* which can contaminate foods such as peanuts, wheat, and corn. Hepatitis C frequently causes chronic hepatitis and cirrhosis, and recent evidence suggests an association between hepatitis C and hepatoma.

319. The answer is C (2, 4). *(Sivak, pp 431–453.)* About 5 percent of gastric ulcers are malignant. Radiologic criteria of ulcer benignity include location near the pylorus, small size, lack of an associated mass, rounded margins, smooth base, and radiation of gastric folds toward the ulcer margin. Exclusion of malignancy usually requires esophagogastroduodenoscopy at the time of diagnosis and repeat esophagogastroduodenoscopy after a course of antiulcer therapy to confirm healing. At endoscopy multiple biopsies should be taken from the margin of the ulcer for pathological examination to exclude malignancy. Healing of the gastric ulcer after a course of antiulcer therapy is a sign of benignity. Risk factors for gastric cancer include atrophic gastritis, pernicious anemia, prior subtotal gastrectomy, and common variable (congenital) immunodeficiency syndrome. Adenomatous gastric polyps, like adenomatous colonic polyps, are precancerous.

320. The answer is E (all). *(Sleisenger, 4/e, pp 1327–1358.)* The differential diagnosis of a lesion of the terminal ileum includes Crohn's disease, intestinal tuberculosis, intestinal lymphoma, periappendiceal abscess, *Yersinia* enterocolitis, and colon cancer. Crohn's disease is an idiopathic inflammatory disease that most frequently involves the terminal ileum. Symptoms and signs may include abdominal pain, fever, diarrhea, gastrointestinal bleeding, tenderness of the right lower quadrant, and a mass of the right lower quadrant. Radiographic findings of terminal ileal involvement include luminal narrowing, cobblestone ulcers, skip lesions, displacement of adjacent bowel, and fistulae. A peri-appendiceal abscess may extend to involve the adjacent terminal ileum. Tuberculosis, histoplasmosis, and lymphoma may involve the terminal ileum possibly because of the high concentration of lymphatic tissue there.

321. The answer is A (1, 2, 3). *(Yamada, pp 1674–1696.)* Patients with the genetic disease familial polyposis coli develop increasing numbers of colonic adenomatous polyps after puberty. Eventually the colon becomes carpeted with colonic polyps. Without surgery patients inevitably develop colon cancer from the adenomatous polyps. Total colectomy is recommended for this disease after puberty. Colectomy before puberty leads to stunted body growth and is not required because colon cancer rarely develops before puberty. Colonoscopy with polypectomy is not a feasible alternative therapy because of the large number of polyps. Subtotal colectomy with an ileorectal anastomosis avoids an ileostomy but requires frequent endoscopic surveillance for colon cancer in the retained rectum.

322. The answer is B (1, 3). *(Beaugerie, Ann Intern Med 117:401–402, 1992. Sherlock, 9/e, pp 249–259.)* In sclerosing cholangitis the bile ducts are irregular with multiple sites of beading and stenosis due to ductal fibrosis and inflammation. These abnormalities are usually demonstrated at ERCP. More than one-half of cases in patients without AIDS are associated with ulcerative colitis and the rest are idiopathic. Clinical findings may include pruritus, abdominal pain, pyrexia, jaundice, and elevated levels of serum alkaline phosphatase. AIDS patients may develop sclerosing cholangitis associated with opportunistic biliary infection by cryptosporidium, cytomegalovirus, and microsporidium. The diagnosis of an opportunistic infection is made by histological demonstration or culture from a ductular aspirate obtained at ERCP or a biopsy obtained at surgery.

323. The answer is A (1, 2, 3). *(Cappell, Am J Gastroenterol 86:1–15, 1991. Jacobson, Ann Intern Med 108:585–594, 1988.)* Cytomegalovirus may produce subclinical disease in healthy adults or they may develop transient fever, malaise, sore throat, and hepatomegaly. Cytomegalovirus remains latent after primary infection and can recur with immunocompromise. With HIV infection, cytomegalovirus may produce colitis, esophagitis, pneumonitis, retinitis, pancreatitis, or hepatitis. Cytomegalovirus frequently produces gastrointestinal ulcers, which may be deep and occasionally cause gastrointestinal perforation. However, cytomegalovirus has not been reported as a cause of colonic pseudoobstruction. Symptoms of cytomegaloviral colitis include gastrointestinal bleeding, abdominal pain, fever, involuntary weight loss, and diarrhea. Cytomegaloviral esophagitis may present with odynophagia (painful swallowing) or dysphagia (difficulty swallowing).

Numerous cases of cytomegaloviral cholecystitis have been reported. Patients present with typical findings of cholecystitis including fever, pain in the right upper quadrant, and a positive Murphy's sign, but they generally do not develop leukocytosis because of their immunocompromised state. Biochemical tests of liver function may be abnormal. Abdominal ultrasonography and computerized tomography typically show a dilated gallbladder with a thickened wall and no gallstones. Cholescintigraphy with radioactively labeled technetium (a HIDA or similar scan) and oral cholecystography result in nonvisualization of the gallbladder. Local cytomegaloviral infection is diagnosed by viral culture or histopathological identification of the virus in tissue.

324–327. The answers are 324-E, 325-A, 326-B, 327-C. *(Sherlock, 9/e, pp 236–248, 425–427, 485–487. Wyngaarden, 19/e, pp 786–788.)* Alcoholic hepatitis typically presents with fever, pain and tenderness of the right upper quadrant, and hepatomegaly in an alcoholic patient. Typically the SGOT (serum glutamic oxaloacetic transaminase, AST) level is much higher than the SGPT (serum glutamic pyruvate transaminase, ALT) level. Although the diagnosis is usually made from these clinical findings, a liver biopsy would show prominent steatosis or fat.

The blood fluke *Schistosoma mansoni* invades the portal vessels, where it stimulates intense inflammation and fibrosis. The portal vessels become pipelike, hence, the name *pipe-stem fibrosis*. Schistosomiasis tends to produce portal hypertension with little derangement of liver function.

Primary biliary cirrhosis is a disease of unknown etiology primarily affecting females. The inflammatory destruction in this disease of small- and medium-sized bile ducts eventually produces a paucity of bile ducts in the late stage of the disease.

Alpha$_1$-antitrypsin disease is a genetic disease in which the normal trypsin inhibitor alpha$_1$-antitrypsin is not produced. Symptoms are produced by hepatic or pulmonic injury. The diagnosis is supported by an absence of the normal spike produced by alpha$_1$-globulins on serum protein electrophoresis. For a definitive diagnosis, the serum alpha$_1$-antitrypsin form is determined by electrophoresis or by monoclonal antibodies. Liver biopsy characteristically demonstrates intracellular granules that are stained by the periodic acid–Schiff reagent and resist digestion with diastase.

328–331. The answers are 328-C, 329-D, 330-E, 331-B. *(Berk, 4/e, pp 3203–3235. Sherlock, 9/e, pp 236–248, 299–306.)* Autoimmune hepatitis was formerly called "lupoid hepatitis" because it shares some features with systemic lupus erythematosus (SLE), such as the presence of an elevated titer of serum antinuclear antibodies (ANA). This disease is treated by corticosteroids to reduce the immune-mediated hepatic injury.

Wilson's disease is a hereditary disease of copper metabolism manifested by pathological deposition of copper in the liver, cornea, and brain. The serum ceruloplasmin level is almost always decreased with this disease. Another screening test is a slit-lamp ophthalmologic examination to detect the brown deposition on Descemet's membrane of the cornea, the Kayser-Fleischer rings.

Hemochromatosis is an autosomal recessive genetic disease of iron metabolism characterized by excessive iron absorption and abnormal iron storage within parenchymal organs, including the liver, pancreas, and heart. Hepatic deposition produces cirrhosis. With this disease, the serum ferritin level and the percentage of iron saturation (serum iron level divided by the total iron-building capacity, expressed as a percentage) are abnormally elevated because of excessive bodily iron. This disease is usually diagnosed by a liver biopsy.

Primary biliary cirrhosis is an idiopathic hepatic disease that primarily affects small- or medium-sized bile ducts. It typically occurs in middle-aged females. Laboratory abnormalities include elevated serum alkaline phosphatase and bilirubin levels. Serum immunoelectrophoresis may demonstrate an elevated serum immunoglobulin M (IgM) level. Patients characteristically develop antimitochondrial antibodies.

332–335. The answers are 332-E, 333-C, 334-B, 335-A. *(Zakim, 2/e, pp 754–791.)* Chlorpromazine, an antipsychotic medication, can produce cholestasis, manifested by an elevation of the serum alkaline phosphatase and bilirubin levels. Patients may develop a flulike syndrome and pruritus. Eosinophilia commonly occurs. Development of this side effect mandates discontinuation of this medication.

Methyldopa (Aldomet) is an antihypertensive medication that may produce an acute hepatitis with significant elevations of the serum glutamic oxaloacetic transaminase (SGOT, AST) and serum glutamic pyruvate transaminase (SGPT, ALT) levels. In most cases, cessation of administration leads to complete recovery, but occasionally chronic active hepatitis may occur.

Estrogens are frequently used in oral contraceptives. Adverse hepatic effects produced by estrogens include hepatic adenomas, focal nodular hyperplasia, and peliosis hepatis. Peliosis hepatis consists of abnormally dilated intraparenchymal vascular channels. Hepatic adenomas are benign tumors of hepatocytes. Estrogens have also been associated with the development of pancreatitis. Thorotrast, a 20% solution of thorium dioxide, was extensively used as a radiographic contrast material between 1930 and 1955. Unfortunately, it is never resorbed and continues to emit radioactive energy. This agent is no longer used because it has been associated with the development of angiosarcomas (hemangiosarcomas). Vinyl chloride workers are also at increased risk of developing this malignancy.

336–339. The answers are 336-D, 337-B, 338-C, 339-A. *(Berk, 4/e, pp 3177–3188. Eastwood, pp 240–247. Sleisenger, 4/e, pp 1134–1152, 1289–1297.)* Sclerosing cholangitis is a disorder of unknown etiology characterized by obstructed bile flow due to irregular beading and dilatation of the biliary tree. About 70 percent of cases are associated with ulcerative colitis. The diagnosis is almost always made by radiographic observation of the bile ducts by endoscopic retrograde cholangiopancreatography (ERCP). A sclerosing cholangitis-like illness has been reported in AIDS patients with biliary infection with cytomegalovirus and *Cryptosporidium.*

In the blind loop syndrome, small intestinal abnormalities such as diverticula, resection, adhesions, or fistulas create intestinal loops that drain poorly and permit bacterial overgrowth. The intestinal abnormalities may be detected by an upper gastrointestinal series with small-bowel follow-through or by a small-bowel series. Bacterial overgrowth may be demonstrated by a ^{14}C-xylose breath test or by a quantitative bacterial culture of a jejunal aspirate.

Celiac disease, or nontropical sprue, is caused by an immunological reaction to gluten, which is a protein present in wheat. Microscopic examination of a mucosal small-bowel biopsy demonstrates blunting of the intestinal villi, lengthening of the mucosal crypts, and severe inflammation.

Pancreatic exocrine and endocrine insufficiency in chronic pancreatitis can result in diabetes mellitus and protein and fat malabsorption. Ingested bentiromide is normally cleaved by chymotrypsin in the intestine to liberate para-aminobenzoic acid (PABA), which is absorbed and excreted in the urine. Abnormally low recovery of PABA in the urine in a bentiromide test suggests decreased chymotrypsin secretion caused by pancreatic insufficiency.

340–343. The answers are 340-C, 341-A, 342-E, 343-A. *(Sherlock, 9/e, pp 236–248, 400–407. Zakim, 2/e, pp 1273–1299.)* Primary biliary cirrhosis is a disease of unknown etiology that primarily affects middle-aged women. Impaired biliary excretion of cholesterol due to progressive bile duct damage leads to hypercholesterolemia and to cholesterol deposition as xanthelasma on the eyelids and xanthomas on the arms.

Excessive copper deposition leads to disease of the liver and basal ganglia in Wilson's disease. Ocular findings include the premature development of large cataracts, called sunflower cataracts, and deposition of a brown pigment in Descemet's membrane of the cornea, a phenomenon called Kayser-Fleischer rings.

Hemochromatosis is an inherited disease characterized by abnormally high iron absorption. Excessive iron is stored in the liver, pancreas, and heart. Subcutaneous iron deposition leads to bronzing of the skin.

344–347. The answers are 344-E, 345-B, 346-A, 347-D. *(Stein, 3/e, pp 337–338, 554–555, 1486–1488, 1495–1496.)* Shigellosis is a severe, acute diarrheal disease produced by a gram-negative bacterium. It causes bacillary dysentery with intestinal ulceration and inflammation. The stool typically contains blood and mucus.

The clinical features of pancreatic cholera include severe watery diarrhea, hypokalemia, and achlorhydria due to secretion of vasoactive intestinal polypeptide (VIP) by a pancreatic tumor.

Vibrio cholerae, a noninvasive pathogen, produces a potent enterotoxin that stimulates adenylate cyclase production and intestinal secretion. The infection causes a severe, watery, secretory diarrhea. The stool osmolarity is similar to that of plasma. Prompt replacement of fluid and electrolyte losses is an essential part of therapy.

A gastrinoma is a tumor that produces gastrin and causes the Zollinger-Ellison syndrome. Patients frequently develop peptic ulcers because gastrin stimulates gastric acid secretion. The large volume of gastric acid production may overwhelm the ability of intestinal secretions to neutralize the acid. An acidic diarrhea results from inactivation of pancreatic enzymes and damage to small intestinal mucosa from the hyperacidity.

Nephrology

DIRECTIONS: Each question below contains five suggested responses. Select the **one best** response to each question.

Questions 348–350

A patient's blood work shows the following: Na^+ 140 meq/L, K^+ 4.0 meq/L, BUN 28 mg/dL, glucose 180 mg/dL, and creatinine 2.0 mg/dL. A 24-h urine collection with a total volume of 1400 mL shows a urine creatinine of 100 mg/dL and urine Na^+ of 70 meq/L.

348. Which of the following is a reasonable estimate of this patient's glomerular filtration rate? (Assume 1 day = 1400 min.)

(A) 50 mL/min
(B) 70 mL/min
(C) 100 mL/min
(D) 200 mL/min
(E) 700 mL/min

349. The fractional excretion of Na^+ (FE_{Na}) is

(A) 1.0 percent
(B) 2.5 percent
(C) 5.0 percent
(D) 10 percent
(E) 50 percent

350. Which of the following is the best estimate of this patient's serum osmolality? (Assume Na^+, its accompanying anion, BUN [molecular weight 28], and glucose [molecular weight 180] are the major contributors.)

(A) 140 mOsm/kg
(B) 200 mOsm/kg
(C) 300 mOsm/kg
(D) 488 mOsm/kg
(E) 1000 mOsm/kg

351. You are asked to evaluate a patient in the emergency room. He was brought by the rescue squad in a comatose state. Serum electrolytes drawn on admission show the following: Na^+ 133 meq/L, K^+ 8.0 meq/L, Cl^- 98 meq/L, HCO_3^- 13 meq/L. An electrocardiogram shows a rhythm with absence of P waves, a widened QRS complex, and peaked T waves. Which would be the most appropriate initial step?

(A) Repeat electrolyte measurements and observe
(B) Attempt cardioversion
(C) Administer intravenous calcium gluconate
(D) Administer hydrochlorothiazide, 25 mg orally
(E) Administer intravenous potassium chloride, 20 meq over 1 h

DIRECTIONS: Each question below contains four suggested responses of which **one or more** is correct. Select

A	if	**1, 2, and 3**	are correct
B	if	**1 and 3**	are correct
C	if	**2 and 4**	are correct
D	if	**4**	is correct
E	if	**1, 2, 3, and 4**	are correct

352. Glomerulonephritides associated with depressed levels of serum complement include

(1) postinfectious glomerulonephritis (e.g., poststreptococcal glomerulonephritis)
(2) membranoproliferative glomerulonephritis
(3) lupus nephritis
(4) IgA nephropathy

353. Multiple myeloma may be associated with

(1) hypercalcemia
(2) the Fanconi syndrome
(3) distal renal tubular acidosis
(4) low anion gap

354. True statements regarding adult polycystic kidney disease (APKD) include

(1) hypertension is a common finding
(2) cerebral aneurysms may be seen in about 10 percent of the cases
(3) the genetic defect in the majority of the patients lies on chromosome 16
(4) the disease is transmitted in an autosomal recessive pattern

355. True statements regarding polyarteritis nodosa (PAN) include which of the following?

(1) Renal arteriography can be helpful in the diagnosis of "classic" (macroscopic) PAN
(2) Hypertension is rare in classic PAN
(3) PAN may be associated with high titers of antineutrophilic cytoplasmic antibody (ANCA)
(4) Steroid therapy is felt to be ineffective in PAN

356. True statements regarding poststreptococcal glomerulonephritis (PSGN) include

(1) it is typically associated with infection by group A beta-hemolytic streptococcus
(2) the latency from infection to renal disease is typically 2 days
(3) complement levels usually return to normal within 6 weeks
(4) most children with PSGN progress to chronic renal failure

DIRECTIONS: Each group of questions below consists of lettered headings followed by a set of numbered items. For each numbered item select the **one** lettered heading with which it is **most** closely associated. Each lettered heading may be used **once, more than once, or not at all.**

Questions 357–360

Match each patient with the most likely renal calculi.

(A) Calcium oxalate stones
(B) Struvite (triple-phosphate) stones
(C) Cystine stones
(D) Uric acid stones

357. Patient with a myeloproliferative disorder

358. Patient with Crohn's disease

359. Patient with recurrent urinary tract infections by *Proteus* species

360. A 20-year-old man with recurrent stones; urinalysis shows many hexagonal crystals

Questions 361–364

In the following patients with the nephrotic syndrome, choose the likely finding on renal biopsy.

(A) Focal and segmental areas of mesangial sclerosis
(B) Diffuse mesangial deposition of acidophilic material with yellow-green birefringence on Congo red staining
(C) Normal glomeruli on light microscopy (LM) with fusion of foot processes noted on electron microscopy (EM)
(D) Diffuse thickening of the glomerular basement membrane on LM with subepithelial dense deposits on EM

361. A 4-year-old child with proteinuria

362. A patient treated with penicillamine for 10 months

363. A 28-year-old HIV-positive patient

364. A patient with familial Mediterranean fever

Questions 365-368

Match each patient with the most likely set of electrolytes and blood gases.

	Serum Electrolytes (meq/L)				Arterial Blood Gas		Urinary Chloride (meq/L)
	Na	K	Cl	HCO₃	pH	P_{CO_2} (mmHg)	
(A)	136	3.2	90	37	7.51	48	5
(B)	138	3.1	113	16	7.32	32	—
(C)	135	5.5	100	8	7.20	20	—
(D)	143	2.9	97	36	7.50	47	50

365. Patient with diarrhea

366. Patient with diabetic ketoacidosis

367. Patient with vomiting

368. Patient with mineralocorticoid excess from an adrenal tumor

Questions 369–371

Match the diuretic with the physiological properties noted below.

(A) Increases reabsorption of calcium
(B) Inhibits the $Na^+/K^+/2Cl^-$ carrier along the thick ascending loop of Henle
(C) May induce a metabolic acidosis
(D) Commonly causes hyperkalemia
(E) None of the above

369. Furosemide

370. Acetazolamide

371. Hydrochlorothiazide

Questions 372–375

Match the drugs below with their characteristic nephrotoxic effect.

(A) Allergic interstitial nephritis (AIN)
(B) Nonoliguric acute tubular necrosis (ATN)
(C) Crystalline nephropathy
(D) Worsening azotemia in a patient with underlying renal insufficiency
(E) Distal renal tubular acidosis

372. Gentamicin

373. Methicillin

374. Acyclovir

375. Tetracycline

Nephrology
Answers

348–350. The answers are 348-A, 349-A, 350-C. *(Rose, Clinical Physiology, 3/e, pp 61–68, 592–593. Rose, Pathophysiology, 2/e, p 68.)* Glomerular filtration rate (GFR) can best be determined by measuring the clearance of a compound (at steady state) that is freely filtered at the level of the glomerulus, is not protein-bound, and is neither secreted nor reabsorbed by the tubules. Therefore, for this compound (C):

$$\text{Amount of C filtered} = \text{amount excreted}$$
$$P_c \times GRF = U_c \times V$$
$$GFR = \frac{U_c \times V}{P_c} \text{ (clearance of C)}$$

Where P_c = plasma concentration of C, U_c = urine concentration of C, V = urine volume. Inulin meets all the above criteria. Determination of inulin clearance, however, can be cumbersome. Therefore, creatinine (Cr) clearance is usually used. The daily production of Cr is relatively constant. It is filtered freely at the glomerulus and not reabsorbed by the tubule (though 10 to 20 percent of the urinary creatinine does come from proximal tubular secretion). Therefore, for this patient:

$$GFR = \frac{U_{Cr} \times V}{P_{Cr}} = \frac{100 \text{ mg/dL} \times 14 \text{ dL } (1400 \text{ mL})}{2 \text{ mg/dL}} = 700 \text{ dL/day}$$

The GFR is then determined by converting to milliliters per minute:

$$700 \text{ dL/day} = 70,000 \text{ mL/}1400 \text{ min} = 50 \text{ mL/min}$$

Measurement of the fractional excretion of sodium (FE_{Na}) can be helpful in distinguishing between prerenal azotemia and acute tubular necrosis (particularly in the oliguric patient). A low FE_{Na} reflects the sodium retention typical of prerenal states. FE_{Na} is the percentage of sodium (Na) filtered at the glomerulus and ultimately excreted in the urine.

$$FE_{Na} = \frac{Na\ excreted}{Na\ filtered} = \frac{U_{Na} \times V}{P_{Na} \times GFR} = \frac{U_{Na} \times V}{P_{Na} \times \dfrac{U_{Cr} \times V}{P_{Cr}}}$$

$$= \frac{U_{Na}/P_{Na}}{U_{Cr}/P_{Cr}}\ or\ \frac{U_{Na} \times P_{Cr}}{P_{Na} \times U_{Cr}}$$

$$= \frac{70 \times 2}{140 \times 100} \times 100 = 1.0\ percent$$

Plasma osmolality is a reflection of milliosmoles (mOsm) of solute per kilogram (kg) of water. The major contributors to osmolality include sodium, its accompanying anions (primarily Cl^- and HCO_3^-), BUN, and glucose. Since BUN and glucose are generally measured in milligrams per deciliter (mg/dL), one has to convert to milliequivalents per kilogram (meq/kg). This can be done by multiplying by 10 and dividing by the molecular weight:

$$Plasma\ osmolality = 2 \times Na + \frac{glucose \times 10}{180} + \frac{BUN \times 10}{28}$$

$$= 2 \times Na + \frac{glucose}{18} + \frac{BUN}{2.8}$$

$$= 2 \times 140 + \frac{180}{18} + \frac{28}{2.8}$$

$$= 300\ mOsm/kg$$

351. The answer is C. (*Rose, Clinical Physiology, 3/e, pp 757–790.*) This patient presents with severe hyperkalemia. Although potassium elevations can occasionally be spurious (e.g., in hemolysis), the changes on this patient's ECG reflect severe cardiotoxic effects from the hyperkalemia. The ECG shows a typical progression in hyperkalemia with peaked T waves followed by widening of the QRS, loss of P waves, and eventually a sine wave pattern. Therapy of severe hyperkalemia includes intravenous calcium gluconate (to normalize membrane excitability), glucose and insulin, sodium bicarbonate (to drive potassium intracellularly), and potassium exchange resins (to remove potassium). Dialysis may occasionally be necessary, particularly in patients with concomitant renal failure.

352. The answer is A (1, 2, 3). *(Rose, Pathophysiology, 2/e, p 166.)* When hypocomplementemia occurs in association with glomerulonephritis, the differential diagnostic list may be narrowed considerably. Specific entities include lupus nephritis, mixed cryoglobulinemia, membranoproliferative glomerulonephritis (MPGN), and postinfectious glomerulonephritis (including poststreptococcal glomerulonephritis, bacterial endocarditis, and the nephritis associated with infected ventriculoatrial shunts). Low levels of complements often result from increased degradation, which in some cases of MPGN may be secondary to the stabilization of C3 convertase by a circulating autoantibody (C3 nephritic factor). IgA nephropathy does not typically present with hypocomplementemia.

353. The answer is E (all). *(Massry, 2/e, pp 738–745. Smolens, Am Kidney Fund Nephrol Lett, vol 4, no 4, 1987.)* Myeloma can be associated with a variety of electrolyte and renal tubular abnormalities. Hypercalcemia is a fairly common finding and is felt to occur secondary to the release of factors such as osteoclastic activating factors (OAF), which stimulate bone resorption. Occasionally these patients may also present with pseudohypercalcemia caused by high levels of calcium-binding paraproteins. In this case, patients are typically asymptomatic because the levels of ionized calcium are normal. Among the tubular defects reported with myeloma, distal renal tubular acidosis, nephrogenic diabetes insipidus, and the Fanconi syndrome are commonly mentioned. These defects are felt to be secondary to direct toxic effects of the light chains (particularly kappa) on the proximal or distal tubules or both. The low anion gap occasionally seen in myeloma (mainly IgG myeloma) is secondary to large amounts of circulating, positively charged paraproteins, which serve as unmeasured cations. (The formula for the anion gap can be derived as follows: since electrical neutrality must be maintained, Na^+ + unmeasured cations = Cl^- + HCO_3^- + unmeasured anions; hence, anion gap = $Na^+ - (Cl^- + HCO_3^-)$ = unmeasured anions − unmeasured cations.) Therefore an increase in unmeasured cations lowers the anion gap. Patients whose paraprotein is negatively charged (such as often with IgA myeloma) should not have a low anion gap unless levels of albumin are very low (because albumin serves as an unmeasured anion).

354. The answer is A (1, 2, 3). *(Rose, Pathophysiology, 2/e, pp 405–410.)* APKD is a fairly common condition that accounts for 10 to 12 percent of cases of end-stage kidney disease. It is inherited in an autosomal dominant pattern; the majority of patients have a defect on the short arm of chromosome 16. The infantile form of PKD, on the other hand, is inherited in an autosomal recessive pattern. Cyst involvement can occur anywhere along the course of the nephron, and progressive cyst enlargement eventually causes the kidneys to become large. Symptoms typically appear in the fourth or fifth decade of life. Hypertension occurs very commonly and in general there is a gradual decline in renal function over time. Flank pain, hematuria (sometimes gross), and urinary tract infections are also commonly seen in these patients. Cysts can also be found in other organs including the liver, pancreas, and spleen. Cerebral aneurysms are also noted in about 10 percent of patients and can lead to subarachnoid hemorrhage. Treatment is generally supportive. Intercurrent episodes of severe flank pain, hemorrhage, or cyst infection often bring the patient to medical attention. With severe cyst infections it is important to treat the patient with antibiotics that are able to penetrate the cyst. Trimethoprim-sulfamethoxazole, chloramphenicol, and the newer quinolones (e.g., ciprofloxacin) are possible choices.

355. The answer is B (1, 3). *(Balow, Kidney Int 27:954–964, 1985. Massry, 2/e, pp 707–714.)* Polyarteritis nodosa (PAN) is a form of systemic vasculitis in which renal involvement is frequent. In the "classic," or macroscopic, form of the disease, medium to small arteries are affected predominantly. Renal damage is felt to be secondary to parenchymal ischemia or infarction, which often leads to a renin-mediated hypertension. Inflammation of the blood vessel leads to aneurysm formation secondary to destruction of the lamina elastica. Demonstration of such aneurysmal dilatation on renal, mesenteric, or hepatic arteriography can be very helpful in confirming the diagnosis. Microscopic PAN involves predominantly the small vessels (capillaries, venules, and arterioles). Hypertension is relatively uncommon; however, glomerular involvement (i.e., glomerulonephritis) is frequent. Laboratory findings may be nonspecific. An elevated sedimentation rate is often noted. Recently, a new serological marker has been discovered that is elevated in various forms of the vasculitides (particularly Wegener's granulomatosis and microscopic PAN). Detection of antibodies to neutrophilic cytoplasmic antigens (ANCA) appears to be a fairly specific and sensitive test in the diagnosis of renal vasculitis. Hepatitis B antigen, rheumatoid factor, and cryoglobulins also have been reported in patients with PAN. The use of glucocorticoid therapy (with and without cytotoxics) has improved long-term prognosis.

356. The answer is B (1, 3). *(Rose, Pathophysiology, 2/e, pp 223–229.)* PSGN usually follows infection with group A beta-hemolytic streptococcus. Patients typically present with hematuria, edema, and often oliguria after mean latency periods of 10 and 21 days with pharyngitis and pyoderma, respectively. The urinalysis characteristically shows an active sediment with proteinuria and hematuria often with red cell casts. Plasma complement levels are low in the majority of cases; however, they should normalize within 6 weeks. The urinary changes, on the other hand, may take much longer to resolve. In severe cases renal biopsy shows diffuse mesangial and endothelial cell proliferation with the characteristic presence of subepithelial humps on electron microscopy. The majority of children recover from the acute episode; however, the prognosis in adults may not be as good.

357–360. The answers are 357-D, 358-A, 359-B, 360-C. *(Massry, 2/e, pp 920–941.)* Nephrolithiasis is becoming an increasingly prevalent problem in Western society. Patients with renal stones often present with signs of partial or complete obstruction, flank or abdominal pain, and hematuria. Calcium oxalate (alone or in combination with apatite) stones are by far the most common as they account for approximately three-quarters of all stones. They are typically radiodense and therefore can often be detected on plain abdominal films. Hypercalciuria (with or without hypercalcemia), hyperoxaluria, hyperuricosuria, decreased urinary citrate, and decreased urine volumes can all predispose to calcium oxalate precipitation. Hyperoxaluria can either be primary (i.e., an inherited enzyme defect) or acquired. The most common cause of the latter is the increased intestinal absorption of oxalate in patients with small intestinal bypass or inflammatory bowel disease (such as Crohn's disease).

Struvite (triple-phosphate) stones are most commonly seen in patients with recurrent infections with uricase-producing bacteria (such as *Proteus*). Uricase-driven conversion of urea to ammonia and CO_2 (and eventually NH_4^+ and HCO_3^-) supports a persistently alkaline urine (pH greater than 7.5), which favors the formation of struvite ($MgNH_4PO_4 \cdot 6H_2O$) crystals. These stones are also radiopaque and occasionally can become quite large within the renal pelvis and calyces (so-called staghorn calculi).

Uric acid stones account for 5 to 10 percent of all stones. In contrast to calcium oxalate and struvite, these stones are usually radiolucent. Hyperuricemia and attendant hyperuricosuria (such as is seen in myeloproliferative disorders, or with defects of purine synthesis) can predispose to uric acid stones. Acid urine and low urine volumes also favor stone formation. Raising urine pH to above 6.0 to 6.5 can be very effective in solubilizing uric acid.

Cystine stones are relatively rare and occur in patients with an inherited disorder of amino acid handling that results in excessive urinary excretion of cystine, ornithine, lysine, and arginine. The urinalysis often shows the distinctive hexagon-shaped cystine crystals.

361–364. The answers are 361-C, 362-D, 363-A, 364-B. *(Rose, Pathophysiology, 2/e, pp 179–296.)* In each of the listed cases, the patient is presenting with the nephrotic syndrome (NS). NS can be defined as urinary protein excretion of greater than or equal to 3.0 to 3.5 g/day (in the adult) usually associated with edema, low levels of albumin, and hyperlipidemia. Proteinuria of this degree almost always indicates glomerular pathology.

When evaluating a patient with glomerulopathy, a routine urinalysis (UA) can be very helpful in selecting a differential diagnostic set. Conditions such as minimal change disease, focal segmental glomerular sclerosis, diabetes, membranous nephropathy, amyloidosis, and pre-eclampsia are usually associated with a nephrotic sediment with heavy proteinuria and little in the way of cellular elements or casts. On the other hand, a nephritic sediment (such as seen with proliferative nephritis) typically contains many red blood cells, often with red blood cell or granular casts with variable amounts of proteinuria.

The most common cause of NS in children is minimal change disease, which represents up to 90 percent of cases. The UA routinely shows proteinuria, with microscopic hematuria present in a minority of cases. On biopsy the glomeruli usually appear normal on light microscopy. The diagnosis is confirmed by electron microscopy, which shows fusion of the epithelial foot processes. Response to steroids is quite good; the great majority of the children have a complete remission by 5 to 8 weeks. Relapses, however, are very common and can be treated with recurrent steroid therapy or, for those with very frequent relapses, cytotoxic agents.

In adults, membranous nephropathy (MN) is the most frequent

cause of idiopathic nephrotic syndrome. The majority of patients with MN have no discernible cause. However, in approximately one-third of the patients, a causative disorder such as chronic hepatitis B infection, malignancy, or certain drugs can be identified. Drugs associated with MN include gold and penicillamine. Pathology may vary according to the stage of the disease, but typically manifests diffuse thickening of the glomerular basement membrane with subepithelial dense deposits on EM. Immunofluorescence (IF) usually shows diffuse granular deposits of IgG and C3.

Focal segmental glomerulosclerosis (FSGS) accounts for approximately 10 to 15 percent of the cases of nephrotic syndrome. Again, the majority of the cases of FSGS are idiopathic, though occasionally a secondary cause can be elicited, such as chronic reflux nephropathy, chronic renal transplant rejection, heroin use, and most recently HIV (AIDS) nephropathy. FSGS is the most common cause of nephrotic syndrome in patients with AIDS and appears to take a particularly aggressive course. Renal biopsy usually shows focal (involvement of some glomeruli) and segmental (involvement of some glomerular capillary loops) areas of sclerosis often associated with deposits of IgM and C3. Epithelial foot process fusion is noted on EM.

Amyloidosis, either primary or secondary, very frequently involves the kidneys. In primary (AL) amyloidosis there is increased production of, and tissue deposition of, fragments of monoclonal light chains (presumably from abnormal plasma cells). Chronic inflammation (from conditions such as rheumatoid arthritis and familial Mediterranean fever) can lead to secondary (AA) amyloidosis partially by the stimulation of secretion of serum amyloid A protein by the liver. Pathologically, one notes diffuse deposition of amorphous acidophilic material within the mesangium, the capillaries, and occasionally the vessels and tubules. These deposits show a characteristic yellow-green birefringence with Congo red staining. The presence of typical fibrils of amyloid proteins on EM confirms the diagnosis.

365–368. The answers are 365-B, 366-C, 367-A, 368-D. *(Rose, Clinical Physiology, 3/e, pp 464–477, 478–555.)* Changes in concentration of serum hydrogen ion are reflected by a reciprocal change in extracellular pH ($-\log[H^+]$, normal values 7.37 to 7.43). *Primary* metabolic acidosis and alkalosis result from a decrease or increase in serum bicarbonate, respectively. The respiratory compensation in these cases acts to return pH toward normal (by decreasing P_{CO_2} in the case of a metabolic acidosis or increasing P_{CO_2} in the case of metabolic alkalosis).

Metabolic alkalosis is associated with an elevated serum HCO_3^- and pH and a compensatory rise in P_{CO_2}. This can result from a gain of HCO_3^- or from loss of hydrogen ions. To maintain the alkalosis, however, the renal tubules must reclaim the generated bicarbonate (the stimulus for which is often provided by concomitant factors such as volume depletion, chloride depletion, potassium depletion, and mineralocorticoid excess). Metabolic alkalosis associated with volume depletion (from conditions such as vomiting and distant diuretic use) is usually reflected by a urinary chloride of less than 15 meq/L. The metabolic alkalosis noted in primary mineralocorticoid excess states will usually be associated with a urinary chloride greater than 20 meq/L.

Metabolic acidosis is associated with a fall in HCO_3^- concentration, low blood pH, and compensatory decline in P_{CO_2}. Metabolic acidosis results from a gain of hydrogen ions, loss of HCO_3^- ions, or the inability of the kidney to excrete the 1 to 1.5 meq/kg per day of hydrogen ions normally generated by the body. Conditions such as lactic acidosis or diabetic ketoacidosis, in which the bicarbonate is replaced by an unmeasured anion (e.g., lactate, beta-hydroxybutyrate), will be associated with a rise in the anion gap (normal 9 to 14). Remember that the anion gap = $Na^+ - (CL^- + HCO_3^-)$. Therefore, in conditions such as diarrhea or renal tubular acidoses, in which Cl rises as HCO_3^- falls, the anion gap will not be elevated. Common causes of high-anion-gap and normal-anion-gap acidoses are listed below:

High-anion-gap acidosis	Normal-anion-gap acidosis
Lactic acidosis	Diarrhea
Ketoacidosis (diabetic, alcoholic)	Renal tubular acidosis
Ingestions	Type I (distal)
Ethylene glycol	Type II (proximal)
Methanol	Type IV
Salicylates	Ammonium chloride
Paraldehyde	Ureterosigmoidostomy
Renal failure (usually late)	Carbonic anhydrase inhibitors
	Chronic renal disease

369–371. The answers are 369-B, 370-C, 371-A. *(Rose, Clinical Physiology, 3/e, pp 389–415.)* Diuretics enhance salt excretion by inhibiting NaCl reabsorption at various tubular sites. Acetazolamide, by inhibiting carbonic anhydrase, decreases Na^+, Cl^-, and HCO_3^- reclamation along the proximal tubule. The ensuing loss of alkali (as $NaHCO_3$) can evoke a metabolic acidosis. Acetazolamide, however, is a relatively weak diuretic, partially because of the ability of more distal sites to increase solute reabsorption.

The loop diuretics (furosemide, bumetanide, and ethacrynic acid) are the most potent diuretics. They inhibit the $Na^+/K^+/2Cl^-$ transporter along the loop of Henle. These agents also inhibit calcium reabsorption at this site and thereby increase calcium excretion.

The thiazide diuretics inhibit Na^+ and Cl^- reabsorption along the distal tubule (and connecting segment) and induce a modest natriuresis. Contrary to the loop diuretics, these agents increase calcium reabsorption, presumably both by a direct distal effect and at the proximal tubule (owing to volume depletion).

372–375. The answers are 372-B, 373-A, 374-C, 375-D. *(Massry, 2/e, pp 812–818.)* Nephrotoxicity can be an important manifestation of drug toxicity, especially since many agents are primarily excreted through the kidneys. The nephrotoxicity of the aminoglycosides (including gentamicin) is well recognized and tends to occur in 2 to 20 percent of patients treated. The patients typically present with nonoliguric renal failure (ATN) several days after initiation of therapy. Risk factors for aminoglycoside nephrotoxicity include increased age, preexisting renal disease, volume contraction, repeated doses, and the use of other nephrotoxic agents. Treatment is generally supportive as the majority of patients will recover renal function after discontinuation of the drug. Rare patients with severe renal failure may require dialysis.

Allergic interstitial nephritis (AIN) is another well-recognized drug effect. Many agents have been associated with AIN including the penicillins (especially methicillin), cephalosporins, sulfa drugs, and diuretics. Characteristically the patients present with rash, fever, azotemia, eosinophilia, and eosinophiluria. The kidneys may show increased gallium uptake and are typically enlarged. Usually the renal function improves after the offending agent is stopped (though this may take several days). The role of steroids in the management of AIN remains controversial.

The antiviral agent acylovir can be associated with acute crystalline nephropathy due to the limited solubility of the agent. It is essential that intravenous acyclovir be given slowly (at least over 60 min) to prevent this effect.

Owing to their decreased anabolism, the tetracyclines are often associated with worsening azotemia when given to patients with renal insufficiency. If a patient with renal failure requires a tetracycline, the preferred one is doxycycline because its ananabolic effect is the least pronounced. Outdated tetracycline has been associated with a proximal renal tubular acidosis, and demeclocycline (another tetracycline derivative) can cause polyuria by inducing a renal concentrating defect.

Oncology and Hematology

DIRECTIONS: Each question below contains four or five suggested responses. Select the **one best** response to each question.

376. Heparin is a naturally occurring mucopolysaccharide that binds to antithrombin III and transforms this molecule into a potent inhibitor of thrombin and other serine proteases. Complications of heparin anticoagulation include all the following EXCEPT

(A) vertebral body collapse
(B) hemorrhage
(C) skin necrosis
(D) thrombosis
(E) thrombocytopenia

377. Marrow-ablative chemotherapy or chemoradiotherapy followed by bone marrow transplantation may be curative in leukemia, lymphoma, and possibly other malignancies. Which of the following diseases may be cured only by ablative therapy and bone marrow transplantation?

(A) Acute lymphoblastic leukemia (ALL)
(B) Acute myelogenous leukemia (AML)
(C) Chronic myelogenous leukemia (CML)
(D) Large cell lymphoma (LCL)

378. Sickle cell disease arises from the homozygous inheritance of a variant gene for beta globin that results in a single amino acid substitution (valine replaces glutamic acid at the sixth position). Sickle beta globin undergoes concentration-dependent intracellular polymerization and sickling with loss of red cell deformability, which leads to hemolysis and vascular occlusive events. All the following statements regarding this disease are true EXCEPT

(A) sudden overwhelming infection may occur
(B) differentiation of crisis pain from other processes requires clinical laboratory studies
(C) hydration and analgesia represent basic management of painful sickle cell crisis
(D) heterozygotes for Hgb S have a decreased risk from malaria, which may account for the prevalence of Hgb S
(E) red cell exchange or hypertransfusion is indicated in children who have had a stroke

197

379. Oncogenes are important in at least some and perhaps many types of cancer. All the following statements regarding oncogenes are true EXCEPT

(A) oncogenes can be identified in the DNA of approximately 60 percent of normal persons
(B) RNA retroviruses may induce oncogenesis by interfering with normal control mechanisms or by inserting transforming viral oncogenes
(C) infection with the type I human T-cell lymphotropic virus (HTLV-I retrovirus) is associated with T-cell leukemia endemic in Japan, the Caribbean, and the southeastern U.S.
(D) chromosomal translocation may result in cancer by altering regulation and expression of cellular proto-oncogenes

380. Vitamin B_{12} deficiency and therapy are correctly characterized by all the following statements EXCEPT

(A) neurological symptoms may precede anemia
(B) only the first stage of the Schilling test is abnormal in patients with bacterial overgrowth
(C) hypokalemia may develop during initial replacement therapy
(D) erythroid hyperplasia is characteristic of megaloblastosis
(E) reticulocytosis occurs on the third to fifth day after initial vitamin B_{12} replacement

381. Severe aplastic anemia is associated with a granulocyte level of <500 cells per microliter, a platelet count of <20,000, and a reticulocyte count of <2 percent in association with profound marrow hypocellularity. All the following statements are true EXCEPT

(A) hepatitis is associated with aplastic anemia
(B) before effective treatment was available, mortality at 12 months following diagnosis was greater than 50 percent
(C) allogeneic bone marrow transplant (BMT) is the treatment of choice in younger patients
(D) aggressive immunosuppressive therapy may achieve remission in lupus-associated but not idiopathic aplastic anemia
(E) blood transfusion may impair engraftment

382. AIDS-related malignancies include all the following EXCEPT

(A) cervical cancer
(B) gastric carcinoma
(C) CNS lymphoma
(D) Hodgkin's disease
(E) Kaposi's sarcoma

383. A 57-year-old man presents with plethora and splenomegaly in the absence of cardiac and pulmonary disease. Complete blood count (CBC) reveals a hematocrit of 62 percent, a white cell count of 24,000/mm³, and thrombocytosis. Red blood cell mass is elevated as determined by isotope dilution. True statements concerning this patient's condition include each of the following EXCEPT

(A) a small minority of patients experience transformation to acute leukemia

(B) there is an increased incidence of peptic ulcer disease

(C) a cerebrovascular event is a common complication

(D) pruritus, particularly after bathing, is a frequent complaint

(E) urine levels of erythropoietin are elevated

384. All the following drugs are contraindicated in patients with glucose-6-phosphate dehydrogenase deficiency EXCEPT

(A) sulfapyridine
(B) nitrofurantoin
(C) colchicine
(D) sulfamethoxazole
(E) phenylhydrazine

385. All the following statements concerning multiple myeloma are true EXCEPT

(A) renal failure develops in approximately 25 percent of patients

(B) hyperviscosity is less common in myeloma than in Waldenström's disease

(C) the anion gap is frequently abnormal in myeloma

(D) pneumococcal vaccination is of limited value

(E) identification of the monoclonal protein spike (M-protein) establishes the diagnosis

DIRECTIONS: Each question below contains four suggested responses of which **one or more** is correct. Select

A	if	**1, 2, and 3**	are correct
B	if	**1 and 3**	are correct
C	if	**2 and 4**	are correct
D	if	**4**	is correct
E	if	**1, 2, 3, and 4**	are correct

386. True statements concerning prostate cancer and its treatment include that

(1) bone metastases are commonly both osteoblastic and osteolytic

(2) 95 percent are adenocarcinomas

(3) tumors are frequently multifocal

(4) radiation therapy rarely causes impotence

387. General use of new chemotherapeutic drugs for cancer follows years of preclinical and clinical research. True statements regarding this research include which of the following?

(1) Phase II trials are undertaken only for drugs that have demonstrated encouraging activity in phase I studies

(2) Phase II trials are usually comparative studies with two or more treatment arms

(3) Phase III drugs are more active than phase I drugs

(4) Randomization of treatment assignment is used in phase III studies

388. Large cell non-Hodgkin's lymphoma and Hodgkin's disease are potentially curable diseases. Statements true of *both* diseases include

(1) 90 percent of cases are of B-cell origin

(2) curative chemotherapy requires multiple drugs

(3) studies of gene rearrangement reveal clonality

(4) radiation may be curative in localized disease

389. A young woman presents with a small breast nodule, which on needle biopsy is found to be an adenocarcinoma. Examination is otherwise unremarkable and laboratory studies including CA-15-3 level are normal. Interventions likely to be curative include

(1) radical mastectomy with full axillary dissection

(2) lumpectomy with axillary sampling followed by radiotherapy

(3) simple mastectomy without axillary dissection

(4) pulse chemotherapy and hormonal therapy without additional local treatment

390. Correct statements about breast cancer include

(1) premenopausal patients with stage I breast cancer may benefit from adjuvant chemotherapy

(2) postmenopausal patients with hormone receptor–positive stage II breast cancer should receive adjuvant tamoxifen therapy

(3) patients with stage II breast cancer and extensive involvement of axillary lymph nodes may benefit from dose-intensive chemotherapy with bone marrow transplantation

(4) radiotherapy of the chest wall combined with axillary and supraclavicular ports is an alternative adjuvant treatment

391. A routine physical examination of an 18-year-old male at school reveals splenomegaly. He denies complaints but CBC shows a modest anemia with increased reticulocytes and spherocytes on blood film. Hemoglobin electrophoresis and Coombs' testing are normal, but osmotic fragility and mean corpuscular hemoglobin concentration (MCHC) are increased. Management of this condition and its complications may include

(1) red cell transfusion

(2) splenectomy

(3) administration of folic acid

(4) cholecystectomy

392. Adjuvant therapy is given to patients who no longer have detectable residual cancer following primary resection of disease but who are considered to be at risk for recurrence. The largest group of patients who receive adjuvant treatment are those with breast cancer. True statements regarding adjuvant treatment of breast cancer include

(1) disease-free survival is improved

(2) overall survival may be improved

(3) younger patients obtain more benefit from chemotherapy, but patients over 50 do better with hormonal treatment

(4) many patients are cured by adjuvant treatment

393. Cytogenetic abnormalities can now be detected in the majority of patients with acute myelogenous leukemia. True statements regarding these abnormalities include

(1) cytogenetic results correlate with morphology

(2) cytogenetic results predict response to treatment

(3) cytogenetic findings resolve at remission

(4) cytogenetic results predict clinical course

DIRECTIONS: Each group of questions below consists of lettered headings followed by a set of numbered items. For each numbered item select the **one** lettered heading with which it is **most** closely associated. Each lettered heading may be used **once, more than once, or not at all.**

Questions 394–398

Match the following descriptions with the appropriate drug.

(A) Methotrexate
(B) Cytosine arabinoside
(C) Nitrogen mustard
(D) Cyclophosphamide
(E) Doxorubicin

394. A synthetic alkylating agent activated by the mixed function oxidases in hepatic microsomes. Hydration and adequate urinary flow help to prevent the cystitis that may result from this drug

395. A synthetic alkylating agent that is so reactive in aqueous solution that it must be used within minutes of solubilization. Extravasation causes a severe chemical burn

396. A folic acid antagonist that is excreted by the kidneys essentially unchanged. Renal function must be assessed, therefore, prior to use. Chronic use may produce hepatic cirrhosis

397. An antitumor antibiotic useful in the treatment of lymphoma, sarcoma, acute leukemia, and breast cancer. Dose-related cardiomyopathy limits the cumulative dose

398. An antimetabolite particularly effective against acute leukemia. Dose-limiting effects include CNS, mucosal, and hepatic toxicities

Questions 399–403

Match the descriptions below with the appropriate pathological RBC inclusions.

(A) Howell-Jolly bodies
(B) Pappenheimer bodies
(C) Cabot rings (ring bodies)
(D) Heinz bodies
(E) Coarse basophilic stippling

399. Appearance in splenectomized patients and in those with hemolytic anemia   A

400. Appearance in megaloblastic anemia; origin unknown   C

401. Iron granulations   B

402. An intracellular precipitate of hemoglobin   D

403. Aggregated ribosomes; characteristic of lead intoxication and thalassemia   E

DIRECTIONS: The group of questions below consists of four lettered headings followed by a set of numbered items. For each numbered item select

A	if the item is associated with	(A) **only**
B	if the item is associated with	(B) **only**
C	if the item is associated with	**both** (A) and (B)
D	if the item is associated with	**neither** (A) nor (B)

Each lettered heading may be used **once, more than once, or not at all.**

Questions 404–408

(A) Small-cell lung cancer
(B) Non-small-cell lung cancer
(C) Both
(D) Neither

404. Resection is the only potentially definitive treatment

405. Oncogene activation/inactivation is common

406. Smoking is a key factor

407. Combination chemotherapy is primary treatment

408. Intensive screening of high-risk persons can significantly decrease death rates

Questions 409–413

(A) Acute lymphocytic leukemia (ALL)
(B) Acute myelocytic leukemia (AML)
(C) Both
(D) Neither

409. Children are most frequently affected and may be cured

410. If patients are untreated or unresponsive to treatment, death usually results within 3 months

411. Histochemical tests are useful in determining subtypes. Affected cells usually stain positively with peroxidase, Sudan black, and esterase stains

412. Chromosomal abnormalities occur and are diagnostic

413. Treatment typically renders patients severely hypoplastic or aplastic for a period of time, and they thus require intensive supportive care

Questions 414–418

    (A) Iron deficiency
    (B) Anemia of chronic disease
    (C) Both
    (D) Neither

414. Increased reticulocyte production *D*

415. Increased free erythrocyte protoporphyrin (FEP)

416. Increased anisocytosis

417. Decreased ratio of iron to total iron-binding capacity (TIBC)

418. Exclusion of diagnosis by serum ferritin level of 150 μg/L *A*

Questions 419–423

    (A) Coombs' positivity (not false positive)
    (B) Stool guaiac positivity (not false positive)
    (C) Both
    (D) Neither

419. May be associated with lymphoma *B*

420. May be related to a drug *C*

421. May be associated with a process that requires red cell transfusion *C*

422. Always associated with shortened red cell survival *B*

423. May be closely linked to increased serum levels of vitamin B_{12} *D*

Questions 424–428

    (A) Thrombotic thrombocytopenic purpura (TTP)
    (B) Chronic idiopathic thrombocytopenic purpura (chronic ITP)
    (C) Both
    (D) Neither

424. Normal or increased numbers of megakaryocytes *C*

425. Steroid therapy *C*

426. Fever *A*

427. Fragmented red cells *A*

428. Presence of serum or platelet-associated antiplatelet antibodies *B*

Questions 429–433

    (A) Hemophilia A (factor VIII coagulant deficiency)
    (B) Hemophilia B (factor IX deficiency)
    (C) Both
    (D) Neither

429. Possible carrier detection by comparison of coagulant factor and von Willebrand factor levels *A*

430. Vitamin K–dependent protein *B*

431. Prolonged template bleeding time *D*

432. Response to cryoprecipitate *A*

433. Response to desmopressin (DDAVP) *A*

Oncology and Hematology

Answers

376. The answer is C. *(Williams, 4/e, pp 1572–1576. Wilson, 12/e, p 315.)* Hemorrhage is the most frequent complication of heparin therapy and may occur even at optimal therapeutic levels. Heparin causes thrombocytopenia in approximately 1 percent of patients and may be associated with diffuse platelet activation and thrombosis. Prompt diagnosis of heparin-associated thrombosis is crucial since continuation of heparin may lead to progressive thrombosis. Heparin use for periods in excess of 2 months may produce osteoporosis. Skin necrosis is associated with vitamin K–antagonist anticoagulation of patients with deficiency of protein C or S activity. In these patients the imbalance between vitamin K–dependent procoagulant and anticoagulant activity is exacerbated during the initial period of vitamin K antagonism, which results in thrombosis. This complication can apparently be avoided by concurrent heparin administration during initial vitamin K antagonism.

377. The answer is C. *(Williams, 4/e, pp 1067–1089. Wilson, 12/e, pp 1571–1575.)* At least 50 percent of children with ALL are cured by current standard-dose therapy, while fewer adults are saved. Treatment of AML is less successful, but at least 20 percent of patients who achieve remission are long-term survivors. Approximately 75 percent of patients with intermediate- and high-grade lymphomas achieve initial remission and 50 percent appear to be cured. CML is only palliated by standard-dose therapies, which have little effect on survival. Cure is currently possible in CML only by marrow ablation followed by allogeneic or syngeneic bone marrow transplantation.

378. The answer is B. *(Williams, 4/e, pp 613–625. Wilson, 12/e, pp 1542–1545.)* Clinical laboratory testing is not useful in the diagnosis of a painful sickle cell crisis. Hemoglobin, reticulocyte number, bilirubin, and lactic dehydrogenase levels, which are typically abnormal in patients with sickle cell disease, do not fluctuate during crisis. Splenic function is an early casualty of sickle cell disease with most splenic function lost in childhood because of repeated thrombosis. Treatment for sickle cell crisis is supportive with intravenous fluids and pain control. Supplemental oxygen is commonly provided. Red cell transfusion is not helpful in the usual crisis, but red cell exchange transfusion may be useful for stroke in evolution or prevention of recurrence. Chest and hepatic crisis may also respond. Aggressive transfusion during pregnancy may be useful in women with sickle cell disease and recurrent abortion. Enhanced production of hemoglobin F via chemotherapy or administration of growth factor may decrease sickling.

379. The answer is A. *(Wilson, 12/e, pp 60–71.)* Oncogenes have been identified in all human and animal tissue studied. The identification of oncogenes may explain the long-observed relationship between various types of cancer and DNA damage such as that from exposure to alkylating drugs or radiation. DNA damage may alter oncogene regulation or expression. Similarly, insertion of viral oncogenes via retroviral vectors may produce malignancy. At least two types of retroviral oncoviruses have been identified. One type interferes with regulation of cellular proto-oncogenes, which results in malignancy usually after a long latent period. The second type of retrovirus serves as a vector for a viral oncogene that may rapidly induce malignant transformation.

380. The answer is B. *(Williams, 4/e, pp 453–481. Wilson, 12/e, pp 1525–1526, 1528–1529.)* Vitamin B_{12} deficiency is an important cause of megaloblastosis and develops in the vast majority of cases as a result of impaired vitamin B_{12} absorption. Dietary vitamin B_{12} is bound to intrinsic factor (IF) secreted by the stomach, and vitamin B_{12} bound to IF is absorbed by ileal mucosa. This mechanism fails if the stomach does not secrete IF or if IF secreted is not available for vitamin B_{12} binding. The latter occurs in pernicious anemia, where an anti-IF antibody blocks vitamin B_{12} binding. Vitamin B_{12} can be stripped from IF by bacterial overgrowth, which occurs in small-bowel diverticula or other blind loops. Diffuse ileal abnormality in Crohn's disease, sprue, or rarely lymphoma or other processes such as tapeworm infestation may also result in vitamin B_{12} deficiency. The cause of vitamin B_{12} deficiency should be determined for optimal management. Detection of IF antibody is diagnostic of pernicious anemia but is found in only a minority of patients. A several-stage Schilling test is undertaken if IF antibody is negative, but only after a period of vitamin B_{12} replacement because megaloblastosis of intestinal mucosa may interfere with vitamin B_{12} absorption. Part I of the Schilling test measures urinary excretion of an oral dose of radiolabeled vitamin B_{12} administered after sufficient parenteral vitamin B_{12} has been given to saturate vitamin B_{12} binding sites so that vitamin

B_{12} absorbed is excreted in urine. If excretion is low, the test is repeated (part II) with the addition of IF. If absorption in Schilling part II remains low, testing is repeated after a course of oral antibiotics. Bacterial overgrowth results in abnormal vitamin B_{12} excretion in both parts I and II of the Schilling test and is corrected by antibiotic treatment. Pernicious anemia results in abnormal excretion in part I that is corrected by the addition of IF in part II.

All cells are affected by vitamin B_{12} deficiency, but because marrow proliferation is continuous, anemia is typically the presenting condition. Occasionally neurological signs of vitamin B_{12} deficiency develop prior to anemia. Response to vitamin B_{12} replacement, as measured by an increase in reticulocytes, occurs within a few days and is occasionally associated with hypokalemia perhaps due to rapid intracellular accumulation of potassium by new cells.

381. The answer is D. *(Williams, 4/e, p p 158–167.)* Blood product support is essential in managing aplastic anemia but transfusion may be associated with alloimmunization and may impair engraftment. Transfusion should be minimized and transfusions from family members avoided if BMT is a consideration. Survival before effective therapies were developed was brief in most patients with severe aplastic anemia as it is in patients failing to respond to current treatment. Immunosuppressive therapy may be successful in severe aplastic anemia regardless of etiological association unless aplasia is due to bone-marrow ablation. BMT is the treatment of choice for younger patients with severe aplastic anemia and for most patients with an identical twin.

382. The answer is B. *(DeVita, 4/e, pp 2093–2108. Wilson, 12/e, pp 1404–1405.)* HIV infection results in progressive deficiency in cellular immunity associated with loss of T4 cells, which specifically bind the virus. In this context a variety of opportunistic diseases including various malignancies may develop. Oncogenetic mechanisms are poorly understood but may involve secondary viral infection in the context of profound immunosuppression with Epstein-Barr virus (EBV) infection that results in B-cell lymphoma or papilloma virus in cervical or anal cancer. Polyclonal "malignant" proliferation in Kaposi's sarcoma may derive from abnormal regulation of cytokine release from HIV-infected lymphocytes or endothelial cells or both. B-cell CNS lymphoma occurs in immunosuppressed recipients of organ transplants in addition to persons with HIV infection. HIV is not typically present in tumor cells, and T-cell malignancies are not dramatically increased in HIV-infected persons. Gastric carcinoma is not associated with HIV infection.

383. The answer is E. *(Wilson, 12/e, pp 1567–1572.)* Polycythemia vera is a chronic progressive disease characterized by an increased production of all marrow elements and splenomegaly. In distinction to the secondary forms of polycythemia, urine and serum levels of erythropoietin are substantially reduced or absent, and in vitro erythroid colonies can be established without erythropoietin. Red blood cell mass, hemoglobin concentration, hematocrit, white cell count, and platelet level are all elevated. Erythrocyte sedimentation rate (ESR) is low and uric acid may be elevated. Bone marrow examination reveals a panmyelosis with absent or markedly reduced iron stores. Progression to marrow fibrosis occurs in up to 20 percent of patients.

Symptoms result from increased blood viscosity with reduced perfusion and include headache, tinnitus, visual alterations, and stroke as well as peripheral vascular ischemia. Histamine levels are markedly elevated, which may explain the high frequency of pruritus, and gastric acid production is increased with increased risk of peptic ulceration. Early satiety and abdominal fullness are due to splenomegaly. The majority of patients die of vascular complications. Acute myelogenous leukemia develops in less than 5 percent of patients. Leukemic risk is increased by chlorambucil, which was once commonly used to control marrow proliferation. Radioactive phosphorus or hydroxyurea or both are now used instead of chlorambucil if phlebotomy is not sufficient to control hematocrit. Effective treatment reduces blood viscosity and restores perfusion. Platelet count may rise markedly during phlebotomy and contribute to vascular events. Iron-deficient erythropoiesis is associated with stiff red cell membranes, which increase blood viscosity. The role of platelets and abnormalities of red cell membranes in the pathogenesis of vascular complications of polycythemia rubra vera is poorly understood but is apparently much less important than red cell mass. Antiplatelet agents increase hemorrhagic risk but have not demonstrated efficacy in preventing stroke and should not be routinely used.

384. The answer is C. *(Wilson, 12/e, pp 1542–1543.)* Glucose-6-phosphate dehydrogenase (G6PD) deficiency is a hereditary disease characterized by decreased enzyme activity with consequent predisposition of red blood cells to hemolyze as a result of oxidant drugs, infection, or acidosis. Hemolysis results from the oxidation of glutathione, which complexes to and precipitates hemoglobin (Heinz body formation). Red cells with Heinz bodies are rapidly removed from the circulation, which results in hemolysis. There are many types of G6PD deficiency and the severity of hemolytic anemia varies markedly. Three common variants of G6PD deficiency are seen: Mediterranean, Central

African, and Chinese variants. The Mediterranean type has the least
stable enzyme with lowest activity and is associated with the most severe hemolytic episodes. The G6PD gene is located on the X chromosome and thus deficiency is sex-linked. Treatment of severe hemolysis
includes blood transfusion, maintenance of good urine flow to avoid
hemoglobin precipitation within renal tubules (which may cause acute
renal failure), and removal of precipitating factors.

385. The answer is E. *(Wilson, 12/e, pp 1410–1417.)* Multiple myeloma
is a clonal B-cell malignancy that results from proliferation of malignant
plasma cells. Differentiation from the more common process of monoclonal gammopathy of unknown significance (MGUS) is important since
treatment for MGUS is not indicated. Infection due to encapsulated
bacteria such as pneumococcus is common due to abnormal humoral
immunity, which explains the lack of response to pneumococcal vaccination in most patients. Late in the course, marrow function is diffusely
abnormal and granulocytopenia may contribute to risk of infection. Renal failure is frequent in myeloma and has various causes. Hypercalcemia due to plasma cell cytokine–mediated calcium release from bone
is perhaps the most common cause of renal failure, but glomerular light
chain deposition (amyloid), recurrent infection, hyperviscosity, and
even direct plasma cell infiltration may contribute. In sufficient quan-
tity, filtered light chains cause dysfunction of the proximal renal tubule
with amino acid and glucose wasting as well as defects in urine concentration and acidification consistent with Fanconi's syndrome. Since the
M-protein is cationic, the anion gap ($Na^+ - [Cl^- + HCO_3]$) is decreased. Due to the physical properties of the proteins involved, hyperviscosity is much more common with IgM-secreting plasma cell disorders.

386. The answer is A (1, 2, 3). *(Wilson, 12/e, pp 1630–1632.)* Prostate
cancers are overwhelmingly adenocarcinomas, are frequently multifocal
within the prostate, and are the second most common cause of cancer
death in men. Tumor spreads by direct extension hematogenously or via
the lymphatics and commonly produces both osteoblastic and osteolytic
bone metastases. Staging is divided into four main groups: stages A and
B designate tumor confined to the prostate and stages C and D tumor
spread beyond the prostatic capsule. Treatment for cancer of the prostate involves surgery, radiation therapy, hormonal therapy, and chemotherapy in various combinations that depend on symptoms, stage,
and previous treatment. Either radiation or surgery can be curative in
the early stage. Impotence is a common complication of both surgery
and radiotherapy.

387. The answer is D (4). *(Wilson, 12/e, pp 1590–1591.)* Chemotherapeutic drugs are examined for possible clinical use in a series of trials. In phase I studies, drugs that have shown promise in the laboratory are evaluated to determine the optimal dose and schedule and clinical pharmacokinetics. Once these characteristics are defined, phase II studies evaluate clinical activity. If useful activity is suggested in phase II, comparison with standard regimens is evaluated in randomized phase III studies.

388. The answer is C (2, 4). *(Williams, 4/e, pp 1031–1088. Wilson, 12/e, pp 1603–1612.)* The curative potential of multiple-agent chemotherapeutic regimens was first demonstrated in Hodgkin's disease, and the potential for cure with such treatment was subsequently shown in non-Hodgkin's lymphoma. Most cases of non-Hodgkin's lymphoma are of B-cell origin as established by surface phenotype or study of immunoglobulin gene rearrangement. T-cell origin can be shown in a minority of patients on the basis of surface phenotype or T-cell receptor rearrangement. The cell of origin for Hodgkin's disease is unknown. Radiation is potentially curative in early stage lymphoma of either Hodgkin's or non-Hodgkin's type.

389. The answer is A (1, 2, 3). *(Wilson, 12/e, pp 1613–1618.)* Local treatments such as radical mastectomy, modified radical mastectomy, simple mastectomy, or lumpectomy with radiation appear equally efficacious in achieving disease control. Node dissection provides staging information of prognostic significance but is not therapeutic. Recurrence in node-positive women is several times more frequent than in women without axillary involvement, and recurrence risk increases in direct relation to the number of nodes involved. CA-15-3, a glycoprotein associated with breast cancer, is often elevated in advanced disease.

390. The answer is A (1, 2, 3). *(DeVita, 4/e, pp 1289–1315. Wilson, 12/e, pp 1612–1621.)* Standard-dose, multiple-agent chemotherapy is a useful adjuvant treatment for premenopausal but not postmenopausal patients with breast cancer and limited nodal involvement. Postoperative radiotherapy of the chest wall has been shown to decrease local recurrence of breast cancer after lumpectomy and following mastectomy in patients with extensive nodal disease, but it has minimal effect on overall recurrence and thus cannot be recommended as an alternative adjuvant therapy. Adjuvant hormonal treatment in postmenopausal patients with hormone receptor–positive primary tumors decreases recurrence of disease and improves survival. Patients with extensive involvement of axillary lymph nodes are at extremely high risk for recurrence of disease but benefit minimally from standard-dose adjuvant chemotherapy. Dose-intensive chemotherapy with bone marrow support may decrease recurrence of disease in these high-risk patients.

391. The answer is E (all). *(Williams, 4/e, pp 558–569.)* This patient has hereditary spherocytosis, an autosomal dominant process in which abnormalities of the red cell skeletal membrane that involve spectrin result in a loss of surface area of red cells with a decreased surface-to-volume ratio and a marked decrease in deformability of red cells. Rigid red cells are trapped in the spleen and lead to hemolysis. Splenectomy corrects hemolysis and is indicated for patients with marked anemia or symptomatic splenomegaly or gallstones. Folic acid supplementation is recommended for all patients with chronic hemolytic syndromes since marrow hyperactivity increases the risk of folate deficiency. Aplastic crisis due to parvovirus infection or other processes may complicate hereditary spherocytosis and red cell transfusion may be required.

392. The answer is A (1, 2, 3). *(Wilson, 12/e, pp 1618–1619.)* The major benefit of current adjuvant treatment in breast cancer appears to be an increase in disease-free survival with less impact on overall survival. There is no clear evidence to recommend current treatment as curative. The role of adjuvant treatment in node-negative breast cancer remains unresolved. Since many such patients will not develop recurrent disease after primary treatment, a major advantage must be conferred on the subset of patients who would otherwise have recurrence to justify the cost and toxicity of treating the entire group. It is conceivable that a more limited occult disease burden in node-negative as compared with node-positive patients may permit greater success with adjuvant treatment in node-negative patients. Additional studies are required to resolve these issues.

393. The answer is E (all). *(Wilson, 12/e, pp 1553–1559.)* There is a close association between specific morphological subtypes of leukemia and cytogenetic abnormalities. Promyelocytic leukemia, t(15;17); myelomonocytic leukemia with eosinophilia, inv 16; and monocytic leukemia, t(9;11) are good examples in which there are distinctive morphological and cytogenetic findings as well as characteristic clinical complications, such as disseminated intravascular coagulation in t(15;17) and skin, meningeal, and mucosal infiltration in t(9;11). Treatment prospects vary widely between leukemic subsets and indicate a need to explore different treatment strategies in subgroups. Cytogenetic abnormalities are no longer found at remission with standard techniques, but more sensitive cytogenetic and molecular probes are being studied for possible use in monitoring remission status.

394–398. The answers are 394-D, 395-C, 396-A, 397-E, 398-B. *(Wilson, 12/e, pp 1587–1593.)* Cyclophosphamide is a broadly active alkylating agent useful in hematological and solid tumor neoplasia. It is metabolized to its active form by liver microsomes. Acrolein is an active metabolite of cyclophosphamide excreted in urine and may cause hemorrhagic cystitis. Toxic risk can be minimized by maintaining a dilute urine and by frequent voiding.

Nitrogen mustard was the first effective chemotherapeutic agent developed. Its major use is in the treatment of Hodgkin's disease. Toxic manifestations other than those listed in the question include nausea, vomiting, bone marrow suppression, and alopecia.

Methotrexate was designed and functions as a folate antagonist. Drug development was encouraged by the observation that exogenous folic acid appeared to accelerate the progression of acute leukemia. Methotrexate has broad activity, including activity against acute leukemia, breast cancer, head and neck cancer, choriocarcinoma, and sarcoma. Major dose-limiting effects of methotrexate include renal and mucosal toxicity as well as bone marrow suppression. Cumulative hepatic toxicity may develop.

Doxorubicin is isolated from *Streptomyces peucetius*. It functions as an inhibitor of DNA synthesis via intercalation of DNA. Side effects other than cardiotoxicity include nausea, vomiting, bone marrow suppression, alopecia, and mucositis. It is a potent vesicant if extravasated.

Cytosine arabinoside (also called *cytarabine* and *Ara-C*) is an analogue of the naturally occurring nucleotide deoxycytidine. Ara-C is activated via salvage pathway enzymes to the active nucleotide Ara-C triphosphate (Ara-CTP), which competes with 2-deoxycytidine triphosphate (dCTP) for the polymerase enzyme. Ara-C is active in acute leukemia. CNS, mucosal, and hepatic toxicities are dose-limiting. Because of its short half-life, and since Ara-C activity is limited to cycling cells, it is given by repeated injection or as a constant infusion. Oral Ara-C is ineffective because the high concentration of cytidine deaminase in the intestinal mucosa converts Ara-C to uracil arabinoside, which is inactive.

399–403. The answers are 399-A, 400-C, 401-B, 402-D, 403-E. *(Williams, 4/e, p 308.)* Pathological red cell inclusions include nuclear or cytoplasmic remnants present in various disease states. Howell-Jolly bodies are nuclear remnants of chromosomes that have separated from the mitotic spindle during mitosis (the results of nuclear fragmentation) or of incomplete nuclear expulsion. They are normally removed by the spleen. Howell-Jolly bodies are found in hemolytic anemia or megaloblastic anemia and following splenectomy. They are prominent in sickle cell disease since these patients have active hemolysis and their disease causes splenic infarction.

Cabot rings (ring bodies) usually appear as singular rings in reticulocytes on Wright-stained peripheral blood films in megaloblastic anemia; their origin is unknown.

Pappenheimer bodies are peripherally located siderosomes that appear as small, dense, blue granules on Wright's stain.

Heinz bodies are precipitated hemoglobin that occur in the context of hemoglobin or enzyme variants. Red cells with Heinz bodies are removed by the reticuloendothelial system.

Basophilic stippling occurs in conditions of abnormal hemoglobin synthesis and represents aggregates of ribosomes. Stippling is a characteristic feature of lead intoxication and the thalassemias.

404–408. The answers are 404-B, 405-C, 406-C, 407-A, 408-D. *(Wilson, 12/e, pp 1102–1110.)* Risk of lung cancer is closely linked to cigarette use. Current treatment is of modest benefit and medical emphasis must remain on prevention via nonsmoking. Intensive experimental screening programs for patients at high risk have been nonproductive since most tumors have early occult dissemination and are not cured by earlier intervention. Although unsuccessful, screening studies were logical since most lung cancers (75 percent) are of the non-small-cell type, which can be surgically cured in the early stage. Primary treatment for small-cell lung cancer, even in the early stage, consists of combination chemotherapy. Patients with limited disease may benefit from concurrent or subsequent radiotherapy. Cells of both small-cell and non-small-cell lung cancer show activity of dominant oncogenes and inactivity of suppressive oncogenes.

409–413. The answers are 409-A, 410-C, 411-B, 412-C, 413-C. *(Wilson, 12/e, pp 1552–1559.)* The peak incidence of acute lymphocytic leukemia (ALL) is between the ages of 2 and 4 years. ALL also occurs in adults, but adult acute leukemia is predominantly myelogenous (AML).

Acute leukemia that fails to respond to therapy is associated with a median survival of approximately 3 months. Death usually results from one of the complications of bone marrow failure, i.e., infection or bleeding. Current therapy achieves complete remission in 90 to 95 percent of children with ALL with a median survival of approximately 5 years. Approximately 50 percent of these patients appear to be cured. Therapy for acute leukemia is divided into several stages: induction, consolidation, central nervous system prophylaxis, and maintenance. Although approximately 50 to 70 percent of patients who have AML will achieve complete remission, the median duration of remission is only 10 to 12 months and fewer than 20 percent of patients are cured.

It is important to distinguish the two major forms of acute leukemia because therapy and prognosis are different. Differentiation can usually be accomplished by examination of Wright-stained smears of peripheral blood and bone marrow. In ALL, the lymphoblasts have a high nuclear: cytoplasmic ratio, scant nucleoli (one or two), and no Auer rods and myeloid elements appear normal. Lymphoblasts stain with para-aminosalicylic acid (PAS) and do not stain with peroxidase and Sudan black. In contrast, myeloblasts contain more nucleoli (two to four) in a homogeneous "ground glass" nucleus. Auer rods may be evident in the cytoplasm and more mature myeloid elements may be abnormal. Myeloblasts stain positively with peroxidase and Sudan black. Esterase stains with or without fluoride inhibition may suggest monocytic differentiation.

Chromosomal abnormalities are common in both ALL and AML and cytogenetic analysis is warranted for diagnostic and prognostic purposes. Most AML patients have a cytogenetic abnormality.

Remission induction therapy results in profound pancytopenia in both AML and ALL. Older induction regimens for ALL were less toxic to marrow but were also less successful.

414–418. The answers are 414-D, 415-C, 416-A, 417-C, 418-A. *(Williams, 4/e, pp 482–506, 540–546. Wilson, 12/e, pp 1519–1521.)* The primary aspect of both iron deficiency and anemia of chronic disease is inadequate synthesis of red cells. Reticulocytes are decreased. FEP levels are increased in both iron deficiency and anemia of chronic disease. Variation in cell size (anisocytosis) is a characteristic finding in iron deficiency but not in anemia of chronic disease. Serum iron may be extremely low in both disorders and has no discriminative value. If TIBC is elevated in association with a low serum iron, the diagnosis of iron deficiency is established. Ferritin is an acute phase reactant, and thus inflammation as well as iron influences ferritin concentration. Ferritin levels below 10 µg/L indicate iron deficiency while those greater than 100 µg/L indicate adequate iron stores.

419–423. The answers are 419-C, 420-C, 421-C, 422-B, 423-D. *(Wilson, 12/e, pp 261–264, 1217, 1533–1537.)* Red cell antibodies may be detected in some patients without hemolysis, but gastrointestinal bleeding always indicates shortened red cell survival. Lymphoma and drugs can each result in both immune hemolysis and gastrointestinal bleeding. Treatment of symptomatic anemia may include red cell transfusion regardless of the cause of anemia, but transfusion in patients with brisk immune hemolysis requires blood-banking expertise to exclude the presence of alloantibodies. Vitamin B_{12} levels are not useful in the evaluation of immune hemolysis or gastrointestinal bleeding.

424–428. The answers are 424-C, 425-C, 426-A, 427-A, 428-B. *(Williams, 4/e, pp 1355–1359, 1378–1380.)* TTP is characterized by microangiopathic hemolytic anemia, thrombocytopenia, and neurological dysfunction with the variable presence of fever and renal disease. The disorder may be either chronic or, more commonly, acute. Patients present with fluctuating neurological abnormalities such as seizures, mental status changes, behavioral disorders, jaundice, purpura, and various manifestations of diffuse microinfarction, such as abdominal pain and complete heart block, which are caused by widespread hyaline occlusion of small vessels. The peripheral smear is consistent with microangiopathic hemolytic anemia; thrombocytopenia, hyperbilirubinemia, leukocytosis, proteinuria, and hematuria are other frequent findings. Therapy involves a combination of glucocorticoids and plasma infusion or plasma exchange. Platelet inhibitors may be useful in some patients. Remission is achieved in 60 to 80 percent of cases but relapse may occur.

Chronic ITP, in contrast, is characterized by thrombocytopenia due to immune-mediated mechanisms. The disease begins insidiously; patients present with cutaneous and mucosal bleeding. Thrombocytopenia is typically isolated, with normal RBC and WBC levels, except in the patient who has had severe bleeding or in the rare patient who presents with both ITP and Coombs-positive hemolysis. Platelet-associated IgG is elevated. Ten to twenty percent of patients recover spontaneously. Treatment includes steroids to suppress the reticuloendothelial uptake of antibody-coated platelets. Patients who fail to respond to steroids or require high-dose steroid therapy to maintain an adequate platelet count are considered for additional treatment. Splenectomy increases platelet count in more than 70 percent of patients and response may be durable. ITP is three times as frequent in women and may respond to the male hormone danazol. The mechanism of action of danazol is unclear, but responses are seen in both men and women. High-dose intravenous gamma globulin is also transiently effective possibly by blocking reticuloendothelial Fc receptors. Vincristine, azathioprine, and other cytotoxic drugs have limited activity in resistant patients. ITP may be more common during pregnancy and transplacental transfer of antiplatelet antibody may cause fetal/neonatal thrombocytopenia with CNS bleeding at delivery. Pathophysiological mechanisms of TTP are less well defined.

429–433. The answers are 429-A, 430-B, 431-D, 432-A, 433-A. *(Williams, 4/e, pp 1449–1471. Wilson, 12/e, pp 1505–1507.)* The von Willebrand factor serves a carrier protein function for factor VIII and levels of the two proteins are similar in normal persons and those with hemophilia B but divergent in patients and carriers of hemophilia A. Vitamin K–dependent proteins include coagulant factors II, VII, IX, and X and proteins C and S. Neither factor VIII nor factor IX is measured in the bleeding time, which is normal in both hemophilia A and B. A markedly prolonged bleeding time in a patient with low factor VIII coagulant level is typical of von Willebrand's disease. Cryoprecipitate contains primarily fibrinogen, the von Willebrand factor, and factor VIII, DDAVP enhances endothelial release of the von Willebrand factor and factor VIII coagulant protein.

Neurology

DIRECTIONS: Each question below contains five suggested responses. Select the **one best** response to each question.

434. A 45-year-old woman presents to her physician with an 8-month history of gradually increasing limb weakness. She first noticed difficulty climbing stairs, then problems rising from chairs, walking more than half a block, and finally, lifting her arms above shoulder level. Aside from some difficulty swallowing, she has no ocular, bulbar, or sphincter problems, and no sensory complaints. Family history is negative for neurological disease. Examination reveals significant proximal limb and neck muscle weakness with minimal atrophy, normal sensory findings, and intact deep tendon reflexes. The most likely diagnosis in this patient is

(A) polymyositis
(B) cervical myelopathy
(C) myasthenia gravis
(D) mononeuropathy multiplex
(E) limb girdle muscular dystrophy

435. A 55-year-old diabetic woman suddenly develops weakness of the left side of her face as well as of her right arm and leg. She also has diplopia on left lateral gaze. The responsible lesion is probably located in the

(A) right cerebral hemisphere
(B) left cerebral hemisphere
(C) right side of the brainstem
(D) left side of the brainstem
(E) right medial longitudinal fasciculus

436. Benign positional vertigo is characterized by all the following statements EXCEPT

(A) vertigo occurs only with certain changes in head position
(B) nystagmus may be purely horizontal, vertical, or rotary
(C) tests of hearing function are invariably normal
(D) induced vertigo and nystagmus last less than 30 s
(E) nystagmus fatigues after repeated recumbency and head tilt

218

437. All the following are recognized neurological complications of HIV infection EXCEPT

(A) dementia
(B) cerebral toxoplasmosis
(C) CNS astrocytoma
(D) myelopathy
(E) chronic inflammatory polyneuropathy

438. A 19-year-old man tells his physician that he has been troubled for 4 days by a severe pain across the top of his right shoulder and the upper part of his right arm. He thought he might have injured the arm but became alarmed when the pain subsided and a progressive weakness developed. All the following comments related to this medical history would be reasonable EXCEPT

(A) he may have received a tetanus toxoid shot in the arm a week before the pain started
(B) the patient is likely to have leukocytosis and an increased sedimentation rate
(C) EMG and nerve conduction studies may identify a local brachial plexus disturbance
(D) recovery of arm strength may take a year or longer
(E) the serratus anterior and deltoid muscles are more likely to be involved than the extensor carpi radialis and interosseous muscles

439. All the following statements concerning chronic subdural hematoma are true EXCEPT

(A) predisposing factors include advanced age, therapy with anticoagulant drugs, and prior head trauma
(B) a common presenting picture is one of focal (lateralizing) signs, such as hemiparesis, aphasia, and homonymous hemianopia
(C) mental status changes can mimic metabolic disturbance, drug intoxication, or Alzheimer's disease
(D) in advanced cases, a dilated pupil will more commonly indicate the side of the hematoma than will a hemiparesis
(E) diagnostic CT or MRI of the head usually obviates the need for cerebral angiography

440. A diagnosis of brain death requires all the following clinical signs EXCEPT

(A) irreversible cessation of respiration
(B) irreversible cessation of cardiac function
(C) pupils that are unreactive
(D) lack of response to oculocephalic testing
(E) lack of decerebrate posturing

441. Which of the following symptoms would suggest that the headaches suffered by a patient were due to migraine?

(A) Numbness or tingling of the left face, lips, and hand lasting for 5 to 15 min, followed by a throbbing headache

(B) An increasingly throbbing headache associated with unilateral visual loss and generalized muscle aches

(C) A continuous headache associated with sleepiness, nausea, ataxia, and incoordination of the right upper limb

(D) An intense, left retroorbital headache associated with transient left-sided ptosis and rhinorrhea

(E) A visual field defect that persists following cessation of a unilateral headache

442. A previously healthy 52-year-old truck driver, while lifting heavy packages, suddenly develops a severe bifrontal headache and a brief period of loss of consciousness without obvious convulsion. On awakening he is brought to the hospital, where he is found to be drowsy and mildly confused with a normal blood pressure. The rest of the neurological examination reveals moderate nuchal rigidity, equal and reactive pupils, full extraocular movements, and no focal motor, sensory, or reflex abnormalities. There are no bruits heard over the orbits or carotid arteries. All the following statements regarding this patient's neurological condition are true EXCEPT

(A) a CT of the head is better than a lumbar puncture as an initial diagnostic procedure

(B) a negative cerebral arteriogram suggests a poorer prognosis in this patient

(C) ophthalmoscopic examination will often reveal hemorrhages that cover the retinal vessels

(D) a new hemiparesis will often occur approximately 7 days after admission

(E) the patient is likely to benefit more from surgical therapy than medical therapy alone

443. Diffuse hyperreflexia in a limb that is markedly atrophic and weak can be seen in which of the following disorders?

(A) Brachial plexus neuropathy involving the upper trunk
(B) Recent cerebral infarction with hemiparesis
(C) Cervical radiculopathy
(D) Multiple sclerosis
(E) Amyotrophic lateral sclerosis

444. A 45-year-old man with a history of heavy drinking is admitted to a hospital with diplopia, mild drowsiness, disorientation, and ataxia of a week's duration. On examination, the patient is found to be inattentive and unable to concentrate. He is disoriented to time and place and periodically falls asleep during conversation. He exhibits horizontal and vertical nystagmus and bilateral gaze palsies. Examination of the limbs reveals a symmetrical polyneuropathy. This diagnostic picture is most consistent with which of the following?

(A) Korsakoff's psychosis
(B) Marchiafava-Bignami disease
(C) Wernicke's disease
(D) Wernicke-Korsakoff syndrome
(E) Alcoholic cerebral degeneration

445. All the following statements about the treatment of Parkinson's disease are correct EXCEPT

(A) selegiline (Eldepryl) works by inhibiting the degradation of dopamine in the striatum
(B) limb and facial dyskinesias are the most common side effects of chronic levodopa therapy
(C) levodopa treatment, while ameliorating symptoms, does not alter the natural history of the disease
(D) bromocriptine works by increasing the release of dopamine from the substantia nigra
(E) use of trihexyphenidyl and benztropine mesylate frequently causes confusional states and hallucinations

446. A patient suffering from narcolepsy is likely to

(1) show early-onset REM (rapid eye movement) sleep after falling asleep
(2) experience terrifying hallucinations while falling asleep
(3) fall asleep while eating, standing, or driving
(4) have attacks of muscle paralysis stimulated by emotional or exciting experiences

447. Segmental demyelination is the primary pathological process in which of the following subacute or chronic polyneuropathies?

(1) Isoniazid (INH) neuropathy
(2) Carcinomatous (paraneoplastic) polyneuropathy
(3) Alcoholic (nutritional) polyneuropathy
(4) Chronic inflammatory polyradiculoneuropathy

448. Correct statements concerning antiepileptic drugs include which of the following?

(1) Ethosuximide is a first-line drug effective in the treatment of typical absence (petit mal) seizures
(2) Phenytoin and carbamazepine are equally effective in the treatment of complex partial seizures
(3) An important side effect of valproate is hepatotoxicity
(4) Phenytoin, phenobarbital, and carbamazepine need be given orally only once a day because of their prolonged half-lives

449. A middle-aged woman with bilateral facial nerve palsy should be evaluated for which of the following diseases?

(1) Sarcoidosis
(2) Acute hepatitis
(3) Lyme disease
(4) Hypoparathyroidism

450. True statements concerning transient ischemic attacks (TIAs) include which of the following?

(1) TIAs are a predictor of cerebral and myocardial infarctions

(2) There are definitive clinical features that indicate which patients with TIAs will develop a stroke

(3) Diplopia, bifacial numbness, and dysarthria imply vertebrobasilar disease

(4) TIAs of the carotid system commonly involve the eye and brain simultaneously

451. True statements concerning pseudotumor cerebri include which of the following?

(1) Visual field testing commonly shows enlargement of the blind spots

(2) Mentation and alertness are often impaired

(3) It is most commonly found in young, obese women

(4) The most feared complication is brain herniation related to increased intracranial pressure

452. Neurological manifestations of vitamin B_{12} deficiency include which of the following?

(1) Paresthesias with sensory loss in the distal limbs

(2) Diplopia with extraocular muscle palsies

(3) Spastic leg weakness with gait instability

(4) Involuntary choreiform movements of the limbs

453. Correct statements concerning Huntington's chorea include which of the following?

(1) It is a hereditary disease with an autosomal dominant pattern

(2) There is a high association with chronic subdural hematoma

(3) Wasting of the head of the caudate nucleus and putamen is seen

(4) Choreoathetosis invariably precedes the manifestations of the psychic disorder

SUMMARY OF DIRECTIONS

A	B	C	D	E
1, 2, 3 only	1, 3 only	2, 4 only	4 only	All are correct

454. In a patient complaining of low back pain radiating down the right leg, which of the following clinical points would suggest a lesion compressing the first sacral root?

(1) Absent ankle reflex
(2) Pain in posterior thigh, posterior calf, and outer plantar surface of foot
(3) Diminished sensation in fourth and fifth toes
(4) Difficulty walking on heel

455. A 65-year-old man with recent onset of Broca's aphasia would likely have which of the following abnormalities on neurological examination?

(1) Decrease in word output
(2) Difficulty repeating spoken words
(3) Weakness of the right face and arm
(4) Severe impairment in writing

456. A person who sustains an injury to the upper trunk of the brachial plexus is likely to show weakness in which of the following muscles?

(1) Deltoid
(2) Triceps
(3) Infraspinatus
(4) Flexor carpi ulnaris

457. Correct statements concerning multiple sclerosis include which of the following?

(1) An attack of optic neuritis is generally required before the diagnosis can be made
(2) Seizures occur in approximately 50 percent of patients over the course of the disease
(3) Peripheral nerve involvement may be the initial manifestation
(4) Cerebellar ataxia may be found combined with sensory ataxia

458. Conditions due to remote effects of neoplasia on the nervous system (paraneoplastic disorders) include

(1) subacute combined degeneration
(2) cerebellar degeneration
(3) Creutzfeldt-Jakob disease
(4) Lambert-Eaton myasthenic syndrome

DIRECTIONS: Each group of questions below consists of lettered headings followed by a set of numbered items. For each numbered item select the **one** lettered heading with which it is **most** closely associated. Each lettered heading may be used **once, more than once, or not at all.**

Questions 459–462

Match each description below with the appropriate dementia-causing disorder.

(A) Hypothyroid dementia
(B) Normal pressure hydrocephalus
(C) Multi-infarct dementia
(D) Creutzfeldt-Jakob disease
(E) Alzheimer's disease

459. Aphasia, agnosia, and apraxia are common; memory loss prominent; familial occurrence well documented; silver-staining neuritic plaques seen throughout cortex

460. Stuttering course; often associated with distinct focal neurological events; pseudobulbar palsy common; hypertension often present

461. Rapid progression; myoclonic jerks; distinctive EEG pattern; occurrence in those receiving injections of human growth hormone

462. Unsteadiness of gait with impairment of balance; urinary incontinence; may follow subarachnoid hemorrhage; CT scan important for diagnosis

Questions 463–466

Match each description with the appropriate type of tremor.

(A) Intention
(B) Enhanced physiological
(C) Rubral
(D) Essential
(E) Parkinsonian

463. Rate of 3 to 5 Hz; motor unit bursts alternate between opposing muscle groups; most prominent in hand and forearm (often unilateral); usually suppressed by willed movement

464. Irregular rate of 2 to 3 Hz; occurs toward end of a precise movement; may be associated with head titubation; often interferes with fine motor activities

465. Rate of 4 to 8 Hz; occurs with action or assumed posture; motor unit bursts usually occur simultaneously in opposing muscle groups; familial form is autosomal dominant; suppressed by drinking alcohol

466. Rate of 8 to 13 Hz; seen with hands outstretched; may be caused by hyperthyroidism, alcohol withdrawal, and lithium toxicity

DIRECTIONS: Each group of questions below consists of four lettered headings followed by a set of numbered items. For each numbered item select

A	if the item is associated with	(A) **only**
B	if the item is associated with	(B) **only**
C	if the item is associated with	**both** (A) and (B)
D	if the item is associated with	**neither** (A) nor (B)

Each lettered heading may be used **once, more than once, or not at all.**

Questions 467–470

(A) Absence (petit mal) seizures
(B) Complex partial seizures
(C) Both
(D) Neither

467. Postictal confusion

468. Automatisms

469. Three-per-second spike and wave discharges

470. Déjà vu experiences

Questions 471–474

(A) Guillain-Barré syndrome
(B) Myasthenia gravis
(C) Both
(D) Neither

471. Ocular and facial muscle involvement

472. Response to edrophonium

473. Respiratory insufficiency

474. Areflexia

Neurology
Answers

434. The answer is A. *(Adams, 5/e, pp 1202–1206.)* Polymyositis is an acquired myopathy characterized by subacute symmetrical weakness of proximal limb and trunk muscles that progresses over several weeks or months. When a characteristic skin rash occurs, the disease is known as dermatomyositis. In addition to progressive proximal limb weakness, the patient often presents with dysphagia and neck muscle weakness. Up to one-half of cases with polymyositis-dermatomyositis may have, in addition, features of connective tissue diseases (rheumatoid arthritis, lupus erythematosus, scleroderma, Sjögren's syndrome). Laboratory findings include an elevated serum CK level, an EMG showing myopathic potentials with fibrillations, and a muscle biopsy showing necrotic muscle fibers and inflammatory infiltrates. Polymyositis is clinically distinguished from the muscular dystrophies by its less prolonged course and lack of family history. It is distinguished from myasthenia gravis by its lack of ocular muscle involvement, absence of variability in strength over hours or days, and lack of response to cholinesterase inhibitor drugs.

435. The answer is D. *(Adams, 5/e, pp 689–693, 1173.)* This patient has weakness of the left face and the contralateral (right) arm and leg, commonly called a "crossed hemiplegia." Such crossed syndromes are characteristic of brainstem lesions. In this case the lesion is an infarct localized to the left inferior pons and caused by occlusion of a branch of the basilar artery. The infarct has damaged the left sixth and seventh cranial nerves or nuclei in the left pons with resultant diplopia on left lateral gaze and left facial weakness. Also damaged in the left pons is the left corticospinal tract, proximal to its decussation in the medulla; this damage causes weakness in the right arm and leg. This classic presentation has been called the Millard-Gubler syndrome.

436. The answer is B. *(Adams, 5/e, pp 264–268.)* Vertigo, which has multiple causes, is defined as an illusion of movement or position and is usually described by the patient as a sensation of spinning or dizziness. It is important for the doctor to clinically distinguish between the relatively benign peripheral causes of vertigo (various types of vestibular or labyrinthine dysfunction) and the central causes, which include posterior fossa tumors such as acoustic neuroma and brainstem lesions due to vertebrobasilar ischemia and multiple sclerosis. Benign positional vertigo is a peripheral disorder marked by recurrent, brief paroxysms of vertigo and nystagmus brought on by specific changes in head position, such as rolling over in bed. There are no associated ear or hearing abnormalities on examination. Bedside diagnosis is aided by the Hallpike (Nylen-Bárány) maneuver, during which the patient is quickly moved from a sitting to a recumbent position with the head hung 30 degrees below the end of the examining table and turned either to the right or left side. In benign positional vertigo, the vertigo and nystagmus begin after an initial latency of several seconds and have a duration always less than 30 s; repeated maneuvers will cause a disappearance (fatigability) of the vertigo and nystagmus. Central disorders of vertigo are characterized by no initial latency period, more prolonged duration of nystagmus, and no fatigability. In benign positional vertigo the nystagmus is usually a mixture of horizontal and rotary. A purely vertical nystagmus does not occur and should make the examiner consider a brainstem origin for the abnormality.

437. The answer is C. *(Adams, 5/e, pp 662–664.)* Neurological complications of AIDS are either due to primary infection with the AIDS virus (HIV) or secondary to immunosuppression and occur in at least one-third of patients with AIDS. A common occurrence in later stages is the AIDS dementia complex, a progressive dementia associated with motor abnormalities and felt to be due to direct infection with HIV. Other CNS complications related to immunosuppression include cerebral toxoplasmosis, primary CNS lymphoma, herpes zoster encephalitis, and infections due to tuberculosis, syphilis, cytomegalovirus (CMV), and cryptococcus. A myelopathy with vacuolar degeneration is common, and a variety of neuropathic conditions have been described, including a distal sensory polyneuropathy and both the acute (Guillain-Barré syndrome) and chronic forms of inflammatory demyelinating polyneuropathy.

438. The answer is B. *(Adams, 5/e, p 1158.)* Local weakness involving one or both arms that begins with severe pain and progresses to weakness as the pain abates may indicate a brachial plexus neuropathy. Although this syndrome can develop without any recognized precipitating cause, it is not uncommon for it to follow viral infection or immunization. The upper part of the brachial plexus is usually involved, and thus the most commonly involved muscles are in the shoulder region (serratus anterior, supraspinatus, infraspinatus, deltoid). There is little or no sensory loss. EMG and nerve conduction studies should provide evidence for a focal lesion of the brachial plexus; myelography is generally not necessary. The prognosis is excellent and no specific treatment is required, though patients must be warned that sometimes it may take up to 2 years for a full return to normal function.

439. The answer is B. *(Adams, 5/e, pp 762–763.)* The diagnosis of chronic subdural hematoma may be difficult because the history is often unrevealing and the symptoms and signs are most commonly nonfocal. Information concerning minor head trauma and anticoagulant drug therapy may often be forgotten by elderly patients and their families. Signs of drowsiness, confusion, apathy, and slow thinking commonly suggest a metabolic or toxic disturbance or a dementing illness such as Alzheimer's disease. These changes in mental status, which may fluctuate, are more common in the presenting patient than lateralizing signs such as hemiparesis. As the subdural hematoma enlarges, the resulting hemiparesis may be either contralateral (from direct pressure on the motor cortex) or ipsilateral (from temporal lobe herniation and compression of the contralateral cerebral peduncle). With progression, temporal lobe herniation will compress the ipsilateral oculomotor nerve, which results in a dilated pupil on the side of the hematoma; this tends to be a better localizing sign than a hemiparesis. Cranial CT (often with the use of contrast) or MRI will clearly demonstrate most chronic subdural hematomas, even if they are isodense. Surgical treatment is usually indicated and consists of drainage of the subdural collection through burr holes.

440. The answer is B. *(Adams, 5/e, pp 303–304.)* The condition of brain death indicates that a patient, despite continued cardiac function, is dead based on neurological criteria and testing. This type of testing is used when a severely brain-damaged patient, artificially maintained on a ventilator, shows no sign of brain function. Diagnosis of brain death requires demonstration of the following: (1) absence of all cerebral functions, i.e., deep coma, lack of convulsions, no decerebrate or decorticate posturing; (2) absence of all brainstem functions, i.e., absence of cranial nerve reflexes (pupillary, corneal, oculocephalic, oculovestibular, oropharyngeal) and presence of absolute apnea; and (3) irreversibility of the clinical state. The last criterion is generally determined by repeat clinical testing at least 6 h after the first examination and by obtaining tests for sedative-hypnotic drug overdose in the appropriate clinical setting.

441. The answer is A. *(Adams, 5/e, pp 152–163.)* The differential diagnosis of headaches associated with neurological or visual dysfunction is important because it encompasses a variety of disorders, some quite serious and other relatively benign. Classic (or neurological) migraine is generally a familial disorder that begins in childhood or early adult life. Typically the onset of an episode is marked by the progression of a neurological disturbance over 5 to 15 min, followed by a unilateral (or occasionally bilateral) throbbing headache for several hours up to a day. The most common neurological disturbance involves formed or unformed flashes of light that impair vision in one of the visual fields ("scintillating scotoma"). Other possible neurological symptoms include numbness and tingling of the unilateral face, lips, and hand; weakness of an arm or leg; mild aphasia; and mental confusion. The transience of the neurological symptoms distinguishes migraine from other more serious conditions that cause headaches. Persistence of a visual field defect, speech disturbance, or mild hemiparesis suggests a focal lesion (e.g., arteriovenous malformation with hemorrhage or infarct). In the case of persistent ataxia, limb incoordination, and nausea, one should consider a posterior fossa (possibly cerebellar) mass lesion. Monocular visual loss in an elderly patient with throbbing headaches should initiate a search for cranial (temporal) arteritis. This should include a sedimentation rate (usually elevated) and a temporal artery biopsy (which would show a giant cell arteritis). Fifty percent of these patients have the generalized muscle aches seen with polymyalgia rheumatica. Unilateral orbital or retroorbital headaches that occur nightly for a period of 2 to 8 weeks are characteristic of cluster headaches. These headaches are often associated with ipsilateral injection of the conjunctivum, nasal stuffiness, rhinorrhea, and, less commonly, miosis, ptosis, and cheek edema. Although both migraine and cluster headaches may respond to treatment with ergotamine, they are generally considered to be distinct entities.

442. The answer is B. *(Adams, 5/e, pp 723–728.)* This patient demonstrates a typical presentation of a pure subarachnoid hemorrhage due to a ruptured saccular aneurysm. Saccular aneurysms are small outpouchings of the arteries that lie in or near the circle of Willis, most commonly located at arterial branchings near the anterior part of the circle. Peak incidence of rupture occurs between ages 35 and 65. Depending on the size and location of the rupture, the patient will present with a severe headache and variable loss or alteration in consciousness, which may improve quickly or proceed to deeper coma and death. An early examination will frequently reveal nuchal rigidity, preretinal (subhyaloid) hemorrhages in the fundi, and a lack of lateralizing signs. An emergency unenhanced cranial CT scan is the diagnostic procedure of choice and will usually reveal collections of subarachnoid, ventricular, or intraparenchymal blood; it may also identify the location of the ruptured aneurysm and any associated hydrocephalus. A lumbar puncture is indicated only if the CT is negative. Four-vessel cerebral arteriography is generally performed in a search for the location of the ruptured aneurysm. A negative arteriogram in the face of subarachnoid hemorrhage is associated with a much better prognosis, and most of these patients survive without rebleeding. A new hemiparesis or other lateralizing finding that occurs 4 to 12 days after initial rupture is indicative of cerebral arterial vasospasm, which is caused by the irritative effects of subarachnoid blood on nearby vessels. Surgery is the preferred treatment of ruptured saccular aneurysms if the patient is medically stable and the aneurysm is surgically accessible. The goal is to clip the neck of the aneurysm and thus prevent further bleeding.

443. The answer is E. *(Adams, 5/e, pp 39–55.)* Diffuse hyperreflexia of an arm or leg indicates upper motor neuron dysfunction at a segmental level above that which supplies the involved limbs. Although weakness can be present with both upper and lower motor neuron lesions, marked muscle atrophy indicates axonal dysfunction in the lower motor neurons that innervate the limb's muscles. Thus, the combination of limb hyperreflexia and significant muscle atrophy can be seen only in conditions that cause both upper and lower motor neuron dysfunction of multiple segments. Amyotrophic lateral sclerosis is such a condition. Both brachial plexus neuropathy and cervical radiculopathy affect only the lower motor neurons and cause segmental weakness, atrophy, and depressed or absent tendon reflexes. Cerebral infarction and multiple sclerosis usually disrupt the corticospinal tracts unilaterally or bilaterally; they cause weakness and spastic hyperreflexia with little or no atrophy.

444. The answer is C. *(Adams, 5/e, pp 851–854, 870–871.)* Wernicke's disease, as exemplified by this patient, is characterized by ocular disturbances consisting of (1) weakness or paralysis of external recti, (2) nystagmus, and (3) paralysis of conjugate gaze. Ataxia and mental confusion complete the clinical picture. Many affected patients also demonstrate a peripheral polyneuropathy. Korsakoff's psychosis, known also as amnestic-confabulatory psychosis, is not a separate disease but a variably present psychic component of Wernicke's disease that involves impairment of retentive memory and learning ability. When both neurological and psychic elements of the disease are present, it is known as Wernicke-Korsakoff syndrome. Marchiafava-Bignami disease, which is seen chiefly in Italian men who are heavy wine drinkers, is associated with bilateral demyelination of the corpus callosum; clinically, this disease is characterized by (1) emotional disorders, (2) loss of mental faculties, (3) convulsions, and (4) a variety of motor disabilities. Alcoholic cerebellar degeneration occurs twice as frequently as Wernicke's disease. It is characterized by a wide-based gait, truncal instability, and limb ataxia usually limited to the legs.

445. The answer is D. *(Adams, 5/e, pp 61–62, 975–982.)* Parkinson's disease (PD) is marked by depletion of dopamine-rich cells in the substantia nigra. The resulting decrease in striatal dopamine is the basis for the classic symptoms of rigidity, bradykinesia, and tremor. By far the most widely used treatment for PD has been the drug levodopa. Levodopa is converted to dopamine in the substantia nigra and then transported to the striatum, where it stimulates dopamine receptors. This is the basis for the drug's clinical effect on PD. Levodopa is usually administered with carbidopa (a decarboxylase inhibitor) in one pill (Sinemet), which prevents levodopa's destruction in the blood and allows it to be given at a dose that is lower and less likely to cause nausea and vomiting. The major problems with levodopa have been (1) significant limb and facial dyskinesias in most patients on chronic therapy and (2) the fact that levodopa only treats PD symptomatically and the disease process of neuronal loss in the substantia nigra continues despite drug treatment.

Other drugs can be used in the treatment of PD. Anticholinergic agents, such as trihexyphenidyl (Artane) and benztropine mesylate (Cogentin), work by restoring the balance between striatal dopamine and acetylcholine. They can have significant anticholinergic effects on the CNS, including confusional states and hallucinations. Bromocriptine and pergolide are dopamine agonists that work directly by stimulating dopamine receptors in the striatum; side effects of these drugs are similar to those of levodopa. Selegiline (Eldepryl), a selective monoamine oxidase-B (MAO-B) inhibitor that blocks the breakdown of intracerebral dopamine, has been used in the symptomatic treatment of PD. Recent studies suggest that this drug is unique in that it may slow progression of PD in its early stages.

446. The answer is E (all). *(Adams, 5/e, pp 345–347.)* The chief and usually first symptom of the narcolepsy syndrome is excessive daytime sleepiness. A patient will have frequent attacks (two to six per day) of

irresistible drowsiness that come on following meals or periods of inactivity. Short periods of sleep follow, which rarely last for more than
15 min. At the end of this time, patients awake feeling refreshed. Attacks of cataplexy are commonly present in patients with narcolepsy.
This disorder is a sudden paralysis or loss of muscle tone brought on by
strong emotion such as laughter or anger. Although the patient may fall
to the ground, consciousness is always preserved. Also commonly seen
with narcolepsy are vivid, often terrifying hallucinations on falling
asleep (hypnagogic hallucinations) and a brief loss of voluntary movements that just precedes or follows sleep (sleep paralysis). It has been
shown that a basic defect in sleep regulation exists in these patients.
Characteristically, normal persons on falling asleep will have 1 to 2 h of
non-REM sleep before they enter their first REM period; during the
night they will then alternate between non-REM and REM periods. Patients with narcolepsy fall into REM sleep very quickly. This "short-
latency," or early-onset, REM sleep can be recorded by polygraphic
recordings in qualified sleep laboratories.

447. The answer is D (4). (*Adams, 5/e, pp 858–861, 1117–1124, 1134,
1140–1143.*) The term *polyneuropathy* indicates a diffuse and symmetrical dysfunction of the peripheral nerves, most commonly in the limbs
but sometimes in the cranial nerves and nerves to the trunk. Clinical
features include distal sensory loss, distal and sometimes proximal
weakness, reflex loss, and autonomic changes. There are two major
pathological processes that can affect the peripheral nerves in polyneuropathy. In segmental demyelination, there is a focal degeneration of
myelin sheaths with sparing of axons. In axonal degeneration, neuronal
disease results in degeneration of axon cylinders along with their myelin. Most polyneuropathies can be classified based on clinical presentation, electrodiagnostic studies (EMG and nerve conduction studies),
and sural nerve biopsy. Axonal degeneration is the pathological substate
of most metabolic and toxic neuropathies with a subacute or chronic
course. Metabolic etiologies include diabetes mellitus, the deficiency
state associated with alcoholism, occult carcinoma, uremia, and vitamin
B_{12} deficiency. Toxic etiologies include various drugs (isoniazid, hydralazine, nitrofurantoin, vincristine), heavy metals (arsenic, lead), and
industrial solvents (*n*-hexane). Chronic polyneuropathies with primarily
segmental demyelination are much less common. Chronic inflammatory
polyradiculoneuropathy (CIP) shows many of the features of the Guillain-Barré syndrome (acute inflammatory polyradiculoneuropathy),
namely, a symmetrical motor-sensory neuropathy, segmental demyelination on electrodiagnostic and pathological studies, and cytoalbumino-

logic dissociation of the CSF. It differs from Guillain-Barré syndrome in that its course is either steadily progressive over many months or relapsing after spontaneous or drug-induced remissions.

448. The answer is E (all). *(Adams, 5/e, pp 293–297.)* Knowledge of drug indications, pharmacokinetics, interactions, and side effects is important for the effective treatment of the epileptic patient. For generalized tonic-clonic seizures and complex partial seizures, phenytoin (Dilantin) and carbamazepine (Tegretol) are considered equally effective; other effective first- or second-line drugs for these conditions include phenobarbital and valproate (Depakene). Choice of initial drug therapy will often depend on expected side effects and individual patient response. For typical absence seizures, ethosuximide is usually preferred; valproate can be used as a second-line drug or when absence attacks are combined with other seizure types. Because of their long serum half-lives, phenytoin, phenobarbital, and ethosuximide can be given in one daily oral dose; carbamazepine and valproate have relatively short half-lives and must be administered in divided doses, usually 3 or 4 times daily. Toxic side effects of the principal antiepileptic drugs should be familiar to all physicians. Phenytoin can cause hypersensitivity reaction (rash, fever, blood dyscrasias), acute toxic effects (ataxia, diplopia, obtundation), and chronic effects (gum hypertrophy, hirsutism, cerebellar degeneration). Main concerns with carbamazepine are sedation, leukopenia, and altered liver functions. Valproate may cause hepatotoxicity and pancreatitis.

449. The answer is B (1, 3). *(Adams, 5/e, pp 619–620, 627–628, 1174–1177.)* Facial palsy as an isolated presenting complaint is common in clinical medicine. It generally indicates peripheral (infranuclear) facial nerve dysfunction and can be recognized by the following ipsilateral signs: inability to wrinkle the forehead, weakness of eye closure, decreased nasolabial fold, drooping of the mouth, and inability to smile. Although idiopathic facial (Bell's) palsy is the most common disease of the facial nerve, less common etiologies should be considered, especially in the presence of bilateral involvement. Sarcoidosis can affect both the peripheral and central nervous system, and the uveoparotid syndrome of sarcoidosis can cause a bilateral facial palsy. More recently, Lyme disease, a tick-borne spirochete infection, has surfaced as a major cause of peripheral facial nerve disease. The most common neurological complications of Lyme disease are meningitis, cranial neuropathies (especially facial nerve), and radiculopathies, although numerous other central and peripheral manifestations have been reported.

450. The answer is B (1, 3). *(Adams, 5/e, pp 703–705.)* TIAs are due to atherosclerotic vascular disease and are reversible neurological deficits that last no more than 24 h and usually less than 30 min. In one study, the 5-year cumulative rate of cerebral infarction was 22.7 percent and, for those with carotid lesions, the rate of myocardial infarction was 21 percent. There are no characteristics that distinguish those patients with TIAs who will go on to stroke from those who will not. TIAs of the carotid system typically result in either ipsilateral monocular blindness or contralateral sensorimotor disturbances; they do not occur simultaneously. TIAs of the vertebrobasilar system are characterized by various combinations of the following symptoms; dysarthria, bifacial numbness, dizziness, diplopia, and weakness or numbness of one or both sides of the body.

451. The answer is B (1, 3). *(Adams, 5/e, pp 547–549.)* Pseudotumor cerebri is a syndrome of unknown origin characterized by extreme elevations of CSF pressure, typically from 250 to 450 mmH$_2$O. Patients present complaining of headache, blurred vision, and dizziness. The neurological examination is significant for papilledema and, rarely, for an abducens palsy or nystagmus. Visual field testing shows enlargement of the blind spots along with peripheral constriction. Otherwise, the examination is usually unremarkable, with preserved mentation and alertness. The only severe consequence of this entity is visual loss in patients who do not respond to either repeated lumbar punctures or lumbar thecoperitoneal shunting. Therapy with steroids or oral hyperosmotic agents may be of benefit but is controversial.

452. The answer is B (1, 3). *(Adams, 5/e, pp 864–867.)* The neurological manifestations of vitamin B$_{12}$ deficiency are most commonly seen in the condition known as pernicious anemia, where there is a chronic lack of intrinsic factor normally secreted by the gastric parietal cells. Patients first complain of paresthesias (tingling, pins-and-needles feeling) in the hands and feet, followed by loss of vibratory and position sensation in the legs; these abnormalities can be correlated with degeneration in the posterior columns of the spinal cord. The gait becomes unsteady and the legs become weak and stiff with associated spasticity, hyperreflexia, and extensor plantar responses; these signs indicate degeneration in the corticospinal tracts (lateral and anterior columns). Together, the clinical picture described is known as subacute combined degeneration. Other neurological manifestations of vitamin B$_{12}$ deficiency include a peripheral neuropathy, mental status changes (somnolence, depression, dementia), and impairment of the optic nerve.

453. The answer is A (1, 2, 3). *(Adams, 5/e, pp 969–972.)* Huntington's chorea is an autosomal dominant disorder characterized by choreoathetosis and dementia. It is believed to be due to an increased sensitivity of striatal receptors to dopamine. Both pathologically and on CT scan a bilateral wasting of the head of the caudate nucleus and putamen is seen. Patients present with disturbances in mood, poor self-control, changes in personality, a gradual fall in intellect, and choreoathetosis. The movement disorder may precede, follow, or occur at the same time as the mental symptoms. Huntington's chorea runs a progressive course; death occurs an average of 15 years after onset. Many of these patients are found to have chronic subdural hematomas related to frequent bouts of head trauma.

454. The answer is A (1, 2, 3). *(Adams, 5/e, pp 180–181.)* Low back pain with radicular pain radiating down the leg (sciatica) is usually due to a herniated intervertebral disk compressing one of the lumbosacral roots, most commonly L5 or S1. The clinical history and neurological examination can often indicate the specific nerve root involved. With lesions of the first sacral (S1) root, pain typically occurs in the midgluteal region, posterior thigh and calf, and outer plantar surface of the foot. Paresthesias and sensory loss occur in the posterior ankle, lateral foot, and outer (fourth and fifth) toes. Muscle weakness, if present, involves the flexors of the foot and toes and is manifested as difficulty walking on the toes. Most patients with an S1 radiculopathy have a diminished or absent ankle (Achilles) reflex.

455. The answer is E (all). *(Adams, 5/e, pp 415–418.)* Aphasia is a cerebral disturbance in language brought on most commonly by vascular lesions in the left, or dominant, perisylvian region. Broca's aphasia—also known as motor, expressive, or nonfluent aphasia—is characterized by markedly decreased word output and slow, disordered speech despite the normal functioning of the muscles of articulation. Repetition of spoken language is always abnormal, while most patients have a correspondingly severe impairment in writing. Comprehension of spoken and written language, impaired in Wernicke's aphasia, is generally preserved in Broca's aphasia. Lesions causing Broca's aphasia usually involve the left inferior frontal gyrus and frontoparietal operculum and adjacent cerebrum. Because of extension of the lesion and surrounding edema to adjacent frontal cortex, there is a frequently associated paresis of the right face and arm.

456. The answer is B (1, 3). *(Adams, 5/e, pp 1156–1157, 1188.)* Knowledge of the anatomical relationships within the brachial plexus is essential for proper localization of a deficit that is causing weakness in an upper limb. The brachial plexus is formed from cervical roots 5, 6, 7, and 8 and the first thoracic root. Roots C5 and C6 merge into the upper trunk, root C7 forms the middle trunk, and roots C8 and T1 merge into the lower trunk. Key muscles affected by upper trunk lesions include supraspinatus, infraspinatus, deltoid, biceps, and brachioradialis.

457. The answer is D (4). *(Adams, 5/e, pp 777–786.)* Multiple sclerosis is a chronic demyelinating disease of the central nervous system characterized by recurrent episodes or attacks of neurological dysfunction related to multifocal disease of the optic nerves, spinal cord, and brain. Following attacks, neurological dysfunction typically improves or remits over days to weeks; new attacks or exacerbations sometimes occur years later. Classic findings include weakness, impaired vision, nystagmus, dysarthria, impaired sensation, bladder dysfunction, and paraparesis. Ataxia is common and may be due to a cerebellar lesion, a lesion of the posterior columns (sensory ataxia), or both. Seizures occur in only 2 to 3 percent of patients with multiple sclerosis. Periphereal nerve involvement is extremely rare and can never be considered as a presenting sign of this disease.

458. The answer is C (2, 4). *(Adams, 5/e, pp 592–593, 1261–1262.)* Carcinomatous cerebellar degeneration is a rare but well-recognized nonmetastatic effect of neoplasia, most commonly associated with lung and ovarian carcinoma and lymphoma. The cerebellar signs, which precede the recognition of a neoplasm in half the cases, include gait and limb ataxia, dysarthria, and nystagmus. The disease is felt to be due to autoimmune factors, based on the finding of anti-Purkinje cell (anti-Yo) antibodies in patient sera. The Lambert-Eaton myasthenic syndrome is marked by weakness and fatigability primarily in the limb girdle and trunk muscles. Ocular and bulbar symptoms are less common. Other features are diminished deep tendon reflexes, dry mouth, and aching pain. As with cerebellar degeneration, neurological symptoms may precede discovery of the tumor (usually oat cell carcinoma of the lung) by months or years. Studies have indicated a defect in the release of acetylcholine quanta from the nerve terminal at the neuromuscular junction. Electrodiagnostic studies (repetitive nerve stimulation at rapid rates) should reveal a characteristic incrementing response.

459–462. The answers are 459-E, 460-C, 461-D, 462-B. *(Adams, 5/e, pp 545–546, 659–661, 959–969.)* Alzheimer's disease, which is the most common degenerative disease of the brain, usually occurs in patients in their late fifties and older. The disease is highlighted by progressive dementia, which begins with memory deficits and personality changes and progresses to involve disorders of cerebral function, including aphasias, agnosias, and apraxias. Pathological changes in the cerebral cortex include neuritic (senile) plaques, neurofibrillary tangles within nerve cells, and granulovacuolar degeneration of neurons.

Multi-infarct, or arteriosclerotic, dementia indicates intellectual impairment as a result of multiple cerebral strokes. Patients usually have a stuttering course with a temporal profile of distinct neurological events (indicating strokes) associated with progression of dementia. Multiple infarcts may also produce a picture of pseudobulbar palsy (i.e., slurred speech, dysphagia, and emotional overflow).

Creutzfeldt-Jakob disease, also known as subacute spongiform encephalopathy, is a nervous system disease marked by a rapidly progressive dementia, diffuse myoclonic jerks, and cerebellar ataxia. Many patients have a distinctive EEG pattern of generalized sharp wave complexes that recur at a rate of one per second. Gibbs has shown that the disease can be transmitted to primates by injecting them with diseased brain tissue. Iatrogenic disease has also occurred in patients who received growth hormone prepared from pooled cadaveric pituitary glands.

Normal pressure hydrocephalus (NPH) is thought to be due to nonprogressive meningeal and ependymal diseases and is characterized by enlarged ventricles with minimal or no brain atrophy. Patients with NPH manifest a clinical triad of progressive gait disorder, urinary incontinence, and dementia. CT scanning or radionuclide cisternography can usually verify the diagnosis of NPH, which may be cured by a ventricular shunt procedure.

463–466. The answers are 463-E, 464-A, 465-D, 466-B. (*Adams, 5/e, pp 83–85.*) Parkinsonian tremor is part of the triad (tremor, rigidity, akinesia) classically seen with Parkinson's disease and drug-induced parkinsonism. It is a rhythmic, coarse tremor (rate 3 to 5 Hz) which, when monitored by electromyography (EMG), shows motor unit bursts that alternate between opposing muscle groups. It is most commonly seen in one or both hands but can also occur in the jaw, lips, or feet. It is known as a resting tremor; that is, it is seen with the limb or body part in repose and is decreased or abolished by willed movement. A "pill-rolling" tremor of the fingers often results and is increased while the person walks.

Intention tremor is a classic sign of cerebellar dysfunction. It is an irregular 2- to 3-Hz tremor seen in the hands during a demanding test such as the finger-to-nose or finger-to-finger test. The tremor, absent when the hands are at rest or at the start of a voluntary movement, is brought on when precise hand movements are required to reach a target. The hand tremor may be associated with a rhythmic head tremor of the same rate (titubation), and both may interfere with the patient's motor and visual activities.

Essential tremor is the most common form of tremor. It is known as familial tremor when it occurs in several family members (autosomal dominant inheritance) and as senile tremor when it first begins in an elderly person. Essential tremor is a type of action tremor because it is brought on during active movement (like reaching for an object); it is also called a postural tremor because it is brought on by sustained postures (like holding the arms outstretched). A rate of 4 to 8 Hz is noted, and an EMG recording usually will document motor unit bursts that occur simultaneously in opposing muscle groups. Tremor of the upper limbs may appear alone or may be associated with or precede a nodding tremor of the head; the lower limbs are often spared. Essential tremor is characteristically suppressed by alcohol ingestion and often responds to treatment with propranolol or primidone.

Enhanced physiological tremor is another type of action or postural tremor with a faster rate (8 to 13 Hz). It is considered to be an abnormal exaggeration of normal (physiological) tremor. Like other postural tremors, it is best demonstrated by holding the arms outstretched. Etiologies include emotional changes (fright, anxiety), metabolic disturbances (hyperthyroidism, hypoglycemia), withdrawal syndromes (sedative drug, alcohol), and drug toxicities (lithium, prednisone, xanthine content of coffee and tea).

467–470. The answers are 467-B, 468-C, 469-A, 470-B. *(Adams, 5/e, pp 276–282.)* Typical absence, or petit mal, seizure is the most characteristic epilepsy of childhood, with onset usually between age 4 and the early teens. Attacks, which may occur as frequently as several hundred in a day, consist of sudden interruptions of consciousness. The child stares, stops talking or responding, often displays eye fluttering, and commonly shows automatisms such as lip smacking and fumbling movements of the fingers. Attacks end in 2 to 10 s with the patient fully alert and able to resume activities. The characteristic EEG abnormality associated with attacks is three-per-second spike and wave activity.

Complex partial seizures, also known as psychomotor seizures, are characterized by complex auras with psychic experiences and periods of impaired consciousness with altered motor behavior. Common psychic experiences include illusions, visual or auditory hallucinations, feelings of familiarity (déjà vu) or strangeness (jamais vu), and fear or anxiety. Motor components include automatisms (e.g., lip smacking) and so-called automatic behavior (walking around in a daze, undressing in public). The brain lesion is usually in the temporal lobe, less commonly in the frontal lobe, and is often manifest as a focal epileptiform abnormality on EEG. Postictal confusion or drowsiness is the rule.

471–474.   The answers are 471-C, 472-B, 473-C, 474-A. *(Adams, 5/e, pp 1124–1130, 1252–1259.)* Guillain-Barré syndrome, also known as acute inflammatory polyradiculoneuropathy, is an acute demyelinating polyneuropathy characterized by diffuse limb weakness that progresses to a maximum deficit over 2 to 3 weeks. As the syndrome develops, typical findings include proximal and distal limb weakness, ophthalmoplegias with facial weakness, areflexia, and frequently, respiratory insufficiency. The CSF shows an elevated protein with normal white cell count (albuminocytologic dissociation) and the EMG/nerve conduction study indicates a demyelinating neuropathy.

Myasthenia gravis is a disease of the neuromuscular junction that results in fluctuating and sometimes persistent weakness of ocular, bulbar, limb, and respiratory muscles. More than 90 percent of patients develop extraocular palsies or ptosis, and 80 percent develop some weakness of the muscles of facial expression, mastication, swallowing, or speech. Diaphragmatic muscle weakness can lead to respiratory insufficiency. Sensory function and deep tendon reflexes are preserved. Weakened muscles usually improve dramatically upon administration of parenteral anticholinesterase drugs such as edrophonium (Tensilon).

Dermatology

DIRECTIONS: Each question below contains five suggested responses. Select the **one best** response to each question.

475. The skin cancer most likely to appear as a painless, pearly, ulcerated nodule with overlying telangiectasias is

(A) bowenoid actinic keratosis
(B) basal cell carcinoma
(C) squamous cell carcinoma
(D) superficial spreading melanoma
(E) glomus tumor

476. All the following skin tumors are caused by human papillomavirus (HPV) EXCEPT

(A) bowenoid papulosis of the penis
(B) condyloma accuminatum
(C) molluscum contagiosum
(D) plantar warts
(E) verruca plana (flat warts)

477. Pyoderma gangrenosum is associated with all the following EXCEPT

(A) inflammatory bowel disease
(B) vasculitis
(C) primary biliary cirrhosis
(D) trauma
(E) lack of response to antibiotic therapy

478. A 15-year-old girl complains of a low-grade fever, malaise, conjunctivitis, coryza, and cough. After this prodromal phase, a rash of discrete pink macules begins on her face and extends to her hands and feet. She is also noted to have small, red spots on her palate. The cause of her rash is

(A) toxic shock syndrome
(B) gonococcal bacteremia
(C) Reiter's syndrome
(D) rubeola (measles)
(E) rubella (German measles)

479. Increased risk factors for the development of cutaneous melanoma include all the following EXCEPT

(A) a changing nevus
(B) a large, congenital melanocytic nevus
(C) multiple dysplastic nevi
(D) a family history of melanoma
(E) type IV heavily pigmented skin

480. A 17-year-old girl noted a 2-cm, annular, pink, scaly lesion on her thigh. In the next 2 weeks she developed several smaller, oval, pink lesions with a fine collarette of scale. They seem to run in the body folds and mainly involve the trunk, although a few are on the upper arms and thighs. There is no adenopathy and no oral lesions. The most likely diagnosis is

(A) tinea versicolor
(B) psoriasis
(C) lichen planus
(D) pityriasis rosea
(E) secondary syphilis

481. All the following statements about aphthous stomatitis (canker sores) are correct EXCEPT

(A) the lesions occur singly or in groups and usually heal in 10 to 14 days
(B) the lesions are often seen in Behçet's syndrome
(C) coxsackievirus is frequently cultured from the lesions
(D) aphthous stomatitis can be associated with Crohn's disease
(E) at least 20 percent of the general population suffer the pain and discomfort of these outbreaks

482. A 45-year-old man with Parkinson's disease has macular areas of erythema and scaling behind the ears and on the scalp, eyebrows, glabella, nasal labial folds, and central chest. The diagnosis is

(A) tinea versicolor
(B) psoriasis
(C) seborrheic dermatitis
(D) atopic dermatitis
(E) dermatophyte infection

483. All the following mucocutaneous findings are associated with HIV infection EXCEPT

(A) morbilliform exanthem
(B) oral hairy leukoplakia
(C) dermatitis herpetiformis
(D) bacillary (or epithelioid) angiomatosis
(E) severe seborrheic dermatitis

484. A 20-year-old white man has noted an uneven tan on his upper back and chest. On examination he has many circular, lighter macules with a barely visible scale that coalesce into larger areas. The best test procedure to establish the diagnosis is a

(A) punch biopsy
(B) potassium hydroxide (KOH) microscopic examination
(C) dermatophyte test medium (DTM) culture for fungus
(D) serological test for syphilis
(E) Tzanck smear

485. Herpes zoster (shingles) is characterized by all the following statements EXCEPT that it

(A) is caused by varicella virus
(B) typically produces grouped vesicles that may ulcerate and scar
(C) has a rate of recurrence of over 20 percent
(D) is not contagious to people who have had chickenpox
(E) has a significant association with malignant lymphoma

486. Psoriasis is characterized by all the following statements EXCEPT

(A) it affects about 2 percent of the population
(B) lesions rarely occur on the scalp, but when they do they cause hair loss
(C) it consists of distinct red scaling papules or plaques on extensor surfaces
(D) the nails may have onycholysis, pits, and splinter hemorrhages
(E) an associated arthritis may occur

487. A 39-year-old woman has had nonhealing painful erosions in her mouth for the past year. She now observes rapidly spreading blisters on her chest and erosions on her scalp; the lesions are flaccid and red at the base. A biopsy report notes acantholysis of the prickle cells and deposition of IgG and complement in the intercellular spaces of the epidermis. Which of the following statements best summarizes both this woman's disorder and the appropriate treatment?

(A) She has bullous pemphigoid and should be treated with potent topical steroids applied every 2 to 3 h
(B) She has bullous erythema multiforme and should be treated with 6-mercaptopurine or methotrexate
(C) She has pemphigus vulgaris and should be treated with oral prednisone, 100 mg or more daily
(D) She has cutaneous lupus erythematosus and should receive oral hydroxychloroquine, 400 mg a day
(E) She has bullous impetigo and needs oral penicillinase-resistant antibiotics for 7 to 10 days

488. Generalized exfoliative dermatitis (erythroderma) is characterized by all the following statements EXCEPT that it

(A) can occur in a patient with psoriasis following the withdrawal of systemic steroids
(B) occurs in association with a T-cell lymphoma
(C) can occur in children with atopic dermatitis
(D) can occur in pityriasis rubra pilaris (a rare papulosquamous disease)
(E) can occur with pemphigus and pemphigoid

489. A 33-year-old fair-skinned woman has telangiectasias of the cheeks and nose along with red papules and occasional pustules. She also appears to have a conjunctivitis because of dilated scleral vessels. She reports frequent flushing and blushing. Drinking red wine produces a severe flushing of the face. There is a family history of this condition. The diagnosis is

(A) carcinoid syndrome
(B) porphyria cutanea tarda
(C) lupus vulgaris
(D) acne rosacea
(E) seborrheic dermatitis

490. A 28-year-old woman who is 3 months post partum notes a distressing loss of scalp hair. The patient takes no medications and says that she feels well. A meticulous physical examination is unremarkable; the scalp and hair appear normal, and there are no bald spots. However, several hairs were easily plucked out and had a small white bulb at the tip. The most likely cause of hair loss is

(A) lupus erythematosus associated with pregnancy
(B) postpartum telogen effluvium
(C) hypervitaminosis due to vitamin supplementation during pregnancy
(D) trichotillomania due to postpartum depression
(E) alopecia areata due to the stress of a new baby

491. The combination of psoralens and long ultraviolet light (PUVA) is effective in all the following diseases EXCEPT

(A) psoriasis
(B) vitiligo
(C) eczema
(D) mycosis fungoides
(E) porphyria cutanea tarda

492. A 22-year-old man from New Jersey has suddenly developed pruritic vesicular rash on his arms, hands, and face. There are linear areas of blisters. The rash appears to be spreading for 2 days. Four days ago he was working in his yard clearing out a wooded area. The diagnosis is

(A) chickenpox
(B) Lyme disease
(C) blister beetle bites
(D) poison ivy
(E) photosensivity reaction

493. Diabetes mellitus is associated with all the following cutaneous signs EXCEPT

(A) bacterial and fungal infections of the skin
(B) necrobiosis lipoidica diabeticorum (NLD)
(C) acanthosis nigricans
(D) brown atrophic macules on the pretibial surface
(E) lichen planus

494. Generalized pruritus without diagnostic skin lesions occurs in all the following conditions EXCEPT

(A) hyperthyroidism
(B) polycythemia vera
(C) carcinoid syndrome
(D) secondary syphilis
(E) pregnancy

495. All the following are cutaneous signs of internal disease EXCEPT

(A) necrobiosis lipoidica diabeticorum (NLD)
(B) granuloma annulare
(C) Paget's disease of the breast
(D) Kaposi's sarcoma
(E) eruptive xanthoma

496. An ill patient presents with a raised, nonblanching, violaceous, widespread rash (palpable purpura). You must consider all the following diagnoses EXCEPT

(A) allergic vasculitis
(B) staphylococcal septicemia
(C) thrombocytopenia
(D) gonococcemia
(E) meningococcemia

DIRECTIONS: Each question below contains four suggested responses of which **one or more** is correct. Select

A	if	**1, 2, and 3**	are correct
B	if	**1 and 3**	are correct
C	if	**2 and 4**	are correct
D	if	**4**	is correct
E	if	**1, 2, 3, and 4**	are correct

497. Skin signs of internal malignancy include

(1) migratory thrombophlebitis
(2) ichthyosis
(3) hypertrichosis lanuginosa
(4) acanthosis nigricans

498. Nail pitting is associated with which of the following skin diseases?

(1) Scleroderma
(2) Psoriasis
(3) Lichen planus
(4) Alopecia areata

499. Cutaneous tumors considered to be premalignant include

(1) actinic keratosis
(2) Spitz tumor (benign juvenile melanoma)
(3) lentigo maligna
(4) seborrheic keratosis

500. A 15-year-old girl has violaceous, lichenified plaques with some excoriations in the antecubital and popliteal areas and the sides of the neck. The face is dry and there is an extra fold under the eyelid. Statements that characterize this disorder include

(1) 90 percent of the patients manifest symptoms before age 5
(2) the majority of patients have a personal or family history of hay fever, asthma, or similar skin problems
(3) the levels of IgE are usually increased
(4) defective cell-mediated immunity is associated with this skin disease

Dermatology
Answers

475. The answer is B. *(Fitzpatrick, 4/e, pp 840–847.)* The question presents the classic description of a basal cell carcinoma. Bowenoid actinic keratosis appears as a keratotic red macule. Squamous cell cancers are the most easily confused with basal cell cancers, but are usually duller with a hyperkeratotic center. Superficial spreading melanomas are normally larger than 1 cm and irregular in border with mixtures of brown/black and white and occasionally blue or red colors. Glomus tumors occur near the nail as a painful, encapsulated, deep nodule.

476. The answer is C. *(Fitzpatrick, 4/e, pp 2609, 2611–2627.)* Molluscum contagiosum is a pearly wartlike growth caused by a paravaccinia virus (poxvirus). More than 50 different human papillomaviruses have been identified in the last few years by gene analysis. These double-stranded DNA viruses belong to the papovavirus group. Anogenital condyloma is usually due to types 6, 11, 16, 18, and 31. Importantly, types 16, 18, and 31 have been associated with premalignant and malignant lesions, such as bowenoid papulosis, cervical dysplasia, and carcinoma in women and occasionally rectal carcinoma and penile carcinoma in males.

477. The answer is C. *(Fitzpatrick, 4/e, pp 1171–1182.)* Pyoderma gangrenosum is a progressive ulcerative lesion with a necrotic base and ragged, overhanging borders. It usually begins as a painful, red nodule on the lower extremities. Because the ulceration involves the reticular layer of the dermis and subcutis, scarring occurs on healing. While it is associated with a variety of diseases, it may occur as an illness confined to the skin in 40 to 50 percent of cases. An interesting feature of pyoderma gangrenosum is the susceptibility of the lesion to occur at sites of trauma. The course of pyoderma gangrenosum is highly variable, although when associated with inflammatory bowel disease, it usually parallels the activity of the gastrointestinal dysfunction. Therapy usually involves high doses of corticosteroids. Cyclosporine is used in resistant cases.

478. The answer is D. *(Fitzpatrick, 4/e, pp 2516–2520.)* The patient presents with the classic picture of measles. The coryza, conjunctivitis, cough, and fever characterize the measles prodrome. The pathognomonic Koplik's spots (pinpoint elevations connected by a network of minute vessels on the soft palate) usually precede onset of the rash by 24 to 48 h and may remain for 2 or 3 days. After the prodrome of 1 to 7 days, the discrete, red macules and papules begin behind the ears and spread to the face, trunk, and then distally over the extremities.

479. The answer is E. *(Fitzpatrick, 4/e, pp 1078–1083.)* All the listed choices are significant risk factors for cutaneous melanoma except dark skin. Melanoma is seen more frequently in fair-skinned persons and rarely occurs in blacks.

480. The answer is D. *(Fitzpatrick, 4/e, pp 1117–1123.)* The description of this papulosquamous disease is that of a classic case of pityriasis rosea. This disease occurs in about 10 percent of the population. It is usually seen in young adults on the trunk and proximal extremities. There is a rare inverse form that occurs in the distal extremities and occasionally the face. Pityriasis rosea is usually asymptomatic, although some patients have an early, mild, viral prodrome (malaise and low-grade fever) and itching may be significant. Drug eruptions, fungal infections, and secondary syphilis are often confused with this disease. Fungal infections are rarely as widespread and sudden in onset; potassium hydroxide (KOH) preparation will be positive. Syphilis usually has adenopathy, oral patches, and lesions on the palms and soles (a VDRL test will be strongly positive at this stage). Psoriasis with its thick, scaly red plaques on extensor surfaces should not cause confusion. A rare condition called guttate parapsoriasis should be suspected if the rash lasts more than 2 months, since pityriasis rosea usually clears spontaneously in 6 weeks.

481. The answer is C. *(Fitzpatrick, 4/e, pp 1393–1395, 2291–2293. Wilson, 12/e, pp 246, 1277.)* Aphthous stomatitis is one of the most common afflictions of the mouth. Between 20 and 50 percent of people suffer occasional or recurrent outbreaks of aphthous ulcers. In one series 50 percent of health professionals questioned stated that they were victims of this disease. Viruses are not cultured from these lesions, although some of them may have a herpetic look to them. Primary herpes simplex virus infection often produces a gingivostomatitis. Recurrent herpes simplex virus infection usually occurs as a group of blisters on an erythematous base at the mucocutaneous junction of the lip or nose.

Coxsackie enterovirus produces lesions on the lips and oral mucosa that are part of hand-foot-and-mouth disease. A brief prodrome of mild fever, malaise, and gastrointestinal discomfort is followed by the evolution of papulovesicular lesions in the mouth. It appears that aphthous stomatitis is most likely to result from immunological damage to the mucous membranes. Whether this is a true autoimmune phenomenon or a secondary reaction to, for example, streptococcal antigens in the mouth, is not clear. In addition, a number of immunological disorders feature aphthous stomatitis. These include Crohn's disease, ulcerative colitis, selective IgA deficiency, pernicious anemia, Behçet's syndrome, and Reiter's syndrome. Although a number of biological response modifiers are being tried, the treatment remains largely symptomatic. Tetracycline suspension held in the mouth for a few minutes before swallowing has been successful for some patients. The lesions may be less painful and heal more rapidly if a steroid in a paste vehicle that will adhere to the oral mucosa is applied to the lesions.

482. The answer is C. *(Fitzpatrick, 4/e, pp 1572–1573.)* The patient has the typical areas of involvement of seborrheic dermatitis. This common dermatitis appears to be worse in many neurological diseases. It is also very common and severe in patients with AIDS. In general, symptoms are worse in the winter. *Pityrosporum ovale* appears to play a role in seborrheic dermatitis and dandruff, and the symptoms improve with the use of certain antifungal preparations (e.g., ketoconazole) that decrease this yeast. Mild topical steroids also produce an excellent clinical response.

483. The answer is C. *(Fitzpatrick, 4/e, pp 636–641, 2637–2689.)* Dermatitis herpetiformis is an autoimmune chronic vesiculobullous disease of unknown etiology. A morbilliform exanthem similar to other viral exanthems is seen in the initial phases of HIV infection. Oral hairy leukoplakia, often confused with oral candidiasis because of its white color, is seen on the sides of the tongue. Its cause is thought to be Epstein-Barr virus. Bacillary, or epithelioid, angiomatosis is a red-blue vascular tumor caused by a bacillus similar to cat-scratch bacillus. This tumor may be easily confused with Kaposi's sarcoma—another vascular tumor commonly seen in AIDS patients (especially homosexual AIDS patients). The incidence of seborrheic dermatitis is three or four times as frequent in AIDS patients and is usually more severe than that seen in the general population. This may be due to an increase in the yeast *Pityrosporum ovale,* thought to be related to seborrheic dermatitis. Psoriasis may also be worse in patients with AIDS. Many other skin infections are common and more severe in AIDS patients (e.g., warts, molluscum contagiosum, and candidiasis).

484. The answer is B. *(Fitzpatrick, 4/e, pp 2462–2465.)* The diagnosis is tinea versicolor, which can be easily confirmed by a KOH microscopic examination. Routine fungal cultures will not grow this yeast. A Wood's light examination will often show a green fluorescence, but it may be negative if the patient has recently showered. A Tzanck smear is used on blisters to detect herpes infection. A punch biopsy would show the fungus but is unnecessary and the fungus might be missed unless special stains are performed.

485. The answer is C. *(Fitzpatrick, 4/e, pp 2543–2572. Rosen, JAMA 269:1836–1839, 1993.)* Most patients who have herpes zoster (shingles) are basically healthy and remain so. However, the disease occurs in 25 percent of patients who have lymphoma, Hodgkin's disease in particular. An affliction chiefly of adulthood, shingles arises from endogenous varicella virus that has lain dormant since the time of its original manifestation as chickenpox. Thus shingles—unlike chickenpox, which is caused by the same virus—is acquired not exogenously but from within. Children who have not been exposed to varicella-herpes zoster virus, when exposed to shingles, can develop chickenpox. There have been only occasional reports to suggest that shingles is directly transmittable and produces shingles in close contacts. Unlike herpes simplex, herpes zoster rarely recurs (10 percent or less).

486. The answer is B. *(Fitzpatrick, 4/e, pp 489–514.)* Psoriatic lesions occur quite frequently on the scalp as well as on the elbows, knees, and sacrum. The scalp lesions are sharply demarcated, as are those on the rest of the skin. These sharply demarcated margins differentiate psoriasis from seborrheic dermatitis, which also commonly affects the scalp. Since the scales may be anchored by hair, they may "heap up" so that localized accumulations are usually felt. In contrast, seborrheic dermatitis does not produce this degree of accumulation; instead, it produces a diffuse, scaly erythema. Hair loss does not usually occur in psoriasis unless the hair is removed by excessive scratching of the lesions. Diagnostic nail changes consisting of onycholysis and pits in the nail plate are often seen. Psoriatic arthritis develops in about 10 percent of patients. Perhaps 90 percent of patients with psoriatic arthritis will at some point exhibit nail lesions.

487. The answer is C. *(Fitzgerald, 4/e, pp 592–619.)* The patient discussed in the question has an advanced stage of pemphigus vulgaris, a disease that is fatal unless properly treated with prednisone. The drug should be given orally, 100 mg daily or more. When affected patients have improved, the dose can be lowered and azathioprine (Imuran), gold, or methotrexate can be added to minimize the need for oral steroids. However, low-dose steroids or immunosuppressive agents early in the course of pemphigus are often unavailing. Approximately 30 percent of patients having this disease die from complications of treatment; of the survivors, many eventually dispense with medication entirely and lead normal lives or require low-dose steroids for maintenance.

488. The answer is E. *(Fitzpatrick, 4/e, pp 527–531.)* The course of exfoliative dermatitis is determined by its cause. In patients with generalized skin disease (e.g., psoriasis), the disease usually responds to appropriate therapy, whereas in systemic disease (e.g., lymphoma), the prognosis is relatively poor. Withdrawal of systemic steroids often results in a worsening of psoriasis and may trigger a pustular psoriasis or exfoliative erythroderma. Although pityriasis rubra pilaris is rare, it will often manifest as an exfoliative erythroderma. Exfoliative dermatitis may occur as a result of a drug reaction, as a manifestation of a generalized preexisting dermatitis, or in association with systemic disease, such as T-cell lymphoma (mycosis fungoides) or leukemia. Approximately 60 percent of patients with erythroderma recover in less than a year, 10 percent have a persistent problem that does not respond to treatment, and up to 30 percent die. It is associated with papulosquamous eruptions, but not with the vesiculobullous diseases (pemphigus and pemphigoid). Toxic epidermal necrolysis and staphylococcal scalded skin syndrome, however, may mimic an exfoliative erythroderma.

489. The answer is D. *(Fitzpatrick, 4/e, pp 727–735.)* Rosacea is a common problem in middle-aged, fair-skinned people. Sun damage appears to play an important role. Stress, alcohol, and heat cause flushing. Men may develop rhinophyma. Low-dose oral tetracycline, erythromycin, and metronidazole control the symptoms. Topical erythromycin and metronidazole also work well.

490. The answer is B. *(Fitzpatrick, 4/e, pp 676–686.)* In the patient presented in the question, the most probable cause of hair loss is normal postpartum telogen effluvium. In the first trimester of pregnancy, telogen hairs (resting hairs) constitute a normal 15 to 20 percent of all hair; later in pregnancy, the telogen hair count may drop to 10 percent. This means that many follicles that normally would have reached the end of their active (anagen) phase are still present at parturition. Telogen counts rise quickly in the postpartum period and sometimes reach 30 to 40 percent of total hair. Telogen lasts approximately 3 months. At the end of this period, there is abnormally heavy shedding while a normal telogen-to-anagen hair ratio is reestablished. A patient who presents with hair loss should be carefully examined for circular bald spots that might indicate alopecia areata or trichotillomania. Trichotillomania, which is loss of hair from pulling, usually causes bald areas with short hairs remaining. Lupus erythematosus and hypervitaminosis can both cause alopecia, but there is no reason to suspect them in this patient. Discoid lupus causes a scarring alopecia.

491. The answer is E. *(Fitzpatrick, 4/e, pp 1728, 1872–1880.)* Psoralens in conjunction with ultraviolet radiation (UV-A, 320 to 400 nm) are frequently employed in treating psoriasis. The combination (PUVA) also has been widely used in treating vitiligo, eczema, and mycosis fungoides. In the presence of psoralen, irradiation with UV-A results in the binding of psoralen to pyrimidine bases in DNA. Although this reaction leads to inhibition of DNA synthesis followed by cell death, recent studies have indicated that PUVA may exert its effect by suppression of the immune response and other effects on cell membranes. This treatment should only be given by experienced dermatologists. Patients who are candidates for this regimen are exposed to a measured dose of ultraviolet radiation following ingestion of the medication. Repeated (PUVA) treatments (two or three times a week) are required to produce disappearance of psoriatic lesions. Possible side effects of this and other types of photochemotherapy include premature aging, cataracts, and skin cancer. Porphyria cutanea tarda and most other porphyrias involve cutaneous lesions as a result of UV-A.

492. The answer is D. *(Fitzpatrick, 4/e, pp 15–35.)* Poison ivy (*Rhus* dermatitis) begins 24 to 48 h after exposure to the oil from the plant in an allergic person. Linear blisters are an important clue to the diagnosis.

493. The answer is E. *(Fitzpatrick, 4/e, pp 2123–2128.)* Lichen planus is not associated with diabetes mellitus. Necrobiosis lipoidica diabeticorum and lipoatrophy are virtually pathognomonic signs. Atrophic brown macules, termed *diabetic dermopathy,* also are classic manifestations of diabetes. Cutaneous bacterial and fungal infections (especially *Candida albicans*) are seen more frequently with diabetes. Although acanthosis nigricans can be seen in several conditions (obesity, gastrointestinal malignancy, acromegaly, nicotinic acid therapy), it is also associated with diabetes mellitus.

494. The answer is D. *(Fitzpatrick, 4/e, pp 416–419.)* A number of conditions are characterized by a generalized pruritus in the absence of recognizable skin lesions. Hyperthyroidism, carcinoid syndrome, and pruritus of pregnancy often are associated with cholestasis, which may be overt; affected patients may manifest jaundice or merely an elevation of serum alkaline phosphatase and bile acids. Syphilis causes a plethora of skin lesions—notably macules or papules in secondary syphilis. Pruritus in the absence of skin lesions is extremely rare in patients who have syphilis.

495. The answer is B. *(Fitzpatrick, 4/e, pp 1187–1191, 1244–1256, 2126–2128.)* Granuloma annulare is a benign dermatosis of unknown cause. It can be localized to a few ringlike violaceous plaques over joints or generalized as smaller lesions (rarer form). Granuloma annulare can start at any age but is frequently found in children and young adults. Diabetes occurs in over 50 percent of patients with NLD. This presents with atrophic, yellowish areas on the skin. The dermatitic rash of Paget's disease of the breast and extramammary Paget's disease is associated with underlying apocrine (mammary) carcinoma. In Kaposi's sarcoma, violaceous tumors are seen in immunosuppressed patients, especially in homosexual patients with AIDS. Eruptive xanthomas (yellow papules with erythematous halos) are seen in diabetes and hypertriglyceridemia.

496. The answer is C. *(Fitzpatrick, 4/e, pp 65, 1994.)* Palpable purpura is one of the most important cutaneous signs of internal disease. Its infectious causes listed in this question are life-threatening and death may occur in a few hours. Gram stain smears of the lesions can often make the diagnosis. In a patient with fever and other signs of infection, one cannot wait for a biopsy diagnosis. Vasculitis is probably one of the most common causes of a palpable purpura. The lesions are palpable because of the inflammatory cell infiltrate. Clotting disorders do not cause palpable purpura.

497. The answer is E (all). *(Fitzpatrick, 4/e, pp 640, 1341–1342, 2051, 2235, 2240.)* When no obvious cause for migratory thrombophlebitis is present, especially when that phlebitis involves areas other than the pelvis, a physician should be suspicious about an underlying malignancy. Often the phlebitis can precede the clinical symptoms and signs of a malignancy by many months. Although carcinoma of the pancreas is the most common tumor with which it is associated, it is by no means the only one. It is unusual to find an operable lesion associated with this sign, so the prognostic significance of the association is grave. Pulmonary embolism is an all-too-common complication. In ichthyosis, the skin appears dry and the stratum corneum sheds rhomboidal scales. In the absence of a family history of this disorder, its development strongly suggests the possibility of an underlying lymphoma. Hodgkin's disease has been the most common malignancy associated with ichthyosis. The increased hair growth associated with the condition hypertrichosis lanuginosa is distinctive. The hair is extremely fine with a silky texture and lightly pigmented. Growth may occur on the trunk, arms, and legs, but the most common sites are the face and ears. Although it can be difficult to differentiate this proliferation of lanugo from the effects seen in women with disorders of male sex hormones, the more florid forms of this syndrome are easily recognized. The mechanisms for the production of the hair growth are unclear, but there is a strong association with cancer involving the breast, bladder, lung, gallbladder, colon, and rectum. Acanthosis nigricans appears as a velvety, brown raised area in the body folds, especially on the neck, axillae, and groin. It has a characteristic appearance on biopsy. Acanthosis nigricans is associated most often with gastrointestinal cancers. It usually appears in people over 40 years of age. Pseudoacanthosis nigricans *must* be ruled out. The cause of the benign "pseudo" forms can be obesity, endocrine abnormalities, and, rarely, drugs (e.g., nicotinamide). It may be confused with lichenification, such as that seen in atopic dermatitis.

498. The answer is C (2, 4). (*Fitzpatrick, 4/e, pp 699, 701.*) Pits are the most common lesion of psoriatic nails and actually represent psoriatic lesions located in the matrix of the nail bed. As the nail plate emerges from the proximal nail fold, the keratotic plug falls off and a pit is formed. The pits typically vary in size, shape, and depth. In alopecia areata, nail pits commonly form in traverse rows. Nail atrophy and dystrophy in lichen planus can be profound, but pits are not characteristically seen.

499. The answer is B (1, 3). (*Fitzpatrick, 4/e, pp 804–807, 1060–1063.*) Lentigo maligna may progress to melanoma and actinic keratosis may change from dysplasia to frank squamous cell carcinoma. Both of these lesions develop in sun-exposed areas of the body. Seborrheic keratoses can become very large but are benign growths. Benign juvenile melanoma has histopathologic characteristics that were originally thought to be indicative of melanoma, but we now know that this is a benign tumor that occurs in children and adults.

500. The answer is E (all). *(Fitzpatrick, 4/e, pp 1543–1564.)* These are characteristics of atopic dermatitis. The cause of this common dermatitis is unknown and appears to relate to genetic and immunological factors; however, there is no clear consensus of the role of allergens in the pathogenesis of atopic dermatitis.

Bibliography

Adams RA, Victor M: *Principles of Neurology,* 5/e. New York, Mc-Graw-Hill, 1993.

Balow JE: Renal vasculitis. *Kidney Int* 27:954–964, 1985.

Bart KJ, et al: The current status of immunization principles: Recommendations for use and adverse reactions. *J Allergy Clin Immunol* 79:296–315, 1987.

Bartlett JG: *Clostridium difficile:* Clinical considerations. *Rev Infect Dis* 12(suppl 2):243–251, 1990.

Beaugerie L, Teilhac MF, Deluol AM, et al: Cholangiopathy associated with *Microsporidia* infection of the common bile duct mucosa in a patient with HIV infection. *Ann Intern Med* 117:401–402, 1992.

Berk JE, Haubrich WS, Kalser MH, et al (eds): *Bockus Gastroenterology,* 4/e. Philadelphia, WB Saunders, 1985.

Braunwald E (ed): *Heart Disease: A Textbook of Cardiovascular Medicine,* 4/e. Philadelphia, WB Saunders, 1992.

Buckley RH: Immunodeficiency diseases. *JAMA* 268:2797–2806, 1992.

Cappell MS: The hepatobiliary manifestations of the acquired immunodeficiency syndrome. *Am J Gastroenterol* 86:1–15, 1991.

Centers for Disease Control (CDC): 1989 Sexually transmitted diseases treatment guidelines. *MMWR* 38:1–43, 1989.

Centers for Disease Control and Prevention (CDC): Probable transmission of multidrug-resistant tuberculosis in a correctional facility—California. *MMWR* 42:48–51, 1993.

Centers for Disease Control and Prevention (CDC): Update: Multistate outbreak of *Escherichia coli* 0157:H7 infections from hamburgers—western United States, 1992–1993. *MMWR* 42:258–263, 1993.

Chow AW, Jenesson PJ: Pharmacokinetics and safety of antimicrobial agents during pregnancy. *Rev Infect Dis* 7:287–313, 1985.

Dobs AS, et al: Endocrine disorders in men infected with human immunodeficiency virus. *Am J Med* 84:611–616, 1988.

Eastwood GL, Avunduck C: *Manual of Gastroenterology: Diagnosis and Therapy*. Boston, Little, Brown, 1988.

Felig P, Baxter JD, Broadus, AE, Frohman LA: *Endocrinology and Metabolism*, 2/e. New York, McGraw-Hill, 1987.

Fishman AP: *Pulmonary Diseases and Disorders*, 2/e, New York, McGraw-Hill, 1988.

Fitzpatrick TB, Eisen A, Wolff K, et al: *Dermatology in General Medicine*, 3/e. New York, McGraw-Hill, 1987.

Greenberger PA, Patterson R: Diagnosis and management of allergic bronchopulmonary aspergillosis. *Ann Allergy* 56:144–148, 1986.

Gross NJ: Pulmonary effects of radiation therapy. *Ann Intern Med* 86:81–92, 1977.

Horan RF, Schneider LC, Sheffer AL: Allergic skin disorders and mastocytosis. *JAMA* 268:2858–2868, 1992.

Houston MC: New insights and new approaches for the treatment of essential hypertension. *Am Heart J* 117:911–951, 1989.

Jacobson MA, Mills J: Serious cytomegalovirus disease in the acquired immunodeficiency syndrome (AIDS): Clinical findings, diagnosis, and treatment. *Ann Intern Med* 108:585–594, 1988.

Kalin MF, et al: Hyporeninemic hypoaldosteronism associated with AIDS. *Am J Med* 82:1035–1038, 1987.

Levine AM: AIDS-associated malignant lymphoma. *Med Clin North Am* 76:253–268, 1992.

Levy MS, Fink JN: Hypersensitivity pneumonitis. *Ann Allergy* 54:167–171, 1985.

Mallette LE, Eichorn E: Effect of lithium carbonate on human calcium metabolism. *Arch Intern Med* 146:770, 1986.

Mandel WJ: *Cardiac Arrhythmias: Their Mechanisms, Diagnosis and Management*, 2/e. Philadelphia, JB Lippincott, 1987.

Mandell GL, Douglas RG Jr, Bennett JE: *Principles and Practice of Infectious Diseases*. 3/e. New York, Churchill Livingstone, 1990.

Marx SJ, et al: Familial hypocalciuric hypercalcemia. *N Engl J Med* 307:416–426, 1982.

Massry SG, Glassock RJ (eds): *Textbook of Nephrology*, 2/e. Baltimore, Williams & Wilkins, 1989.

McCarty GA: *Arthritis and Allied Conditions*, 11/e. Philadelphia, Lea & Febiger, 1989.

Med Lett Drugs Ther: Gonadorelin-synthetic LH-RH. 25:106, 1983.

Middleton E, et al (eds): *Allergy: Principles and Practice,* 4/e. St. Louis, CV Mosby, 1993.

O'Byrne PM, Dolovich J, Hargreave FE: State of art: Late asthmatic responses. *Am Rev Respir Dis* 136:740–741, 1987.

Patel HP, Anhalt GJ, Diaz LA: Bullous pemphigoid and pemphigus vulgaris. *Ann Allergy* 50:144–149, 1984.

Patterson R (ed): *Allergic Diseases: Diagnosis and Management,* 4/e. Philadelpia, JB Lippincott, 1993.

Reynolds JC, Parkman HP: Achalasia. *Gastroenterol Clin North Am* 18:223–255, 1989.

Roitt IV, Brostoff J, Male DK: *Immunology,* 2/e. St. Louis, CV Mosby, 1989.

Rose BD: *Clinical Physiology of Acid-Base and Electrolyte Disorders,* 3/e. New York, McGraw-Hill, 1989.

Rose BD: *Pathophysiology of Renal Disease,* 2/e. New York, McGraw-Hill, 1987.

Rosen S: Shingles, sorrows, salves, and solutions (grand rounds at the Clinical Center of the NIH). *JAMA* 269:1836–1839, 1993.

Schiff L, Schiff ER: *Diseases of the Liver,* 6/e. Philadelphia, JB Lippincott, 1987.

Sherlock S: *Diseases of the Liver and Biliary System,* 9/e. Cambridge, MA, Blackwell Scientific, 1993.

Schlant RC, Alexander RW, O'Rourke RA, et al (eds): *Hurst's The Heart,* 8/e. New York, McGraw-Hill, 1994.

Singer DE, et al: Screening for diabetic retinopathy. *Ann Intern Med* 116:660–671, 1992.

Sivak MV Jr (ed): *Gastroenterologic Endoscopy.* Philadelphia, WB Saunders, 1987.

Sleisenger MS, Fordtran JS: *Gastrointestinal Disease: Pathophysiology, Diagnosis, Management,* 4/e. Philadelphia, WB Saunders, 1989.

Smolens P: The kidney in dysproteinemic states. *Am Kidney Fund Nephrol Lett,* vol 4, no 4, 1987.

Somberg JC, Muira D, Keefe DC: The treatment of ventricular rhythm disturbances. *Am Heart J* 111:1162–1176, 1986.

Stein JH, Hutton JJ, Kohler PD, et al: *Internal Medicine,* 3/e. Boston, Little, Brown, 1990.

Stiehm ER, et al: Intravenous immunoglobulins as therapeutic agents. *Ann Intern Med* 107:367–382, 1987.

Stites DP, Terr AI (eds): *Basic and Clinical Immunology,* 7/e. Norwalk, CT, Appleton & Lange, 1991.

Sussman GL, Tarlo S, Dolovich J: The spectrum of IgE-mediated responses to latex. *JAMA* 265:2844–2847, 1991.

Wellens HF, Bar LW, Lie KI: The value of the electrocardiogram in the differential diagnosis of tachycardia with a widened QRS complex. *Am J Med* 64:27–33, 1978.

White PC, et al: Congenital adrenal hyperplasia. *N Engl J Med* 316:1519–1524, 1580–1586, 1987.

Williams WJ, et al (eds): *Hematology,* 4/e. New York, McGraw-Hill, 1990.

Wilson JD, Braunwald E, Isselbacher KJ, et al (eds): *Harrison's Principles of Internal Medicine,* 12/e. New York, McGraw-Hill, 1991.

Wyngaarden JB, Smith LH Jr (eds): *Cecil Textbook of Medicine,* 19/e. Philadelphia, WB Saunders, 1992.

Yamada T, Alpers DH, Owyang C, et al (eds): *Textbook of Gastroenterology.* Philadelphia, JB Lippincott, 1991.

Zakim D, Boyer TD: *Hepatology: A Textbook of Liver Disease,* 2/e. Philadelphia, WB Saunders, 1990.